Tales from the Towers

The unofficial story behind Alton Towers,
Britain's most popular theme park

By Nick Sim

"I expect to be at Alton next week...I am sure I do not need much inducement to stay, for I am nowhere so happy."

Augustus Welby Northmore Pugin, November 1845

Tales from the Towers

For Natalie

Writing this book would have been impossible without her strength and inspiration.

For Steven

Who I hope will grow up to love Alton Towers just as much as his dad does.

For Mum and Dad

Who took me on that fateful trip to Pleasurewood Hills.

And for Charles Talbot, John Talbot, Augustus Welby Northmore Pugin, Henry Chetwynd-Talbot, Charles Henry Chetwynd-Talbot, John Broome and John Wardley

The men who helped turn Alton Towers into a place that has entertained tens of millions of people.

Copyright © 2013 by Nick Sim

Published by Theme Park Tourist
http://www.themeparktourist.com
13 Gladstone Road, Ipswich, Suffolk, IP3 8AT

Cover artwork by Simon Goodway
http://www.simongoodway.com

ISBN: 978-1492377160

First Edition
Printed in Great Britain

Contents

Acknowledgements 6

Foreword 8

1. From country estate to tourist magnet 12

2. All the fun of the fair 54

3. The stately home that's anything but stately.........................77

4. The house of wax takes over 129

5. The Secret Weapons.......................................170

6. Merlin's magic wand..194

7. Waking up the neighbours................................. 223

8. The business of theme parks.............................. 249

9. When things go wrong...................................... 282

10. Creating the magic.. 295

11. What might have been...................................... 308

Acknowledgements

Writing a book about a tourist attraction that has been welcoming guests for more than one-and-a-half centuries is a challenging undertaking. I'm grateful to a number of people for their help in pulling together the information required.

John Wardley, who is bombarded by interview requests on a regular basis, was gracious enough to find time to answer my questions about the many projects that he undertook at Alton Towers and elsewhere – despite being busy enjoying his hard-earned retirement.

Staff at Staffordshire Moorlands District Council, Bedford Borough Council, Stafford Borough Council, Wandsworth Borough Council and Derbyshire County Council offered invaluable (and completely free) assistance in locating planning documents that provided vital information.

Several former staff members at Alton Towers shared their recollections, including Alistair Farrant's amusing anecdotes about portraying Henry Hound. Many others wish to remain anonymous.

Doug Barnes, the owner and producer of the Season Pass Podcast, was kind enough to allow me to use material from the show's interviews with John Wardley. For anyone with an interest in theme park history, the show is highly recommended.

The community members of the Towers Times, Towers Street, Towers Nerd and CoasterForce websites have graciously offered help and advice throughout the project. Chris Johnson, in particular, was kind enough to share his own interview with Wardley.

Acknowledgements

Adam Perry, who runs the excellent Alton Towers Memories website (altontowersmemories.net), provided some invaluable information on the use of the Towers during the Second World War.

When looking for details of the development on the Alton Towers mansion and gardens, I found that most of the work had already been done by Michael J. Fisher in his extraordinary *Alton Towers: A Gothic Wonderland*. For serious history buffs, this is an essential read.

Several of the excellent photos included within the book were kindly provided by Brian Negus, Dave Smith, Nick Laister, Glen Fairweather and Matthew Wells.

The nurses and doctors at Ipswich Hospital, notably Dr Rubin Soomal, have kept me healthy and fit for long enough to complete this book, as well as enabling me to see my son crawl, swim and laugh for the first time. My family and I are eternally grateful for this.

Finally, writing this book would have been impossible without the help of my wife Natalie, who performed seemingly impossible tasks such as tracking down plans stored on micro-fiche decades ago and long since filed away.

Foreword

When I was six years old, my parents took me to Pleasurewood Hills in Corton, Suffolk. Boasting a small roller coaster, a chair lift and a selection of flat rides, it was the first theme park that I'd ever seen. While it was hardly Disneyland, visiting the park was a life-changing experience for me at that age. Theme parks appeared to be small patches of heaven right here on earth, where the only purpose was to have fun.

Every year on the first Saturday of the May/June half-term school holidays, we would return to see Woody Bear and his friends at Pleasurewood Hills. I would count down the days for months beforehand. Although the trip itself seemed to race past, there was always the consolation of visiting the information centre before we left. There, I could pick up leaflets for theme parks all over the country, with exotic names such as The American Adventure, Camelot and Chessington World of Adventures. I would take these home and pore over them, before folding sheets of plain A4 paper into three parts and scrawling my own maps for fictional parks that I hoped to one day build myself.

There was one leaflet that took pride of place in my collection every year: the one for Alton Towers. Usually fronted by a picture of the gothic mansion that lends the park its name, as well as the Corkscrew roller coaster that had helped establish it as Britain's leading theme park, these seemed to depict a magical place beyond my wildest dreams. While visiting Disneyland in California was firmly at the top of my wish list, Alton Towers developed into an almost mythical dreamland in my mind.

In the end, due to the distance from my home in Ipswich to Staffordshire and the cost of taking a family of five on a trip to the park, I didn't actually visit Alton Towers until the end of my first year at university in 2001. I was expecting to be underwhelmed – surely nowhere could live up to the idealised vision of the park that my childhood imagination had generated? I needn't have worried. Rides such as Nemesis and Oblivion blew my mind, and I've been back every year since.

At some point during one of my regular visits, I began to realise what an extraordinary story must lay behind Alton Towers. How had the imposing mansion come to be, with its seemingly random array of rooms, chapels and sprawling corridors? Who was behind the stunning gardens, and the many unusual structures within them? And how on earth had anyone been permitted to build a theme park on the site, when planning consent would surely be refused today? I resolved that one day I would write a book about the park, and try to answer those questions myself.

Years went by. I built a successful career in telecommunications research, married my beautiful wife Natalie, bought a house and paid off the mortgage, and started a website at themeparktourist.com that now brings in millions of visitors every year. Although the Alton Towers book project remained in the "someday/maybe" section of my to-do list, alongside running a marathon and visiting the Tokyo Disney Resort, it was always somewhere off in the distance. I imagined that I would spend ten years or so gathering the information, interviewing hundreds of former staff members, and gradually piecing together the story.

Of course, with Natalie and I determined to travel the world before we hit 30 and nurturing a plan to turn the website into a full-time business, things kept getting in the way. Then, my health situation suddenly changed dramatically, and it became clear that I may not have the luxury of pulling together the book over the course of a decade. If I was going to write it, it had to be now.

My original plan had to be condensed into a four-month period, during which I underwent continuous, intense chemotherapy and went on three family holidays and numerous other excursions. Inevitably, then, some corners had to be cut. I couldn't possibly interview hundreds of people – instead, I relied on information from existing sources such as newspapers, books and a handful of knowledgeable former employees of the park.

Despite my long-held ambition to write the book, I realised immediately that I knew almost nothing about the history of Alton Towers, besides a vague recollection that it had once been home to the Earls of Shrewsbury (gleaned not from the careful study of history books, but from the Hex – The Legend of the Towers ride). Given this starting point, and the enforced timetable for the project, it is absolutely inevitable that some factual errors are going to have found their way into the book. Hopefully, these do not affect my retelling of the overarching story behind the park, which is genuinely fascinating.

If you do spot any such errors, feel free to report them to me via themeparktourist.com. Please also take a look at the accompanying pages on the website, which feature a number of images that couldn't be incorporated into the print or digital versions of the book. These can be found at http://www.themeparktourist.com/tales-from-the-towers/.

John Wardley says that during his long and illustrious career as an attraction designer, he hoped to take riders on an "adventure". I'll never follow in Wardley's footsteps as I dreamed as a child – I simply don't have the required talents. However, our website has helped a few million theme park visitors save money and have a better time on their trips. And

Foreword

I hope that, in some small way, reading this book takes you on an adventure of your own.

Nick Sim
July 31, 2013

1. From country estate to tourist magnet

Most modern theme parks have an iconic structure at their centre, designed to impress guests and draw them deeper into the park. Walt Disney pioneered the concept at Disneyland, where Sleeping Beauty Castle awaits visitors as they march down Main Street, USA from the park's entrance. Walt Disney World's Epcot boasts Spaceship Earth, a massive geodesic sphere with a diameter of 165 feet. As recently as 2010, the rival Universal Orlando Resort installed a towering recreation of Hogwarts Castle as part of the Wizarding World of Harry Potter expansion at Islands of Adventure. While these creations are visually striking, they all share one thing in common: they are works of fiction, designed specifically to entertain.

At Alton Towers, though, a *real* Gothic mansion dominates the view as visitors enter the park via Towers Street. Overlooking a lake, and surrounded by acres of landscaped gardens, the Towers have attracted millions of tourists to rural Staffordshire over a period of more than one hundred and seventy years. However, the history of the site stretches back much further than this. Few theme parks can trace their roots back for thousands of years, but Alton Towers is a fascinating exception.

As long ago as the first century BC, an Iron Age fort sat on Bunbury Hill, now the site of the Towers. Local legend holds that this was the site of a brutal battle in 716AD between the Saxon Kings Coelred of Mercia and Ine of Wessex, centred around a fortress on the hill. Ine's Rock, which can still be found in the Towers' grounds, is said to have been the location for Ine's preparations. The fighting itself was reputedly so gruesome that by the late nineteenth century the site was referred to as "Slain Hollow". It ended in a stalemate, with an Anglo-Saxon sword and a Celtic axe-head being found in the vicinity in 1834.[1]

The fort was enhanced to become a castle by the eleventh century, with the estate being awarded to the knight Bertrum de Verdun in the twelfth century after he had fought in the Crusades. Ownership passed by marriage to Thomas de Furnival in 1318, when he married Joan de Verdun.[2] Finally, the estate came into the hands of the Talbots – the family who were to eventually shape it into the tourist magnet that it continues to be to this day – when Sir John Talbot married de Furnival's eldest daughter, Maud, in 1406. In 1442, Talbot became the Earl of Shrewsbury, a title which had been forfeited by the previous holder, Robert de Montgomerie, after he rebelled against Henry I more than three centuries earlier.

The Talbot family has a colourful history, with several of the earls meeting sticky ends. The first earl was captured in France in 1429 by Joan of Arc, before being released and returned to Ireland. He was back in France by 1453, though, when he was killed at Castillon. His son, John, died seven years later at the Battle of Northampton during the Wars of the Roses. The sixth earl, George, was trusted to hold Mary Queen of Scots in custody while she was imprisoned at Tutbury Castle during the sixteenth century. In 1667, the eleventh earl, Frances, was fatally wounded in a duel with the Duke of Buckingham, who had been engaged in an affair with his wife.

The Earls of Shrewsbury were prominent figures in English society, but the Alton estate was just a part of their property holdings. Heythrop in Oxfordshire was the family's principal residence by the eighteenth century, while the Alton site held nothing more than a modest hunting lodge. Alveton Lodge

(Alveton was the ancient form of Alton) was part-occupied by tenant John Burton and his family, and seemingly rarely used by the earl. The rectangular structure's only stand-out feature was a tower with a spiral staircase, which is still in place today and is among the elements that lend Alton Towers its name.[3]

It was the fifteenth earl, Charles, who finally recognised the site's potential. While the valley that now holds the gardens was little more than a rabbit warren at the turn of the nineteenth century, Charles saw the opportunity to convert it into something much more attractive. Opting to devote more time to Alton, he employed garden architects Robert Abraham and Thomas Allason, and began a process that took decades to complete.

Evidently, Alton Lodge was not a grand enough name for the residence of an earl. By 1811, the building's name had been changed to Alton Abbey. Despite the religious connotations, the name is likely to have been chosen simply for reasons of fashion rather than as an indication that the site held any religious significance.[4] While its name was lost, parts of the Lodge survived the extensive renovations that were commissioned by the earl. The Burtons' home was demolished, but much of what remained received a Gothic makeover to fit in with extensions that were built to the north and west. Alton Abbey was twice the size of its predecessor, boasting an impressive entrance hall, a dining room, a drawing room, a long gallery, a chapel, a conservatory and a library.

By 1814, Charles had moved his family to Alton Abbey, and begun the transformation of the valley into acres of landscaped gardens. The earl's vision extended beyond his own lifetime - by this stage, he was sixty one years old and unlikely to see his plans through to completion. Alongside the alterations to the house, he also turned his attention to installing a variety of unusual and imposing structures in the gardens. Many of these can still be seen today.

Consistency wasn't always Lord Shrewsbury's focus, and he often ignored advice from leading artists and architects to pursue his own agenda. He frequently changed his mind, although this did not stop a huge volume of work from taking place over the next decade. Diverting water from a spring several miles away in Ramshorn, he added a series of lakes and water courses to the previously dry valley. The eclectic gardens had diverse themes – perhaps a portent for a site that would eventually become one of Europe's most popular theme parks.

In the early years of the gardens' development, when the greenery had not yet had time to mature, the man-made structures stood out even more than they do today. They included an imposing Gothic Prospect Tower, built on a large rock on the valley's northern side and completed by 1823. This offered stunning views across the gardens towards the Towers. Another major building, the Flag Tower (which now hosts mobile telecommunications equipment), took more than a decade to complete after construction commenced in 1810, and was missing several key features from the original design when it was finally finished.

The distinctive Pagoda Fountain was envisaged by prominent garden architect John Claudius Loudon as having a total of six storeys, adorned with gas-lit Chinese lamps. The final model, designed by Robert Abraham, wasn't completed until the 1830s, several years after the fifteenth earl's death in 1827, and featured just three storeys and no lamps. Like many other structures in the gardens and the fountains, extensive use of cast iron was made in its construction, with the famous Coalbrookdale Iron Company being employed to carry out the work.

Cast iron was again used to create the seven domes of the Garden Conservatory, another addition during the earl's spending spree. The initial design and architect were both changed, resulting in materials being procured at high cost and then going unused. The domes were finally cast in 1824, with the conservatory having originally been proposed during the previous decade.

Perhaps the strangest addition was a recreation of Stonehenge. While it bears little resemblance to the real prehistoric monument in Wiltshire, it was intended to impress visitors with its scale, with each of the huge stones weighing around nine tons each.[5]

Frustrated that he had been consulted by the earl, only for many of his suggestions to be changed or ignored, Loudon wrote a review of the Alton Towers gardens in his *Encyclopaedia of Gardening* (1834).[6] The architect offers up a detailed description of the sights that awaited visitors to the gardens during the period surrounding the fifteenth earl's death:

By the road leading from Uttoxeter, we came unexpectedly close to the house, and near the head of the north side of the valley, which contains the chief wonders of the place. The first objects that met our eye were the dry Gothic bridge, and the embankment leading to it, with a huge imitation of Stonehenge beyond and a pond above the level of the bridge alongside of it, backed by a mass of castellated stabling. Farther along the side of the valley, to the right of the bridge, is a range of architectural conservatories, with seven elegant glass domes, designed by Mr. Abraham, richly gilt. Farther on still, to the right, and placed on a high and bold naked rock, is a lofty Gothic tower, or temple, on what is called Thomson's rock, also designed by Mr. Abraham consisting of several tiers of balconies, round a central staircase and rooms; the exterior ornaments numerous, and resplendent with gilding. Near the base of the rock is a corkscrew fountain of a peculiar description which is amply supplied from an adjoining pond. Behind, above, and beyond the range of conservatories, are two lakes; and beyond them is another conservatory, curiously ornamented. Below the main range of conservatories is a paved terrace walk, with a Grecian temple at one end, and a second terrace containing a second range of conservatories.

The remainder of the valley, to the bottom, and on the opposite side, displays such a labyrinth of terraces, curious architectural walls, trellis-work arbours, vases, statues, stone stairs, wooden stairs, turf stairs, pavements gravel and grass walks, ornamental buildings, bridges, porticoes, temples, pagodas, gates, iron railings, parterres, jets, ponds, streams, seats, fountains, caves, flower-baskets, waterfalls, rocks, cottages, trees, shrubs, beds of flowers, ivied walls, rock-work, shell-work, root-work, moss houses, old trunks of trees, entire dead trees, etc., that it is utterly impossible for words to give any idea of the effect. As the sandstone rock protrudes from the sides of the valley in immense masses, abundance of use has been made of it to form caves, grottoes, caverns, and covered seats; it has even been carved into figures: in one place we have Indian temples excavated in it, covered with hieroglyphics; and in another, a projecting rock is formed into a huge serpent, with a spear-shaped iron tongue, and glass eyes! There is a rustic prospect tower over an Indian temple, cut out of solid rock, on the highest point of the north bank; and, in the lowest part of the valley there are the foundations and two stories (executed before the death of the late earl) of an octagon pagoda... The pagoda, the Gothic temple, the range of gilt conservatories, and the imitation of Stonehenge form the leading artificial features of the valley. The valley itself is upwards of a mile in length: It gradually widens from its commencement at the stone bridge with the pond above it, till it terminates by opening into the wide valley containing the Chumet [sic], there a considerable stream, and a navigable canal.

If his [the earl's] *object were originality, and that of a kind which should puzzle and confound, he has certainly succeeded; and, having attained the end which he proposed, as far as respects himself, he is to be considered eminently successful.*

Loudon, though, was unimpressed by the gardens' cluttered appearance, with the thousands of trees that had been planted not yet having matured. In 1834's *An Encylopaedia of Cottage, Farm and Village Architecture and Furniture*, he wrote:

The scenery of the valley of Alton Towers is not here presented as a model for imitation. On the contrary we consider the great part of it in excessively bad taste, or rather, perhaps as the work of a morbid imagination joined to the command of unlimited resources. Though he consulted every artist, ourselves among the number, he seems only to have done so for the purpose of avoiding whatever an artist might recommend. The result...was one of the most singular anomalies to be met with among the residences of Britain, or, perhaps of any other part of the world. An immense pile of building in the way of house, with a magnificent conservatory and chapel, but with scarcely a habitable room; a lofty prospect tower not built on the highest part of the ground; bridges without water underneath; ponds and lakes on the tops of hills; a quadrangular pile of stabling in the middle of the pleasure ground.

Following Charles' death, the title of Earl of Shrewsbury was handed down to his nephew, John Talbot. While the sixteenth earl's principal residence remained at Heythrop, he continued to invest significant resources at Alton, both in completing projects started by his uncle (such as the Pagoda Fountain) and in commissioning his own expensive additions to the house and gardens.

One of John's first installations was a tribute to his predecessor, a replica of the Choragic Monument which was built in 344BC in Athens as a tribute to Lysicrates. Unlike the original, it was made of cast iron, and hosts a bust of the fifteenth earl. An inscription reads "He made the desert smile", a reference to the extraordinary transformation of the valley below.

Disaster struck the earl in 1831, when Heythrop was gutted by a fire. Salvaging whatever works of art, furnishings and other effects that he could, the earl moved his family to Alton. Unlike his uncle, "Good Earl John" (as he came to be known) had children, and he was determined to provide for them a home in keeping with their lofty status. An avid collector of art, he also needed extra space to display his treasures. In 1832, he renamed Alton Abbey to its current name, Alton Towers. Over the next two decades, he would spend more than one million pounds (a vast sum of money at that time) on doubling the building's size, as well as further enhancing the gardens.[7]

The expansion work took place in almost every direction, including downwards. Coal vaults and cellars were excavated beneath the building, and new floors were added on top of existing ones. Two coach houses were converted into an Armoury and a billiard room, while a sprawling Picture Gallery was constructed in order to display the earl's collections. A central element of the expanded building was the Octagon Gallery, so named for its distinctive shape. While the Octagon likely dates from 1824, it became more significant when it was linked to the Armoury via the Picture Gallery to create an impressive new entrance route to the house.[8]

The earl hired Thomas Fradgley, a respected architect who had overseen projects in the surrounding area, to head up the work on the Towers. One of Fradgley's main roles was to construct an impressive new chapel, which was several times larger than the existing one.[9] With the Catholic Emancipation Act having been passed in 1829, the Catholic Lord Shrewsbury was able to play a greater role in public life – and the chapel would be a focal point for the Catholic population surrounding Alton. Indeed, it served as the local parish church until 1840. The old chapel, meanwhile, was converted into the Plate Glass Drawing Room – so named because of its use of single sheets of plate glass, a novelty at the time.

Fradgley's biggest addition to the building was the West Wing, which hosted several libraries, a Music Room, the State Bedroom and Dressing Room, the State Boudoir and a romantic Poet's Bay. Contemporary drawings show that the interiors of these rooms were lushly finished, at great expense.

The earl continued to update the Towers' gardens, including the addition of the Swiss Cottage in 1835. This hosted a blind Welsh harper, Edward Jervis, who would play to entertain the family and their visitors. Built by Thomas Fradgley, the brick structure boasted a thatched roof which has long since been replaced by tiles.

Most visitors sang the praises of the gardens. By now, though, some of the trees were beginning to grow very large, and were obscuring important views. "The trees and shrubs have grown too large for the terraces, walks, walls and buildings" noted Gardiner's Magazine in 1840, with garden architect W.A. Nesfield writing in 1844: "In truth the entire ornamental ground, i.e. including the approaches and drives at Alton Towers, is overloaded with foliage to the utter ruin of the scenery which might be so dealt with as to produce a most satisfactory variety of interest." [10]

While the sixteenth earl made huge changes to the Towers and the gardens, perhaps his biggest undertaking was the gathering of the huge selection of artwork, armour and sculptures that he used to fill the grand spaces he had created.

Building on the initial collections procured by his uncle, he eventually amassed a staggering seven hundred pictures, which were displayed throughout the house in its lengthy galleries and ornately-decorated rooms.[11] This included more than two hundred paintings that formerly belonged to the mother of Napoleon Bonaparte, the former French emperor who had died in exile in 1821 following his disastrous war with Russia and subsequent brief return to power.

The Talbot family had played an active role in military conflicts during medieval times, and this was celebrated in the Armoury. There, a vast collection of suits of armour and weaponry awaited visitors, designed to impress them on their way into the Towers. More than twenty artificial figures stood clothed in full suits of armour, while smaller sections of other suits were also on display. Gruesome weapons, such as maces and axes, completed the scene.

The Towers' libraries, while hosting more than four thousand books, were relatively lightweight in comparison to the collections of other landed gentry at the time. Nevertheless, there was a wide selection of scholarly works, along with a handful of novels and works on Catholic theology.

It was the earl's Catholic faith that was to guide the direction of the next phase of Alton Towers' development. Freed from the repression that had plagued his ancestors, he was able both to take up his seat in the House of Lords and to play an active role in the revival of the Catholic faith in Staffordshire and elsewhere. At that time, the Gothic Revival movement was portraying the Gothic style of building as the only "true" physical representation of Christianity. The earl was about to engage with one of its leading proponents, who altered the look of the Towers forever.

Hidden Secret: Head down to *Le Refuge* in the gardens. Notice the classical-style columns? These were almost certainly removed from the original entrance hall to Alton

Abbey. Considered worthy of preservation, they were installed in the garden alcove instead.[12]

The son of a French immigrant, Augustus Welby Northmore Pugin was born in 1812. His father was an artist and illustrator, and the young Pugin soon demonstrated his own creative flair. By the tender age of fifteen, he was already designing furniture for Windsor Castle. While not born into Catholicism, he converted in his twenties and by the time he was first engaged by Lord Shrewbury he was heavily involved in both practicing and writing about Gothic architecture.

The design of large swathes of Alton Towers is often attributed to him, but Pugin did not actually visit the property until 1837.[13] This, of course, was more than two decades after work to extend the Lodge and create the gardens had begun, and five years after the renaming of the building to the Towers. While Pugin's influence was broad and he often disapproved of the approach of the architects who came before him, in many areas his work actually combined with or built upon what was already there.

Pugin was a notorious workaholic, and was frequently engaged in multiple concurrent projects that necessitated travel all over the country. Lord Shrewsbury, meanwhile, was abroad for much of the year, despite the vast sums of money he was spending on his English home. Thus, Pugin was forced to carry out much of his work at a distance from his patron, corresponding via letters. Not all of this communication was cordial – Pugin was a firm believer in the "True Principles" of Gothic architecture, and was not afraid to push back on the earl's ideas – particularly if they involved cost-cutting measures that would compromise Pugin's designs. Although they fell out on occasion, the earl seems to have been willing to forgive Pugin's stubbornness, and they became close friends despite their differing social statuses.

Between 1837 and his death in 1852, Pugin carried out extensive alterations and additions to the Towers. One of the first was the construction of the Talbot Gallery, which was built between 1839-40. Located to the west of the Octagon (which now hosts the pre-show for Hex – The Legend of the Towers), it necessitated huge changes to the existing structure. The end result was an impressive axial system that connected the Armoury and Picture Gallery with the new gallery. From the entrance to the Armoury to the distant end of the Talbot Gallery, visitors would have to walk a distance of some 480 feet, while gazing upon a spectacular array of armour, artwork and furnishings

At the heart of the Octagon, Lord Shrewsbury requested that Pugin install a statue of the first earl, known as the "Grand Talbot". The architect acquired a wooden horse to seat the figure, as well as the appropriate armour. Guests who encountered it were left in no doubt as to the heroic nature of the Talbot line, with the rider's sword inscribed with the phrase (in latin) "I am (the sword of) Talbot, for the vanquishing of my enemies." [14]

One of Pugin's most celebrated projects at the Towers was his conversion of the newly-expanded chapel into a Gothic masterpiece. From 1839-40 he installed a reredos (a frame of elaborately carved wood) along with an intricately-decorated altar screen. A later phase of work, completed in the years leading up to Pugin's death, involved an overhaul of the chapel's ceiling, as well as the installation of decorative panels and a frieze.

In-between the two phases of work on the chapel, Pugin was also responsible for fortifying the Towers, which were very vulnerable to attack during periods of civil unrest. In 1841, he had written: "Who would hammer against nailed portals when he could kick his way through the greenhouse?" [15] When riots took place in Stoke during August 1842, the architect installed a barbican to protect the approach to the Towers' entrance, and excavated a deep ditch which ran along the length of the north front of the building. A drawbridge allowed entrance to the east side of the Towers and the newly-updated chapel. [16]

The biggest disagreements between Pugin and Shrewsbury were over the conversion of the former entrance hall into the lavish Great Dining Hall. Pugin envisioned an enormous, imposing space along the lines of a medieval banqueting hall. The earl, however, was wary of the costs involved and the project did not get underway until 1849, some six years after it was first proposed. When it was finally completed midway through the next decade (largely to Pugin's original design), the hall boasted a ceiling decorated in gilt and painted wood, from which hung an enormous brass chandelier. This can now be found in the Houses of Parliament, although the chain remains at Alton Towers.

The architect had by 1851 built a formidable reputation. He took part in the Great Exhibition at Crystal Palace, displaying items from Alton Towers in the Medieval Court. The world appeared to be at his feet.

Pugin had, though, been warned by doctors to contain his workload, and it was perhaps inevitable that he suffered a breakdown in early 1852. After spending time in the notorious Royal Bethlem Hospital (commonly known as "Bedlam"), he eventually died at his home in Ramsgate on September 14, 1852 at the age of forty. He had packed an extraordinary amount of activity into his short life, being married three times (his first two wives died), siring eight children and working on a huge variety of buildings including the Palace of Westminster and Big Ben. He continued to exert an influence long after his death.

Both Pugin and Lord Shrewsbury passed away before the completion of the Great Dining Hall. The earl succumbed to malaria in November 1852, having contracted the disease during one of his lengthy stays abroad, this time in Italy. Between them, Pugin, his benefactor and the fifteenth earl had created an external structure, interior and surrounding gardens that were already renowned throughout the country. Within a few short years, though, Alton Towers would begin a period of decline that lasted for over a century.

Even as work continued during the 1830s and 1840s to develop the building and its gardens, Alton Towers had begun its evolution into a tourist attraction. As early as 1837, E. Rhodes' Derbyshire Tourist's Guide makes reference to "obtaining tickets to the house and gardens".[17] At this stage, though, admission appears to have been restricted to members of the upper classes, with Rhodes warning that "tickets of admission are given out only to persons coming in private carriages or with clergyman. All others, because of vandalism in the house and gardens, it has been thought necessary to ban."

Just as coastal resorts such as Blackpool had been transformed by the arrival of railways, the development of the Churnet Valley Railway opened up Alton Towers to a wider audience. Linking Alton with mainline stations in major towns, the line opened in 1849.[18] The gardens were opened to visitors from Monday to Friday, with the interior of the house being opened up on Tuesdays and Thursdays.

By 1851, horse-drawn buses were ferrying passengers between the recently-built Alton Station and the Alton Towers estate.[19] Trains were by this stage running to Manchester, a major urban centre, although it would still be some years before the full potential of the Towers and gardens as a commercial tourism business would be realised.

Still, as early as May 1856 Alton Towers was advertising in the Times newspaper, promising that:

Alton Towers and Gardens will be open to visitors on and after Monday, the 19th of May, under the following regulations:

On Tuesdays, Thursdays and Saturdays, the house and gardens will be open to visitors without tickets. On Mondays parties will be admitted by tickets only. The gardens will be open from 12 to 5, and the house from 2 to 5.

In case of unfavourable weather the house cannot be shown. As large parties cause much inconvenience, it is requested that no party may consist of more than 10 persons.

No excursion parties of any kind will be admitted into the grounds, unless previous permission has been obtained, and application for such permission must be made at least seven days before to Mr. James Whitaker, the head gardener, explaining the number and object of the proposed party, so that if the object be approved, preparations may be made for their reception. - The Times, May 13, 1856

A report from The Times itself, published in July 1857 (after the sixteenth earl's death), offers an impression of what awaited those who made the trip:

The entrance hall is an apartment as large as a modern mansion, and nearly 60 feet in height. Hung round with weapons, stags' heads, and hunting trophies, it gives the visitor a good idea of the noble suite of apartments which are to follow, and can be seen from the door, for communicating with the hall is the armoury, and joined to that again is the picture gallery, forming one magnificent vista nearly 500 feet in length, and lofty in proportion.

The armoury is a splendid chamber, with a vaulted roof of carved and polished oak, and with every minor fitting, even to the doors and door locks, in keeping with its severe and massive style of decoration. It is adorned with a collection of antique weapons and armour, second in extent, rarity and value only to those of Meyrick and the Tower of London. Twenty-four figures, sheathed from head to foot in complete mail, stand in niches on each side of the hall, and look so formidably grim and silent, that one can fancy vengeful eyes are watching from behind the barred visors, and though of course not frightened, would prefer not being left alone with them. The rest of the hall is filled with dismembered portions of cap-à-pie suits, rich to look at and uncomfortable to wear, with halberds, maces, half-pikes, balls, wheel-guns, and double axes, all presenting the same general bloodthirsty features, and expressively constructed to gash and maim on the smallest provocation.

A fine old screen of pikes and parisans divides the armoury from the picture gallery, a spacious building 120 feet long and 30 feet high. It is lit from the roof, and all its decorations are rich and beautiful, harmonizing well with the fine paintings, mosaics and sculptures which adorn its entire length.

The picture gallery opens into the octagon chamber, a copy of the Chapter-house at Salisbury. One noble column supports the groined roof, over which its enriched capitals radiate in all directions. By the side of the column is a representation of the tomb of the first earl - old John Talbot - Shakespeare's favourite hero, with his mailed feet resting on a couchant hound.

From this the visitor turns into the tribute of the Talbot gallery, then to the Talbot gallery itself, then to the Talbot corridor, which leads to the State bed and dressing rooms, the library (two spacious chambers), the ante-library, the poet's bay, small dining-room, drawing-room, music-room, and so on from room to room till the visitor is bewildered amid countless chambers, all of which are furnished in a style to extort both admiration and wonder. It is useless to attempt describing how the rooms are situated, or even all the rooms in the place. We have the suite of Doria rooms, the Arragon rooms, the chintz rooms, the red bedrooms, the yellow bedrooms, the plate-glass rooms, the south rooms, the fleur de lis rooms east and west, the Sussex and billiard rooms, the upper red bedrooms, and so on till you wonder what on earth they were all built for, and under what possible combination of circumstances (unless the whole county were entertained) they could all be used.

The State bedrooms deserve special notice; their fittings are so gorgeous and magnificent as to almost dazzle the eyes.

No merely verbal description will convey an adequate idea of the rare beauty of the pleasure grounds. Though the ground they cover is little more than 50 acres in extent, yet the paths through them are so winding and so diversified as to appear almost endless. Both sides of the steep ravine down which they extend are divided into a series of terraces, each of which is named and distinguished for some surpassing natural or architectural beauty. Grottoes, fountains, temples, rockeries, statues, refuges, conservatories, and pagodas are disclosed by every winding path or stand out boldly on little eminences overlooking the deep ravine.

Such is a cursory mention of the principal objects in the gardens, which have been described by Loudon "as the finest combination of garden building with garden scenery anywhere existing in Europe." For some years past they have been considered as public grounds to all the surrounding neighbourhood, and thousands of visitors from the manufacturing districts daily availed themselves of the privilege during the summer. No tickets were required, and everyone went in or out as he liked. With a most unusual amount of consideration for the visitors, the predecessor of the late Earl allowed a house for the sale of refreshments to be built in a secluded part of the grounds, where refreshments of all kinds are sold at a moderate fixed rate. Gradually the mansion itself was thrown open - at first on tickets, and then freely to all who came - and though hundreds daily wandered through its beautiful saloons, a shilling's worth of loss or damage was never sustained. - The Times, July 8, 1857

Following the death of John Talbot, the title of Earl of Shrewsbury passed to his cousin, Bertram. Aged just twenty, Bertram attempted to continue the work on Alton Towers that had been undertaken by his predecessor and Augustus Pugin. In this, he was aided by Pugin's son Edward, who continued to work on the Great Dining Hall and a variety of other rooms, following his father's plans.

While Bertram had been groomed by his much older cousin to take over the role of earl from an early age, his was never likely to be a long reign. His health had been faltering for some years, and the seventeenth earl would die in Portugal of a pulmonary disease at the age of just twenty-four. The Times broke the news on August 18, 1856:

Intelligence has reached England of the death of the young Earl of Shrewsbury, which took place at Lisbon on the 10th inst... On arriving at Lisbon his progress to Cintra was delayed by the breaking out of the cholera in Lisbon and the neighbouring districts. He therefore took up his abode at the Hotel Braganza at Lisbon, where he had a return of the more serious symptoms of his malady, under which he rapidly sank.

Bertram, being of such a young age, had not fathered a son, and the senior line of the Talbot family came to an abrupt end on his death. Wishing for Alton Towers to remain in Catholic hands, Bertram named the infant son of the Duke of Norfolk as its new owner in his will. He also left one year's wages to each of his upper servants, and half-a-year's wages to his under servants.[20] They would need the money, for Alton Towers was to be unoccupied for three years while a bitter legal battle raged over its ownership.

In May 1857, The Times reported on "The Great Shrewsbury case", which had been brought before the House of Lords. The principal challenger to the will was Henry John Chetwynd-Talbot, who was already in possession of nearby Ingestre Hall and claimed to be the rightful heir to the Earl of Shewsbury.

As it directly involves the first and oldest earldom in the land, and indirectly affects estates of the annual value of 40,000l [pounds], our readers will readily believe us when we say that the Shrewsbury case will rival in interest and importance the great Douglas and Berkeley cases.

The printed document formally asserting the claim on the part of his Lordship was laid upon the table of the Upper House on Thursday last. It consists of 41 pages of genealogical and other matter, and is entitled "The Case of the Right Hon. Henry John Chetwynd, Earl Talbot, claiming to be Earl of Shrewsbury."

It first recites the terms and limitations under which the earldom was originally conferred in 1442 upon John Talbot, the great Earl of Shrewsbury, and General of the English army in the wars with France, and carries down the pedigree, step by step, through seven generations, from father to son, in a direct line, until the elder branch of the first earl's family became extinct on the death of Edward, eighth earl, without issue male, on the 8th February 1617.

It then shows how, on the failure of the elder line, the earldom descended upon the heirs male of Sir Gilbert Talbot, of Grafton, K.G., as representative of Gilbert, third son of the second earl, and was enjoyed by them successively down to the year 1856, when it became extinct by the death of Bertram Arthur Talbot, the late earl, at Lisbon.

It further recites that Earl Talbot now claims to be entitled to the earldoms of Shrewsbury, Wexford and Waterford, as nearest heir male of the said Sir Gilbert Talbot, through the second marriage of his son John, and consequently as the nearest heir male of the body of the first earl.

We understand that the opponents of his Lordship's claim are three in number - first, the Duke of Norfolk, as guardian of the interests of his infant son, to whom the late earl bequeathed his magnificent property at Alton Towers; secondly, the Princess Doria Pamphili of Rome, as only surviving child of John, 16th earl; and thirdly, Major Talbot, of Castle Talbot, county Wexford, as a rival claimant to the title. - The Times, May 25, 1857

Ultimately, Henry John Chetwynd-Talbot was victorious. He was named the Earl of Shrewsbury, and took possession of Alton Towers in 1860. There was one major problem facing him, though – the Towers were now all but empty.

'The magnificent contents of Alton Towers, the princely seat of the Earl of Shrewsbury, which will be sold by auction by Messrs. Christine and Manson.' So runs the grandiloquent advertisement which announces that one of the noblest families in the English peerage is extinct, its effects for sale, and the manor over which the premier earls of England have held right and jurisdiction since the days of Henry II, is about to pass into the keeping of strangers' hands. – The Times, July 8, 1857

Henry's legal victory granted him the title of eighteenth Earl of Shrewsbury, as well as ownership of the Alton Towers building and surrounding estate. It did not, though, extend to possession of the moveable contents of the Towers, which had not been contested and were left to the son of the Duke of Norfolk, Lord Edmond Howard. They were sold in the spectacular Great Sale of 1857, which saw more than four thousand lots being auctioned off over a period of more than a month. Beginning on July 6 and not concluding until

August 8, the sale emptied the Towers of the many treasures that had been acquired by the fifteenth earl and his successor.

The Times previewed many of the items that would be on sale in its June 29, 1857 issue:

By order of the executors of the late Earl of Shrewsbury the superb contents of Alton Towers, for many years a source of delight to tourists from all parts of England and other countries, and of excursionists residing in Staffordshire and the neighbouring counties, will in a few days be disposed of by public auction.

The Towers are now closed to the general public, and admission can only be obtained by catalogues. Under one of the conditions of sale no lot can be removed during the time of sale, and therefore the contents of the Towers may be inspected by all lovers of the beautiful in art until Saturday the 8th of August.

It would be futile, in the limited space at our disposal, to attempt anything like even an outline of the treasures thus to be brought to the hammer. We find that the sale of the pictures will last six days, and that there are upwards of 700 lots, including the collection of Madame Letitia Bonaparte, mother of Napoleon I.

The great part of these pictures are hung in a noble gallery, 150 feet long, lighted from the ceiling, which is of oak and supported by light arches springing from the corbels of Talbot dogs holding the arms of the family. The collection of arms and armour is, perhaps, as a private collection, unrivalled for extent and for historic interest.

The sculpture includes a magnificent seated statue of Raffaelle, six beautiful statues of the seasons, and a number of colossal, heroic and life-size busts of mythological deities and modern celebrities. The collection of porcelain is exceedingly rich and varied.

There is, too, an almost endless variety of the finest old bugle, marquetrie, Florentine, mosaic marble, and carved oak furniture. The service of silver and silver-gilt plate weighs upwards of 10,000 ounces. - The Times, June 29, 1857

The four thousand books in the Towers' library were not part of the main auction. Instead, they were transported to Sothebys in London to be sold off separately.

The scene during the opening days of the sale, which saw visitors admitted to the Towers on an unprecedented scale, is brought to life by another Times story, this time from July 8, 1857:

Rusties, holyday-seekers from the manufacturing districts, country gentlemen, and agents from London jostle and crowd about the grand saloons and galleries. Some examine the various lots, note their numbers, and speculate upon their prices; others wonder in dumb admiration of the splendour around, or regale furtively upon the contents of heavy baskets which they lug about the palace, while Ruth and Giles, who till then never sat on anything softer than a dairy stool or five-barred gate, recline with easy luxury upon the embroidered couches in the Music-room.

No place is shut against the curious or closed to the depreciating eyes of would-be purchasers. The late earl's bedroom, plain, quiet, and unostentatious amid the general magnificence, is still crowded as forming an important part of the show. Even the noble chapel, with its high vaulted roof and stained glass windows, which seem to hush the very daylight into a mournful silence, resounds with loud talking and the tread of feet as visitors pour in and out each hour.

High towers and chambers, the Doria apartments and suite of Arragon saloons, conservatories, galleries, and corridors, all, from roof to basement, are thrown open to the public and become as thoroughfares, for the "magnificent contents of Alton Towers are on view."

The sale commenced on Monday and will continue for the next five weeks, when Alton Towers will be stripped and desolate and closed for many years to come.

Let them place in the best light the massive armour of the renowned John Talbot, the suit in which he fought his way through France by the side of stout John Folstoffe, in which he encountered Joan of Arc, and died full knightly under the walls of Poitiers. It is a mere suit of armour now, and the poetical associations of an extinct line go for naught, for the last heir male of the Shrewsburys has been laid at rest for ever, and the "magnificent effects" of Alton Towers are for sale. – The Times, July 8, 1857

The following week, the sale continued with the disposal of the collection of armour and weaponry. This attracted considerable interest, bringing in a total of £1,700:

The sale of the collection of armour and arms commenced on Monday, and was continued yesterday and today, and brought to a close this afternoon. The attendance of buyers was numerous, and included agents on the part of the Government from the Tower of London. The interest attaching to the sale seems to increase, and the number of visitors during the last few days who have perambulated the grounds is very large. The railway has each day brought thousands from different parts of the country.

The sale of the porcelain, sculpture, marbles, and marble tables in the Talbot Gallery, the Picture Gallery, and the Conservatory will commence tomorrow, and the general impression is that for several of the articles there will be great competition and high prices realized. The marbles include the celebrated mosaic Roman table, with exotic birds in the centre, said to be the most splendid of its kind in the empire. - The Times, July 16, 1857

Many of the items that made Alton Towers such a spectacular place to visit were removed and sold during the auction, including some that had yet to even be installed, such was the unfinished nature of the Towers at the time. Some of the lots were bought by the Duchess of Sutherland, who probably moved them to Trentham Hall – an estate that later nearly became a sister park to Alton Towers during the 1980s.[21]

Some significant decorations were not sold. This included the great chandelier in the dining room, which was to remain in place until the next great fire-sale almost seven decades later. The interior of Alton Towers, though, would never look the same again.

Henry Chetwynd-Talbot arrived at Alton Towers on April 13, 1860, with a reputation as a popular landlord. Setting off from Ingestre with his family and close friends in six carriages, he was met west of Uttoxeter by around 300 officers and men from the Queen's Own Yeomanry Calvary, along with 120 mounted tenants from his existing estate at Ingestre and his newly-acquired one at Alton. By the time the procession reached Uttoxeter, it was a quarter-of-a-mile long. In the town, it was greeted by bunting, flags and pealing church bells. When it reached the Towers, the procession was a mile long. In total, more than 40,000 people turned out at the estate to witness the spectacle.

The new earl had, however, spent a tremendous amount of money on the legal fight over Bertram's will. His primary residence remained at Ingestre, and the cost of restoring Alton Towers' interior to its previous level was prohibitive. Instead, in the years leading up to his death in 1868, he refurnished it in eclectic style, with little consistency and a lower overall quality than before.

Perhaps impressed by the turnout for his arrival, Henry soon began to further develop Alton Towers as a tourist attraction. While this was beneficial for the local economy and for the enjoyment of those who visited the estate, the earl's primary motivation is likely to have been his own financial considerations. Simply put, he needed money to maintain the Towers and gardens, and to replace the furnishings that were lost in the Great Sale.

Again, the railway played a vital role. The North Staffordshire Railway company began offering day trips to the Towers, incentivising the earl to open up the grounds by paying him a portion of the proceeds. This enabled Lord Shrewsbury to hire forty men to maintain the gardens helping to keep them in good condition.[22] One visitor in June 1868 was suitably impressed:

On entering the gardens, the walks appear to diverge in all directions. The usual route now is along the main line, a noble serpentine walk, continuous to the extent of between two or three miles, making the entire circuit of the gardens and arboretum. Near the entrance stands the beautiful Choragic Temple, which Mr Rhodes observes, is as beautiful of that of the Sibylis at Tivoli. It is a copy as large as the original of the celebrated Choragic Monument at Athens, erected in honour of the Lysicrates, three hundred and thirty years before Christ.

Language indeed would fail to convey an adequate idea of the glory of such a scene as we now, "looked on", which is more "like the baseless fabric of a vision" than a reality, a mere creation of the mind that seems "not of earth, and yet it is on it". - Derbyshire Times, June 6, 1868

Posted in the same newspaper was an advert from Palmer's Cheap Day Trips, which was offering "the most delightful excursion of the season" to the Towers. "Cheap Excursion Trains" ran from Sheffield and Chesterfield to the gardens, with entry tickets on sale for 6 pence each.[23]

While the Armoury, Picture Gallery, Octagon, Talbot Gallery and other areas of the house were now lacking the permanent art installations that they had once held, they were still an impressive setting for temporary exhibitions. In 1865, such an event was put on to help raise funds for the completion of the construction of the Wedgwood Institute (a school of art and science) in nearby Stoke.

The Art Exhibition having been determined upon, a difficulty presented itself; there was not in any of the Pottery towns a building suitable for an exhibition on the scale and of the character contemplated. In this emergency application was made to the Earl of Shrewsbury for the use of Alton Towers, and permission having been readily given, the committee at once proceeded energetically in their endeavour to make the exhibition worthy of the occasion.

Alton Towers itself is peculiarly appropriate for an exhibition of this character. The wild and diversified scenery of which it is the centre and the charmingly picturesque gardens, pleasure grounds, and cascades by which it is surrounded combine to invest the place at this season of the year with extreme beauty.

The Exhibition is comprised in the "Armoury", which is at the entrance, the "Picture Gallery", the "Octagon Room" and the "Talbot Gallery", a noble suite of apartments in a continuous line, nearly 450 feet in length.

The collection in the Armoury is most interesting; here are some 300 specimens of electro-types of armour, sent from the South Kensington Museum, casts of others from the vestibule of the Louvre, and the Museum of Artillery in Paris, these having been taken by the permission of the Emperor.

The "Octagon Room", as containing the specimens of old Wedgwood ware, must be regarded as the most interesting feature of the Exhibition. Here are to be seen specimens of Wedgwood ware in many forms, illustrative of the progress of the manufacture from its earliest stage as developed by Wedgwood himself.

Such is a very hasty sketch of this Exhibition. That the Exhibition does the promoters of it credit, and is worthy of the object for which it was originated, there seems to be no doubt; there is a good prospect, too, that its success will be equal to its excellence. - The Times, July 11, 1865

Following Henry's death in 1868, his son Charles John became the nineteenth Earl of Shrewsbury. He continued his father's development of the tourism business, although he was not averse to hosting charity events, either. In 1870, he wrote to the editor of The Times to "communicate to the public, through the medium of your paper, the result of throwing open the house and gardens last week at Alton Towers, in aid of the general fund for the sick and wounded of both armies." A total of three hundred pounds was raised from the event, with the railway companies donating their profits.[24]

The earl was praised for allowing the public into the estate, with some suggesting that other noblemen should follow his example:

Until about a couple of years ago the grounds of Alton Towers were closed to ordinary visitors. The "herd profane" were not suffered to penetrate the sacred precincts of the Vale of Tempe, or to disturb the invisible gods "walking in fair procession" on the soft lawns, or among the "pinnacled crags". They were left to their mines and forges and workshops. The beauties of nature were not for them.

But the present Earl of Shrewsbury and Talbot, who, as Viscount Ingestre, showed that he knew something of the wants and difficulties of working people, held a different opinion. Calling to his assistance Mr Cook, the well-known excursionist, he decided upon throwing open the whole of the grounds at Alton Towers on certain days during the summer and autumn months. The results have been most encouraging. At present there is an average weekly attendance of ten thousand visitors, the number on the day of our visit being between two and three thousand; and it is gratifying to record that the noble proprietor of this splendid domain has expressed his entire satisfaction with the good order displayed by the crowds that flock to gaze upon the varied charms of his famous grounds.

Perhaps the example of the Premier Earl may not be lost upon other landed proprietors. Certainly the lesson is worth studying. - The Graphic, July 29, 1871

As at the modern theme park, special events were used to pull in guests. An 1875 flower show drew a relatively negative review from the Staffordshire Daily Sentinel, which noted that "with regard to the flower show, there were no features calling for very special notice", but also conceded that "perhaps the correct idea is that the flower show makes a sort of fixture day for those who have heard of Alton but have never been, to go, or those who, having been, have a desire to re-visit the place." Evidently, not all of the visitors stayed in the grounds of Alton Towers: "Not a few also, we must confess, seemed to have been disposed to test the quality of the beer supplied at the Shrewsbury Hotel, Talbot, and other inns. While there was, to put it mildly, a good deal of hilarity, there did not seem to be any rudeness or riot, but a thorough, hearty, determined merriment." [25]

Visitors were not always so well-behaved. A letter sent to a Staffordshire newspaper in the 1890s complained of frisky couples "frolicking in the shrubbery and littering the lawns with ginger beer bottles and pork pie papers". [26]

It was the twentieth earl, Charles Henry, who really seized upon the idea of attracting huge crowds to the Towers by putting on lavish celebrations. Having taken on the title in

1877, he worked with organisers James Pain and Sons of London to host a series of "Grand Fetes" throughout the late nineteenth century and early twentieth century. These were major events, designed to attract tens of thousands of people.

While the Towers and gardens themselves remained popular attractions, Pain and Sons introduced a number of other elements to entertain the vast crowds. This included music and dancing, horse-jumping competitions, donkey racing and circus-style novelty acts. The Towers would be illuminated by thousands of lights in the evening, before a spectacular fireworks display took place.

Pain and Sons scoured the globe for unique performers to appear at the fetes. In 1892, for example, "Victorina, the strongest athlete on earth" demonstrated his ability to catch a cannon ball fired from a "real cannon with real gunpowder". A year later, the line-up included Sante, "the man with the iron head", whose act saw "granite blocks (obtained locally) broken on his head by sledge hammers". Mademoiselle Onri, meanwhile, slid down a high wire over the lake in front of the Towers, suspended only by her hair. Over the same lake, Ella, Zuila and Lulu – three "charming" ladies – walked along a wire 500 feet across and 75 feet high without the aid of a safety net. The second, evening performance of the high wire acts took place in darkness, with the performers illuminated only by limelights mounted on boats on the lake.[27]

Performing animals also played a part in the celebrations. In 1895, the "Three Roys" showed off their "educated dog", a number of "clever dogs" appeared under the direction of Mr. Grosvenor McCart and Mademoiselle Paula "handled several large boa constrictors and crocodiles dexterously". Humans matched their feats, though, with American rifle expert Mademoiselle Winona and the Paddock troupe of trick cyclists also wowing the audience.[28] If that wasn't entertainment enough, guests could look at a collection of instruments of torture, acquired by Lord Shrewsbury during a trip to the Royal Castle in Nuremberg in 1892.[29]

As it does at today's theme park, new technology and trends played a role in the Grand Fetes. This included the operation of an electric searchlight, mounted on the Flag Tower in 1894.[30] A year later, the new craze for "Living Pictures" (theatrical scenes populated by stationary actors who do not speak or move) came to Alton Towers, proving to be "very much to the taste of the lookers on".[31]

The illumination of the Towers was a major undertaking, requiring dozens of Pain's employees to set up over a period of several weeks. The result was spectacular, and "could be seen for miles around". By 1894, The Mercury reported that "this is the last time the building will be illuminated, owing to the tremendous work it entails." [32] This proved to be inaccurate, though – a year later, the Towers and grounds were again "illuminated with thousands of fairy lamps of many colours, though not upon so large a scale as customary, by reason of the all-spoiling rain." [33]

Fireworks displays are still a major attraction at Alton Towers in modern times, and guests would gather in huge numbers during the Grand Fetes to witness pyrotechnics such as "batteries of coloured roman candles", "electronic streamers", "swarms of writhy fiery cobras" and "flights of whistling rockets". The grounds would then stay open until late, with the last guests filing out at around 11pm.

Substantial funds were invested not just in laying on the Grand Fete events, but in ensuring that they were marketed effectively. A large, visually striking advert in the August 2, 1901 edition of The Mercury offers a comprehensive preview of that year's fete:

On 6th and 7th August comes Alton Towers fete
That old-established fixture, Alton Towers fete
And the principal attraction at Alton Towers fete

Will be Wild Wolves from Russia for Alton Towers fete
Their first performance in England being at Alton Towers fete
The Band of H.M. Scots Guards plays at Alton Towers fete
The Latest Opera Pieces at Alton Towers fete
Whilst horses jump for £100 at Alton Towers fete
And Ladies ride the Jumpers at Alton Towers fete
Then comes the Donkey Race at Alton Towers fete
Ladies mounted on Donkeys racing at Alton Towers fete
Whilst Pain's Daylight Fireworks at Alton Towers fete
Explode like aerial cannons at Alton Towers fete
A real live Man Monkey at Alton Towers fete
Is coming to make the people laugh at Alton Towers fete
Old English Pastimes also at Alton Towers fete
The Zento Lady Cyclists coming to Alton Towers fete
And a graceful Lady Bender at Alton Towers fete
Besides the three pretty "Rosebuds" Alton Towers fete
Will have the Rozells Comical Gymnasts
Alton Towers fete
Something new and startling at Alton Towers fete
Will be Marti Julietta at Alton Towers fete
Additional music given at Alton Towers fete
By the Kingsley Band and others at Alton Towers fete
The world famous Gardens open for Alton Towers fete
Marvellous High-wire Walker at Alton Towers fete
The Patriotic Fireworks at Alton Towers fete
Portraits in Fire of the King and Queen at Alton Towers fete
Bombardment of Taku, and other big things at Alton Towers
fete
Refreshments by Midland Catering Co. at Alton Towers fete
Fresh Spring Water for Abstainers at Alton Towers fete
One Shilling admission to Alton Towers fete
Children passed at half the price to Alton Towers fete
The whole Programme on each of the days at Alton Towers
fete
From 11am and 9.30pm at Alton Towers fete
And Cheap Trips from everywhere to Alton Towers fete

*Keep that Tuesday and Wednesday perfectly free for Pain's
Great Fete!* - The Mercury, August 2, 1901

The Grand Fetes would attract large crowds – in 1894, "on
the first day the attendance was very large, and it was
estimated that some thirty thousand persons were present." [34]
The make-up of the crowds was diverse, as reported by the
Nottingham Evening Post in 1895:

*To the student of human nature Alton Towers upon a fete day
is indeed a happy hunting ground, in which he may find wide
scope for the exercise of his faculties of observation. Here are
gathered together a truly heterogeneous assembly - such a
one as would have rejoiced the heart of Dickens and
furnished him with "types" innumerable.*

*It is essentially a festival of the masses. Everywhere the
British working man and his feminine counterpart are in
evidence, though the middle-class element is by no means
lacking. Sallow operatives from Nottingham, Birmingham
and Derby rub shoulders with fresh-complexioned farm
labourers from the agricultural districts, glass-workers from
Tutbury, and artisans hailing from the extensive area
rendered distinctive the appellation of the Potteries.*

*There is no mistaking the holiday feeling which is abroad.
Even if it rains - as it frequently did yesterday, and that in no
uncertain manner - while the sphere of enjoyment is
necessarily lessened, the spirits of the people do not appear
to be materially affected.* - Nottingham Evening Post, August
7, 1895

The earl himself was not afraid to engage in a little self-
promotion during the fetes, perhaps to remind the attendees of
who was responsible for their enjoyable day out. In 1893,
"amidst a splendid display of fireworks appeared a colossal
portrait of the Earl of Shrewsbury and Talbot, surmounted by
the coronet and monogram, 'S.T.' and sported by the motto
'Welcome to Alton Towers'." [35]

While the Grand Fetes were still being held as late as 1901, the boom in tourism at Alton Towers was beginning to subside. This was largely driven by the cancellation of the agreement between the railway company and the earl in 1900, which led to a drop in visitors to the estate. In June 1901, the Grantham Journal reported: "The Earl of Shrewsbury and Talbot has determined to close Alton Towers Gardens to the public after the present season. This decision has been arrived at in consequence of the little use to which the right of admission has been put." [36]

The grounds had evidently been reopened to the public by 1907, when "excursionists from the Staffordshire Pottery districts" were still visiting Alton Towers "by the thousands in the summer".[37] By 1910, however, the estate had once again shut its gates to visitors, much to the frustration of local businessmen who relied upon the tourists that it brought to the area.[38]

The loss of business from the railway companies wasn't the only reason behind Alton Towers' decline. The earl's personal problems also played a huge role, and were played out in the newspapers of the time in a manner not entirely dissimilar to present-day celebrity scandals.

The twentieth earl and his countess separated in 1896, although they did not divorce. Instead, the earl continued to keep Ingestre as his main residence, with Lady Shrewsbury permitted to reside at Alton Towers "whenever she might desire". The earl agreed to pay his wife an allowance of £4,000 a year, and to fund the maintenance of the Towers and gardens. The Countess promised in a letter to her husband at the time that "I am willing to live apart from you and not in any way molest you or bring proceedings against you, or attempt to interfere with you, if you will make no public scandal, and if you will in no way molest or interfere with me, and not attempt to force me to cohabit with you."[39]

Despite Lady Shrewsbury's apparent wish to avoid it, "public scandal" was headed her way. In 1903, she claimed, the earl tried to entice her to leave Alton Towers by offering to increase her allowance.[40] When she refused, he unilaterally cut her allowance by £1,000, and – she alleged - allowed the house and surrounding gardens to be neglected. Determined to claim what she felt she was entitled to, the Countess dragged Lord Shrewsbury through the courts, in a blaze of publicity which offered the general public a rare insight into the lives of the social elite.

A large crowd gathered in London's Chancery Court No. 1 to see the earl and his wife take the stand in November 1905.[41] Newspapermen were among them, with the Daily Express reporting: "Beyond a few friends of the litigants it was a somewhat commonplace crowd that packed every vantage point in the fog-dimmed little court. It is not every day that the domestic details of a countess' household are laid bare to the public, or that a countess herself appears as a witness." [42]

During her testimony, the countess "drew a brilliant picture of the Alton Towers of ten years ago. How its magnificent flowerbeds were one of its distinctive features. How it possessed forty guest chambers, and an abundance of plate and linen for the entertainment of the guests. How a staff of twelve gardeners and eight "potters" were employed in the gardens. How there were extensive conservatories, and everything in the house as comfortable as it could be."

She then detailed the present contrast. "In the place of the gardening staff of twenty there are a man and a boy. The forty guest-chambers and the splendid reception rooms are looked after by a caretaker assisted by his wife and daughter. The beautiful flower beds are overrun with grass and weeds."

Alton Towers, said the countess, was "going to rack and ruin".[43]

Lady Shrewsbury herself admitted that she only lived at the Towers for around four months of the year. She was furious when in 1902 she arrived at the estate with her daughter, Lady Viola, and was unable to get in. "My daughter and I drove up and we were told that the Towers was not available. Lady Viola went in by the back door and opened the front entrance for me. The door was banged in my face. I asked the housemaid why she had locked it, and she said she had been ordered to admit no one to the house. There were no preparations for our arrival. The silver and the house linen were locked up. The lamps were not usable. That was the occasion when Lady Viola had to dig potatoes, and get them out herself. We had to break open cupboards to get the things we wanted for our use." The revelation that the daughter of a countess had had to dig her own potatoes was major news at the time. So was the claim that, a year later, she had to break in through a window to gain access to the Towers.

Responding to his wife's allegations, Lord Shrewsbury spent "an uncomfortable morning" in the witness box, not helped by physical discomfort caused by gout ("it was obvious from his constant change of position that he was in pain").[44] On the subject of the potatoes, he was defiant: "I did not know they had gone to Alton. Somebody else could have been got to dig up the potatoes. Plenty of people want work there." [45] He later had to sit and listen as his housekeeper provided precise details of the contents of the house, such as the presence of "177 table napkins and 17 dozen rubbers and dusters". The Countess, meanwhile, "smiling as though she knew her fight was almost won", watched her husband squirm.[46]

The earl's defence – that his wife had voluntarily given up £1,000 of her allowance when it was decided that the couple's son should enter the Home Guards – was rejected. He was ordered to pay the full allowance of £4,000, and to keep Alton Towers in "habitable repair". By this time, though, the fortunes of England's landed gentry were beginning to decline. Court order or not, the house and gardens continued to suffer from a lack of investment.

The earl had seemingly lost all interest in Alton Towers, preferring instead to dabble in commercial enterprises such as his Talbot motor car company. He eventually decided to sell much of the land surrounding the house, and this he did via an auction in 1918. The countess continued to live in the house after the earl's death in 1921 for a further two years, but in 1924 the property was sold to a consortium of local businessmen operating as Alton Towers Limited. Having been in the hands of the Talbot family for almost seven hundred years, the Towers had passed into new ownership.

Alton Towers Limited, run by Charles Cowlishaw, planned to operate the estate as a tourist attraction, and hoped to protect the building itself from housebreakers who had destroyed many other grand properties. The interior had been partially emptied once again, however, with an auction commencing not long after the site was acquired, as directed by the executors of the late earl's will. Although not quite on the same scale as the Great Sale of 1857, it still saw nearly 4,000 lots being sold over a period of eleven days. The Times reported:

The outstanding feature of the forthcoming sale will be the furnishings of the mansion suites - tables, chairs, cupboards, sofas, screens, bureaux, cabinets and so forth, English French and Dutch, a vast quantity of decorative china, decorative objects, and a considerable number of modern books and periodicals. The linen and clothing - among the latter a "Father Christmas dress", furs, etc. - will occupy the whole of one day, and the estate effects, including 1,200 new pheasant-rearing coops, will take up another day, and apparently every movable item in the great mansion will be submitted to the auctioneer's hammer. - The Times, January 12, 1924

Cowlishaw was at least successful in buying a number of items of furniture in the sale, ensuring that they remained at the Towers.

A major shareholder in the company that had acquired Alton Towers was William Stansford Bagshaw, who had also purchased shares for his sons Dennis and Anthony – who were to play a big role in its future. The firm immediately hired gardeners to restore areas that had been in decline for the past two decades, and soon reopened them to the public.

The Towers themselves now stood empty, but the rooms still maintained many of their elegant fixtures and fittings. They provided an impressive setting for a number of cafes, which were installed in the dining room, the "T" room and the music room to serve refreshments to visitors.

The newly-reopened Alton Towers proved to be just as big a magnet for tourists as it had been during the previous century. From the time it reopened until the outbreak of the Second World War, it enjoyed a boom in attendance. While much of this was still supported by the railway, increasing ownership of cars meant that many guests started to arrive by road, too. In August 1931, the Derby Evening Telegraph reported on a "Midlands invasion by road and rail", which saw more than 20,000 visitors descend upon the Towers (10,000 arriving by train). 725 motor cars, 235 motorcycles and 108 charabancs (open-topped vehicles that carried sightseeing groups) were counted on the grounds during the August Bank Holiday Monday.[47] Similar attendance figures were reported in 1934, with 500 cars and 60 coaches (by now rivaling the railways in the tour business) being counted.[48] To cope with the increase in traffic, work had to be carried out on local roads, and the railway station's platforms were extended.[49]

While the Grand Fetes were no more, Alton Towers Limited continued to provide additional entertainment beyond the gardens, which were still the main attraction. This included regular concerts by well-known bands, theatrical performances and motorcycle races around the grounds.

By 1929, Alton Towers was boasting in advertisements that it offered "adequate catering, free parking, grounds for cars and charas, boating and fishing on the lakes and ample shelter in case of inclement weather." The advert quoted Popular Gardening Magazine as saying that "The Gardens are considered one of the most extraordinary combinations of garden scenery with garden building in Europe." [50]

Special events continued to be hosted in the grounds, such as the Womens Institute Pageant that attracted 6,000 spectators and 1,500 participants in June 1928.[51] The women involved put on a performance to show how England was built up over successive ages by different races and civilisations, with ten episodes being acted out that covered a range of events from the time of the Romans to the eighteenth century.

The rail companies began to innovate in the 1930s, when they designed trains suitable for "observation purposes" and began to offer rail "cruises". Starting at urban centres such as Birmingham, Coventry, Nottingham, Sheffield and Stoke-on-Trent, these cruises would wind their way through areas such as the scenic Peak District, travelling at reduced speed past the most beautiful stretches. Passengers would then disembark at Alton Towers, spending a couple of hours there before returning to their home town.[52]

Just as they do today, the owners of the Towers had to invest in new attractions to keep visitors returning year after year. Rather than a thrilling new roller coaster, the big addition in 1933 was an "immense rock garden". Publicity materials at the time promised that "tons of rock, carefully selected for its age, beauty and colour-giving propensities, have been taken from various parts of the Alton grounds in order to convert a natural abyss into a huge and magnificently designed natural scene. Cascades and waterfalls tumble with increasing sparkle over the wonderfully contrasting hues of natural rock. Wonderful rock formations, which have lain hidden for centuries, are now exposed so that all may see them. Rock plants, many of which are rare and which have been collected from the furthest corner of the globe, abound among the boulders. Many stately and beautiful trees shape a background to this magnificent panorama, which cannot fail to delight any lover of nature." [53]

Alton Towers continued to operate until the outbreak of the Second World War, with a 1938 advert promising that "The Towers will be floodlit, and the Gardens and Walks to the Station will be illuminated each Sunday during September", with dancing in the Talbot Gallery every Sunday.

The success of the tourism operation spared the Towers the fate of many other country houses, over four hundred of which were completely destroyed between 1920 and 1955 as the rise of the middle classes reduced the influence of rich landlords.[54] However, while the gardens thrived during the inter-war years, the house itself fell into an increasing state of disrepair.

The contents of the house had already been cleared in the sale of 1924, and there is evidence that the new owners also stripped out oak paneling, doors and even stone from the Towers after taking ownership of the property.[55] The roof – which had leaked in places for many years – continued to cause problems, with flooding damaging rooms on the upper levels.

When Britain entered the Second World War following the invasion of Poland by Germany, the house and its grounds were requisitioned by the army for use by an Officer Cadet Training Unit. Just as it had again become a successful

From country estate to tourist magnet

attraction, the Towers now faced an uncertain future.

Alton Towers, as pictured in Morris's Seats of Noblemen and Gentlemen (1880)

The Pagoda Fountain, as seen today. Image: Natalie Sim

The Garden Conservatory in 2013. Image: Natalie Sim

An advert for Alton Towers in The Times, March 27, 1929

For more images, visit
http://www.themeparktourist.com/tales-from-the-towers/

2. All the fun of the fair

Cadets arriving at Alton Towers to undergo training during the Second World War would typically arrive by train, walking up to the Towers while their bags were transported by a truck. The stunning setting of the estate was to become their home and workplace for a lengthy period, although they were allowed to visit nearby towns and villages. The site of hungover cadets, who had sloped out to the Shrewsbury Hotel or another drinking establishment the previous night, was not uncommon on a Sunday morning.

While parts of the Towers building were in use during the war, the majority of the cadets that were based at the estate were stationed in huts located in an area outside the main building, where Cloud Cuckoo Land stands in today's theme park. The brick-built structures boasted single beds, washing areas and toilets, with hot water and wardrobes being welcome luxuries.[56] Much of the building was simply closed, particularly those areas that were affected by leaky ceilings. However, some of the larger rooms were put to use. The library, for example, was a common room. Fittingly, guns were stored in the armoury, and the chapel was used for its original purpose – hosting religious services.[57]

Other areas of the grounds were used for training purposes, with "jungle" warfare being practiced in the gardens, "river crossings" over the waterways and lakes and an assault course located in the Deer Park. The steep Steps Walk was used for a morning run, to keep the cadets in top physical condition. The pretty lake, previously used for gentle boating activities, was now the setting for assault boat training, ahead of the amphibious landings that would be necessary to liberate mainland Europe from the Nazis. Hungry after their exertions, cadets could grab meals and light refreshments from the Swiss Cottage.[58]

Once their training was completed, the newly-commissioned officers could look forward to a farewell party, at least some of which were hosted in the Music Room. Alton Towers had played its part in preparing men for the very real dangers that awaited them in the fight against fascism.

Following the end of the war in 1945, the army did not immediately hand back Alton Towers to its private owners. Instead, it continued to be used for training purposes for a number of years, and was normally closed to the public.

Occasionally, however, the army did host special events that saw the Towers once again welcoming visitors. One such event, held over the Whitsun weekend in 1946, saw cadets acting as guides and staffing the entrances. Military bands performed concerts, while children could look forward to thrilling rides on assault craft similar to those used in the Rhine crossing on the lake.[59] The small admission charge was donated to the Army Benevolent Fund.

Motor racing events continued to take place at the Towers, pulling in large crowds. These races were not limited to professionals as they would be today – instead, anyone with a suitable motorbike or car could join the line-up.[60] In the case of motorcycle races, participants were typically drawn from the Auto Cycle Union, which had more than 50,000 members by the 1950s.[61]

Over the years since the wartime occupation of the Towers, there has been considerable controversy over who was responsible for the subsequent decline of the building into a near-ruined state. The owners pointed their fingers squarely at the army, with an official guide from the 1970s claiming that

"Before the war, visitors were able to see the inside of the mansion, but this, apart from those parts which house the model railway, the gift shop, a bar and a cafeteria, is unfortunately now in ruins. This was brought about by the fact that the Towers was requisitioned at the beginning of the war and used as an officer cadet training unit. It was not derequisitioned until 1951 - six years after the army had finished with it, and the combined effects of this neglect on top of the rough treatment the building had had throughout the war made it impossible to restore it." [62]

It is undoubtedly true that the army did not hand back the Towers to its owners until some six years after the end of the war. Dennis Bagshaw, one of the major shareholders, negotiated compensation from the Ministry of Defence, but this was claimed to be insufficient to carry out the expensive repairs needed.[63] The materials required would also have been in short supply during the post-war years.

The army, with more pressing matters at hand, did not carry out extensive maintenance on the building during the war. Leaking roofs continued to cause problems, and many rooms were simply abandoned for a period of more than a decade. The cadets, though, lived outside the building, which meant that overuse and "rough treatment" were not likely to have been a problem (although it has been claimed that soldiers machine-gunned one of the estate's conservatories during "one particularly boisterous evening" [64]). The National Monument Record, produced in 1951, features photos of internal areas of the building, showing that many were still in reasonable condition with stained glass and other decorative features still in place.[65]

So how did the house end up in its current state, stripped of almost every internal feature that made it such a spectacle for visitors in years gone by? The simple answer is that the owners saw it as a potential goldmine during a period when many of the materials used to build it – such as lead and copper – were now rare and valuable, having been used up for the war effort. In 1952, they carried out a comprehensive asset-stripping operation that lasted for just three months, tearing out internal features and carting them away in laden-down vehicles to be sold.[66]

First, the lead was stripped from the roofs and sold to recoup the cost of buying the house from the previous owners, the Cowlishaws. This led to widespread flooding, which provided the pretext for what happened next – almost anything that could be removed, was. Thousands of feet of timber, wall coverings, flooring, fireplaces, glass and even plumbing were pulled out and sold. Pugin's magnificent altar screen was destroyed simply to gain access to the oak wainscot behind it.[67] Items that were too heavy or awkward to remove, or of little financial value, were dumped in the east wing of the house and burned where they lay. The house was left without floors or staircases, meaning that most areas would be off-limits to visitors for years to come. In any case, there was very little for them to see other than empty shells and bare walls.

Had the army held on to the property for a little longer, the fate of Alton Towers could have been very different. 1953 saw the passing of the Historic Buildings and Monuments Act, which was designed to provide for "the preservation and acquisition of buildings of outstanding historic or architectural interest and their contents and related property." [68] By the time the act was passed, the "contents and related property" of Alton Towers were beyond rescue, and the house itself was in danger of complete collapse.

Fortunately for the owners, the Towers mansion was not the main attraction for visitors. Stripped of its contents once in 1857, and again in 1924, it was still an impressive building before the 1952 operation, but the real draw was the gardens.

While the army had used areas of these for training, it had also retained a small staff of gardeners throughout the war. The gardens were in much better condition than the house when they were handed back in 1951.

Having been left without a source of income for more than a decade, and with only limited compensation being offered by the Ministry of Defence, the original Alton Towers Limited went into voluntary liquidation. The company formed to replace it – also known as Alton Towers Limited – had a familiar look when it began trading in 1952. The Bagshaw family, which oversaw the asset-stripping process, remained the major shareholders.[69]

Even as they were tearing apart the house, the Bagshaws began the process of hiring gardeners and restoring the grounds. By the summer of 1952, the process was complete and Alton Towers was once again open to the public.[70]

On the first day that it reopened, May 25, 1952, Alton Towers attracted some 5,500 guests.[71] This was an impressive figure, although it was significantly lower than the enormous holiday crowds that descended upon the estate during summers in the 1920s and 1930s. The gardens continued to be popular, but the business-minded owners believed that the key to growing the attendance figures was to install additional attractions. Thus began a process which ended several decades later with the full conversion of the site into a theme park.

Marketing materials from the 1950s continued to focus on the gardens and related outdoor activities, with Alton Towers being billed as "The Rose Garden of England".[72] The still water in front of the Towers was immediately restored to its previous function as a boating lake, and guests could also fish in some areas of the grounds. As they had been during the Grand Fetes and the inter-war years, bands were hired to perform at weekends. Having continued even during the army occupation, motor racing events also remained popular.[73]

Just as they are now, the owners of the property were keen to extract as much cash as possible from guests on top of the modest entrance fee. The Swiss Cottage in the gardens continued to operate and other refreshment outlets were soon established, including a bar and café in the Towers building.

The railway continued to be an important transport link, but private car ownership was now on the rise and an increasing number of guests now made their way to Alton Towers in their own vehicle. The estate's rural location meant that the once-quiet roads surrounding it would now be choked with traffic on busy days, leading to conflicts with local residents that continue to this day.

The first big addition to Alton Towers following the war was also the first permanent ride to be installed on the site. Opened in 1953, the miniature railway served a dual purpose. Firstly, it offered guests pleasant views of the gardens, with its track passing by lakes and rhododendrons. Secondly, it acted as a transportation link across the vast estate, carrying riders from the area that is now Mutiny Bay to the Gothic Prospect Tower in the valley.

Just as theme parks today "borrow" ideas from their competitors, Alton Towers' installation of the miniature railway is likely to have been inspired by the success of similar rides at other stately homes. A miniature railway had been operating at Trentham Gardens, located less than twenty miles away, since 1934, taking guests on a journey alongside the picturesque Trentham Lake. After its closure in 1987, the trains from this line were moved to Alton Towers, where one of them, "The Trentham Flyer", continued to run.

The original locomotive on the Alton Towers railway was acquired from Lilleshall Hall in Shropshire, where it had been operating from 1929 until the outbreak of the Second World War.[74] Costing £400 to build (around £20,000 in today's money), it had been manufactured by the Baguley company of Burton-on-Trent, who built many similar trains for other attractions. At the Towers, the train chugged up and down a shuttle-style circuit (rather than a loop), although the route was to evolve substantially over the following four decades.

Rides on the railway were not included in the admission cost, so a small hut was constructed on each platform to sell single and return tickets. The railway was not run directly by Alton Towers Limited, with the concession being farmed out to other operators instead. It proved to be a very popular addition, and was still prominently promoted in guides for the park well into the 1970s.

The miniature railway survived the transition from pleasure garden to theme park in 1980, becoming just another attraction in Alton Towers' line-up. Its circuit was shortened to make room for the sprawling log flume a year later, but as late as 1993 a second track was built to allow two-train operation using the engine acquired from Trentham. It finally reached the end of the line, though, at the end of the 1996 season, when it was shuttered and never reopened. Parts of the track remained in place until the Haunted Hollow walkthrough was constructed in 2007.

Hidden secret: Take a look at the Mutiny Bay Sales and Information booth. This was once one of the Miniature Railway's stations.

The desolate Towers building was largely deserted throughout the early 1950s, but the owners recognised that it still had the potential to host indoor attractions. These offered the opportunity to further increase revenue and drive attendance. More importantly, they would also give guests something to do when it rained. With the gardens being completely exposed to the elements, a major indoor addition was just what was needed to head off guest dissatisfaction on days of inclement weather.

In 1957, the once-magnificent chapel that had been designed by Pugin as a place of Catholic worship little more than a century earlier became the home of what was billed as the "world's largest" model railway. Such attractions were common at seaside resorts, but Alton Towers sought to build its own on an impressive scale.

As with the miniature railway, guests had to pay a separate admission charge to view the model railway. It was run as an independent business by Aubrey Percy Bentley, who handed it down to his son in 1964.

The 1957 park guide boasted that the layout of the model railway covered some 800 square feet, with 22 locomotives, 105 goods wagons and 33 passenger coaches on show, all electronically controlled.[75] All this had taken nearly three years to build, with Bentley and his father working sixteen hours a day. Thousands of tiny trees were used to line the model's circuits, and real water was employed to create rivers and lakes.

The owner of the model railway continued to expand it, and by 1964 it was: "Truly magnificent in its scope; this railway has everything. 50 engines, hundreds of coaches and goods wagons; an Alpine Village, 3 stations, waterfalls, lake and automatical signals. Boys (and their dads) love it. It is perhaps the most astonishing piece of model railway engineering in the world." [76]

A 1960s guide to the attraction describes the scene inside the chapel: [77]

On entering the building, one is presented with a view extending along the 50 foot length of the layout, showing how each system is planned.

On the first level British Railways are featured, on the next, Italian State Railways, and, on the uppermost level, trains typical of American practice are run.

All the scenic features of the Alton Towers model railway from locomotives and buildings to diminutive people and animals, are to the same scale - 4 millimetres to one foot.

On the lower mountain slopes and the shores of the Talbot Lake is the Alpine village - "Alton-in-the-Alps". The realism and charm of this village is enriched by the model chapel with its tolling bell. A group of Swiss houses and a windmill with its sails slowly turning complete this attractive feature.

Like the miniature railway, the model railway survived for more than a decade after the conversion of Alton Towers into a theme park. By 1993, the then-owners of the Towers – the Tussauds group – were taking a more sympathetic approach to the building. It was decided to restore the chapel, including the ceiling decoration that had been undertaken by Pugin (this was hidden under a false ceiling at the time). The model railway suffered the same fate as many of the previous contents of the Towers – it was dismantled and sold at auction.

Hidden secret: Take a look at the floor in the abandoned chapel. You can get a sense of the scale of the model railway, which has left a permanent outline on the floor.

It is not uncommon for modern theme parks to combine rides and attractions with animal exhibits. Flamingo Land and Chessington World of Adventures in the UK both feature zoos, as do Disney's Animal Kingdom and Busch Gardens Tampa in Florida. The same could be true of Alton Towers, had one of the park's more unusual 1950s additions remained in place.

In 1959, the area of the park close to the Dovecote (near what is now the entrance to Hex) became home to the Alton Towers Zoo. This hosted a variety of exotic species, including chimpanzees, flamingos, bear cubs and a leopard. Footage of the zoo suggests that the animals' accommodation was somewhat basic, with wire fences and cages in place of the naturally-themed, glass-fronted enclosures that are typical of modern zoos.

The park brought in well-known actor Sir Bernard Miles to open its new attraction. The thespian was famous for the catchphrase "It looks good, tastes good...and by jolly it does you good!", which he had coined in an advert for Mackeson stout. Two chimpanzees were pictured in a promotional image for the zoo with Miles, each holding empty Mackeson glasses, suggesting that they had a taste for it, too.

In an embarrassing incident a few years after the zoo opened, its animal inhabitants performed a mass break-out and escaped into the surrounding countryside. Reportedly, all of them were quickly recaptured, with the exception of two rare anteaters.[78]

Perhaps unsurprisingly given this incident, the zoo was a short-lived attraction at Alton Towers. It closed in the early 1960s, and although the park still hosts a handful of species today, it has never again attempted to build a full-blown animal park.

The 1960s saw Alton Towers continue to expand its offerings, adding a number of temporary and fixed attractions that reduced the emphasis on the gardens. In some ways, the site began to evolve into a permanent version of the Grand

Fetes, with a diverse array of entertaining elements designed to appeal to a broad spectrum of the public.

Some of the new additions were similar in style to attractions that can be found at traditional seaside resorts, including pony and donkey rides and a paddling pool, which was originally located in the Ingestre Lake (now home to Battle Galleons) until a dedicated pool was built nearby.

Advertisements, by now being run in national newspapers, continued to focus on the gardens: "Passing through the gates, one enters a different world, a world of terraced walks, lakes, cascades, fountains, caves, grottoes, conservations, a Chinese Pagoda and Temple, extensive woodland and rock walks and breath-taking views at almost every turn." [79] However, an increasing portion of these adverts was given over to additional attractions such as the miniature railway, the boating lake, a stream traction engine museum, an on-site pottery studio and a putting green.

Food and drink were on offer at several outlets, including the Swiss Cottage, the Towers Cafeteria and the new Talbot Cafeteria. The Armoury, which now hosts the queue line for Hex, was converted into an enormous gift shop.

Although its zoo had proven to be a spectacular failure, Alton Towers didn't shy away completely from installing animal exhibits in the 1960s. Towards the end of the decade, the park installed a pool near the main lake. This became home to a trio of playful sea lions, who proved to be very popular with guests. Feeding time was a major fixture, with large crowds forming to watch the mammals gobble down fish. Guests had to be wary of getting too close, though – reputedly, one of the sea lions was fond of spitting at them.[80]

Located on what is now Towers Street, the pool remained in place even after the sea lions finally left the park in 1990, before being filled in several years later.[81] It wasn't the only animal enclosure to be installed after the demise of the zoo, with an aviary and a monkey exhibit also remaining well into the 1970s.[82] A small aquarium, hosting tropical fish, was also opened during the seventies, remaining open until 1994.

By far the most significant addition during the 1960s was the fairground that was located behind the Towers, in the area that now hosts Cloud Cuckoo Land (the temporary structures erected there by the army during the war by now having been torn down). It arrived at the start of the decade, and was primarily run by Brian Collins, whose family were well known funfair operators. Along with a constantly-changing line-up of rides, the fairground also offered games of skill (of the type which can still be found at the park today) and an amusement arcade.

The fairground proved to be an immediate hit, although Alton Towers appears to have been wary of "lowering the tone" for guests who had come to visit the gardens. In a 1961 advert, it boasted: "The Amusement park is a recent addition which is rapidly acquiring popularity, although discreetly situated behind the Towers, completely out of sight of the gardens." [83]

The rides in the fairground were models designed for travelling fairs, so it was easy for its operators to swap them out and bring in new ones. This meant that there would usually be something new for returning visitors to experience, although it also dictated that there would be little in the way of theming, with the rides instead sitting on a largely nondescript patch of land.

There was no flat entry fee, with guests instead paying for each individual attraction. Many of the off-the-shelf rides in the fairground were well-known models designed for families, such as carousels with ornately-crafted horses and bumper cars ("dodgems"). The chair-o-plane (or "waveswinger") offered a virtually identical experience to the Twirling Toadstool that now sits on the same Cloud Cuckoo

Land site, with guests dangling in seats suspended by chains from a rotating central structure. The Peter Pan Railway (which saw individual trains travelling around a basic circuit), and the Happy Caterpillar ride (a caterpillar-themed train that bounced as it moved in a tight circle) rounded out the kids' line-up.

Several of the rides were of a more thrilling nature, and were in fact not too dissimilar to some of the flat rides that operate at Alton Towers today. One of these was the Loop-O-Plane, which operated at the park for several seasons and bears comparison to the modern-day park's Submission (albeit on a smaller scale). Originally developed by Lee Ulrich Eyerly as early as the 1920s, it was conceived as playing a role in the training of pilots. However, when it was demonstrated in public, Eyerly quickly realised that it had far greater potential as an amusement park ride. It consisted of two gondolas attached to arms, which rotated to send guests through a 360 degree loop.[84] Its fearsome appearance and intense ride experience meant that many potential riders were scared off, but it seemingly drew satisfactory crowds at Alton Towers.

One of the rarer rides that enjoyed a stay at the fairground was the Razzle Dazzle, widely regarded as the world's first "white knuckle" attraction after its invention in the early twentieth century. It incorporated both rotational and tilting motion, and was a forerunner to many modern rides. It was often jokingly referred to as a "oncer", as most riders were only willing to brave it a single time. Eventually renamed as the Alpine Tippler (complete with scenes of mountains painted on its boards, in an early example of "theming"), it can now be found in the Hollycombe Collection in Hampshire, and is the only surviving example of its type.[85]

Another ride that was designed to quicken the pulses of those who braved it was the Waltzer, examples of which still operate at many seaside amusement parks and travelling funfairs today. It consisted of a number of individual cars, which rotated independently as they raced around a circular circuit. The undulating floor and the varying weights of the riders meant that the spinning of the cars was not predictable, making every ride slightly different.

Seizing upon the popularity of the fairground, Alton Towers installed its first permanent attraction. The Fun House was located in the building that now hosts the park's 4-D cinema, with its primary attraction being the imposing, vertical Giant Slide. It also featured a large "joy wheel" that was turned by a showman, with guests being challenged to stay standing in it for as long as possible. The Fun House remained in place for over a decade until its eventual conversion into a theatre.

Hidden secret: Take a look at the building that is used to sell the Driving School attraction's on-ride photos. This was once the site of the fairground's Penny Arcade.

Besides the fairground, the other major crowd-pleaser opened during the 1960s was Alton Towers' Aerial Cable Car system, which debuted to much fanfare in May 1963. As with the miniature railway before it, the attraction doubled as both a transportation system and a visually spectacular ride, running along a similar route from what is now Mutiny Bay to the Gothic Prospect Tower. It was the predecessor to today's Skyride, which still provides an important means of whisking guests around the sprawling grounds.

The attraction was installed by Anthony Bagshaw, and manufactured by Chairlifts Ltd., a subsidiary of the British Ropeway engineering company, which also built the cable car ride at now-rival Drayton Manor. As with the other rides at the park, it carried a separate fee. The 430 yard circuit offered some spectacular views, as the park's marketing materials proclaimed: "You are bound to enjoy the thrilling ride over and among the treetops, lakes and woodland glades with

sleigh's brakes, sending them careening into cushioned pads at the base of the chute.

In the same year, a go-kart circuit was also opened at the park, with guests paying a fee to race around it for a few laps. Again, this was used on special event days to host "grand prix"-style championships.

A slightly more educational addition was the Planetarium, which opened in the central courtyard that is enclosed by the Towers. Featuring commentary from Patrick Moore, the renowned astrologer (known to many children of the 1990s as the "GamesMaster" in the Channel 4 television show), it displayed scenes of planets and stars. A flat temporary roof was constructed in part of the derelict House Conservatory to house guests. It was eventually closed in 1987.

While it is now devoid of attractions, the lake in front of the Towers had been in continuous use throughout the estate's time in private ownership. Rowing boats were still available to hire during the 1970s, and a motor boat chugged up and down. Guests could also hire five-seater motor boats of their own on the nearby Ingestre Lake, with "car-type" steering to try and minimise the chance of collisions.[90]

Hidden secret: Take a look at the sculpture located inside the Oblivion ride building. It was partially-made using the projector from the shuttered Planetarium.

After so many decades of neglect and pillage, the seventies also finally saw the first attempts to rescue the Towers themselves. Granted Grade II Listed Building status, the rooms were cleared of tons of rubble that had accumulated over the past two decades. New floors, made of concrete and steel rather than the original timber, were installed so that the public could once again enter the main state rooms.[91]

A plaque was installed reading: "The Restoration of Alton Towers building was commenced in 1975 under the direction of D.S. Bagshaw." Ironically, this was the same Dennis Bagshaw who had overseen the asset-stripping operation in 1952 that had left the Towers so badly in need of a rescue operation.

The gift shop in the Towers' Armoury expanded its line-up to include "ornaments of all sorts, jewellery, china, brass and leather ware, toys and books for the children, postcards, souvenir guides, Kodak films and many other items." Nearby, the 800-seater Talbot Restaurant (now a Burger Kitchen outlet) offered main meals, snacks and hot drinks. The Springfield Restaurant, now Oblivion's shop, was privately-owned by Dennis and Isabel Morris, and was used to host at least one wedding reception.[92]

Sporting events continued to use the estate as an attractive backdrop, particularly motor races. The 1978 RAC Rally's circuit, which began at Birmingham's Civic Centre, took in the West Midlands Safari Park and Trentham Gardens on its way to Alton Towers. Drivers had to navigate 2,000 gruelling miles in total – 5 of them at the Towers.[93]

Late in the preceding decade, the owners had also branched out into offering the first on-site accommodation at the park. A far cry from today's Alton Towers Hotel and Splash Landings Hotel, the International Caravan Park was somewhat basic, but still attracted plenty of tourists.

The Grand Fetes had drawn tens of thousands of visitors to the Towers towards the end of the previous century. 1974 saw the debut of a new series of annual events that did not quite rival the fetes in scale and scope, but still pulled in vast crowds. These were the Mirror Days, "garden parties" promoted in the Daily Mirror Newspaper's gardening section by renowned horticulturalist Xenia Field.

Mirror Days had already been held at other locations, but the first one at Alton Towers on June 16, 1974 proved to be so successful that all of the subsequent ones were held there. Having gained admission for the specially reduced price of 25 pence for adults or 12.5 pence for children, attendees could look forward to a line-up of bands, fancy-dress contests and flower sales.

Ahead of the following year's event, Field was expecting attendance to be high: "Start early - that's my advice if you're coming to our Garden Party at Alton Towers. There is plenty of room but we're anxious to avoid any build-up of traffic." Field herself was on hand to help sell some 6,000 plants, with "a splendid batch of mixed colours and varieties" on offer.[94] The gardening theme extended to the children's fancy dress parade, with kids asked to dress up as a plant of their choice.

Whereas the Grand Fetes had boasted an international line-up of performing artists, there was no mistaking the quirkily British nature of the Mirror Days. This is epitomised by the "wellie-flinging" finals that were the highlight of the 1976 celebrations. More than 25,000 people had entered the Mirror's contest to prove that they could hurl a Wellington boot further than anyone else, with the twenty finalists doing battle in the grounds of the Towers. Some of the entrants had real pedigree, with the husband and wife international hammer and discus throwing pair of Howard and Rosemary Payne among the line-up. The winners could look forward to a £250 continental holiday, with tankards for the male finalists and goblets "for the girls".[95]

The Mirror Days made use of the swathe of new permanent attractions that had been installed during the 1970s, including a competition in the new skateboarding area that opened in 1978 and bobsleigh and go-karting contests the following year. Guests could look forward to a long day, with the gates being open from 8am "until dark". In keeping with the gardening theme, they were asked to wear a flower, with prizes on offer for the best buttonholes.

Celebrity appearances were common, with pop star Scott Fitzgerald, comic Arthur Mullard and football stars Gordon Hill, Howard Kendall and Jimmy Greenhoff among those persuaded to join the festivities.[96] The real stars, though, were the "Supergirls" and "Mirrorbelles" in the beauty pageant, which was billed as the main event.

"The Mirror is looking for a Supergirl. A Supergirl who will become a top model. A girl of the Seventies who will influence our lives and our clothes in the way models Jean Shrimpton and Twiggy did. She'll be our princess, with all the beauty needed to look stunning in clothes. Above all, she will be a girl with that touch of something special that will put success at her fingertips." So screamed the Mirror's advert for its annual contest in 1975 – clearly, political correctness was not high on the paper's agenda during this era, with intelligence not among the judging criteria. Instead, the lucky public could look forward to seeing "gorgeous girls on parade in a paradise setting".[97] The winner would claim £100 prize money and a rose bowl in 1974, but this had doubled to £200 by 1978.

By 1979, the price of admission had almost tripled to 70 pence for adults and 25 pence for children, reflecting the growing roster of attractions. The "Fun Diary" for the day included: [98]

11.00am - Xenia Field's African Violets offer and introduction to Mirror Girl competition
12.15pm - Pushball tournament
12.30pm - Beauty Contest preliminary heats
12.40pm - Chest expander championship
1.15pm - Bobsleigh championship
2.00pm - Children's Fancy Dress contest
2.15pm - Kart Grand Prix

2.30pm - Xenia Field Rose buttonhole contest
3.00pm - Beauty Contest finals

In July 1980, Xenia Field broke the news in her column that the Mirror Days were no more: "I am very sorry that we shall not be able to hold our big day out at Alton Towers this year. The many attractions that have been introduced have made it difficult to accommodate our usual programme. Even though we won't have the pleasure of being with you, I should point out that Alton Towers will still have plenty to offer." [99]

Indeed, Alton Towers did have plenty new to offer in 1980. Driven by the efforts of a controversial entrepreneur, the estate now boasted a flat entry fee that covered all of its attractions, and an iconic new ride was pulling in vast numbers of guests. The theme park era had begun.

The Miniature Railway in action.
Image: Matthew Wells

The model railway was a popular fixture in the chapel.
Image: Matthew Wells

The original Cable Car attraction.
Image: Nick Laister Collection / joylandbooks.com

The Chair-o-Plane ride thrills guests in the fairground.
Image: Nick Laister Collection / joylandbooks.com

For more images, visit
http://www.themeparktourist.com/tales-from-the-towers/

3. The stately home that's anything but stately

One man was the driving force behind the conversion of the quiet, sedate Alton Towers of the post-war years into a thriving theme park packed with thrill rides. That man was John Broome, a flashy, ambitious property developer who would go on to have an extraordinary career in the leisure industry marked by lofty highs and disastrous lows.

Born in 1943, Broome was the son of a former Oldham Athletic footballer who eventually became the headmaster and owner of a preparatory school near Chester. His father packed him off to a private boarding school near Fleetwood, and at an early age he began to show the entrepreneurial spirit and willingness to take huge financial risks that lay behind his future successes and failures.

Aged just 16, Broome attended a public auction for a detached house. Despite possessing meagre savings of just £122 in his Post Office account, he lodged the winning bid of £2,200. His parents were presented with the bill for a house that they did not even know existed. While a publicity handout later claimed that "the beating he received taught him the folly of approaching business with a cavalier attitude", Broome himself said of the incident "I don't think my father and mother were angry, merely dismayed. It was more a case of 'They've got a right one here'." [100] Unlike some of the leaps of faith he made later in life, the gamble paid off. The young property developer converted the house into three flatlets and let them out, paying back his parents within two years.[101]

After completing his studies, Broome joined the staff at his father's school, teaching geography, history and economics. He still had ambitions in the property market, however, and continued to buy and convert properties himself. "Between the ages of 19 to 23 everyone thought there was something wrong with me," Broome said in a 1982 interview. "While other lads were having a roaring time, I never went out. I completely cut myself off. After teaching I'd get home, snatch tea, and work on converting property. I did it all myself - plumbing, electrics, painting. After five years of this, I decided writing homework on the blackboard while thinking of my next deal was not a good mix." [102]

By the time he entered his thirties, Broome had built up a multi-million pound fortune on the back of his property exploits. As well as buying Stretton Hall in Cheshire as a luxury home, he acquired a fleet of expensive vehicles including a Rolls-Royce Corniche, a BMW, a Mercedes Estate, a Range Rover and a £500,000, seven-seater helicopter which he used "as nonchalantly as a bus."[103] He was prone to ostentatious displays of wealth, such as buying the first car phone in Chester and hiring a personal pilot for his chopper.[104]

While he enjoyed his success and the cash that came with it, Broome was not one to rest on his laurels: "Retire? Yes of course I could. But what would that make me? A big fat hippo incapable of doing anything. Wealth does not come into it. I want the excitement of business, of employing people, and of building something that will outlast me." [105]

In 1973, Broome married Jane Bagshaw, daughter of the then-owner of Alton Towers, Dennis. At the time, his father-in-law was juggling a day-job as an estate agent with his management duties. While large numbers of visitors were being drawn to the gardens and a handful of other attractions, Broome felt that the potential of the business was not being fully tapped, describing it as a "middle of the road leisure op".[106]

"Stately homes were not professional leisure operations" in those days, according to Broome. "They opened for secondary reasons such as cash flow, tax advantages and to obtain grants. At stately homes you see small children traipsing around with middle-aged parents." He was equally dismissive of rival attractions: "Teenagers go alone to arcades, and safari parks do not have 'repeat' business. Once a family has had monkeys sitting on their car bonnets, market research shows they do not return a second time." He was determined to offer a "complete day out for the family".[107]

Initially, Broome's involvement in the family business was limited. He purchased a trackless train with four coaches for £25,000, and obtained a concession to run it in the park's grounds. Over the next few years, he gradually bought up other concessions, including those for the fairground, cable cars and miniature railway.[108] By the end of the decade, he had dropped his involvement in local politics to focus on Alton Towers, and had been appointed as its chairman.[109]

Walt Disney had established the concept of the theme park in 1955 with the opening of Disneyland in California. While many had questioned the wisdom of spending vast sums of money on what was initially viewed as little more than a funfair, Disney had proved them wrong. The park had turned around the fortunes of the struggling company, and a second theme park, the Magic Kingdom, opened in Florida in 1971. Other companies soon tried to copy Disney's template, and America developed a thriving theme park market. Despite this, by the 1970s Britain had yet to follow suit, with rides being largely restricted to seaside resorts and travelling funfairs – partly due to car ownership and road infrastructure in Britain lagging behind the US.

Broome, a fan of American ideas, spotted the opportunity, and travelled to the United States and other countries to analyse the parks' operations and business models. He became convinced that he could convert Alton Towers into the UK's first theme park, and make a fortune in the process. In his words, he wanted to turn it into "the stately home that's anything but stately". Many dismissed the idea as unrealistic, but local journalist John Abberley recalls of a meeting in the late 1970s that "there was something in his manner which suggested that he knew where he was going with Alton Towers." [110]

Having formulated his plans and secured financing, Broome decided that 1980 was to be Alton Towers' first year as a theme park. He closed the fairground, with its travelling rides being left in place initially behind a boarded fence. Only the permanent attractions – the Fun House, the Penny Arcade and the Astroglide, remained in operation. The rest were eventually moved to other locations, with the Waltzer finding a home on Clacton Pier and the Water Chute being installed at Southport's Pleasureland. [111]

Broome also shuttered 30 of Alton Towers' bars – a major source of income – on a "hunch". Alcohol was now restricted to a few high-end restaurants. He later said of the move: "I don't drink much, but that did not affect my decision. Nor was rowdiness the cause, but rather the hundreds of disappearing dads. Fathers would bring the families, and then slip off to the bars. Alton, I decided, is fun for all the family - and that includes dads. I believe that an entertainment place for a family should mean a child of two being able to wander around in complete safety. If not, the place will falter in the end." [112]

The biggest change was to the park's entrance fee, which rose to £2.50 for adults and children alike. However, rather than guests having to pay for each attraction individually, all of them were now included in the single, flat price. While Disney had introduced a similar system of "unlimited use" tickets in the late seventies as it prepared to open Epcot at Walt Disney World, the concept was a revelation in England. "You can budget for a day," Broome said, "and ride as many times as you like."

To headline the new venture, Broome needed a major attraction that could spearhead the park's marketing campaign and stand out as being unique within the UK. Disney had established the concept of an E-Ticket attraction (one that, before unlimited use tickets were introduced, would cost more to ride than others), but building the kind of custom, vastly expensive dark rides that dominated the Disneyland line-up was not a viable option for a start-up theme park in the Staffordshire countryside. Nor was the park's budget likely to stretch to cover the impressive theming that surrounded Disney's roller coasters, such as the Matterhorn Bobsleds and Space Mountain.

Instead, Broome was looking for a ride that he could lease, rather than purchase. This ruled out the custom-designed coasters that were being produced by firms such as Arrow Development for Disney and its competitors in the US. He had also identified a site not far from the old fairground (in the area now known as the Dark Forest) where the attraction could be situated, and this was limited in size. The ride would have to fit into its not-too-spacious footprint.[113]

Broome turned to Dutch firm Vekoma. Founded as a manufacturer of agricultural and mining machinery in 1926, it was by now producing "off-the-shelf" amusement park rides for the travelling funfair circuit in Europe. In the late 1970s, it was making its first tentative steps into the roller coaster market, with the double-looping MK-1200, better known as the Corkscrew. Designed to be put together and taken down quickly, it was also of a relatively compact design.

The first Corkscrew roller coaster had debuted at Knott's Berry Farm, not far from Disneyland, in 1975. Built by Arrow Development, it is widely credited as being the first modern roller coaster to feature an inversion. In fact, it featured two, in the form of the signature "corkscrew" element. Vekoma's ride was very similar, adapting Arrow's design to meet the needs of travelling showmen.

Alan Brown, working for Broome as Alton Towers' General Manager at the time, travelled to Vekoma's factory in Vlodrop, Holland. There, the first prototype of the Corkscrew was waiting for him in the yard. "It hadn't been painted, so it was all rusty and looking rather terrible." Still, Brown was satisfied by the experience on offer: "It was quite a thrilling ride, for those days." [114]

In 1979, Broome persuaded a group of German financiers to fund the installation of a Corkscrew model at Alton Towers, at a cost of £1.25 million. Work to prepare the site began three days before Christmas, with the aim of getting the ride open in time for the start of the park's first season as a theme park in April 1980. The coaster itself arrived in pieces in dozens of containers shipped from Holland, and construction was completed in time for the busy Easter holidays.

Broome was determined to make a big splash with the Corkscrew, and Alton Towers billed it as "Europe's first double-looping roller coaster". This wasn't strictly true: Vekoma had already sold an identical model to German duo Oskar Bruch and Fritz Kinzler, which had operated at the Annakirmes fair in Düren, Germany in August 1979 before being sold to Traumlandpark. Another version of the ride, dubbed Tornado, was also installed at Walibi in Belgium in 1979. Meanwhile, nearby Blackpool Pleasure Beach had been inverting riders twice on its Revolution roller coaster for a year before the Corkscrew opened – although, technically speaking, they passed through the same loop twice, in forwards and backwards directions. Broome could, though, justifiably claim that the Corkscrew was the first ride of its type in the UK.

Ahead of the ride's debut, a crew from the BBC's *Nationwide* programme, which covered news and current affairs, visited the park to try out the Corkscrew. A dispatch rider on a motorcycle was on hand to whisk the footage off to the studio in London. He made it just in time for the Corkscrew to feature on the show, which was broadcast directly after the evening news – a prime slot. The sight of riders spiralling upside down on the new coaster helped hugely to raise awareness of Alton Towers' new status as a theme park, and further television appearances followed.

April 4, 1980, the opening day for the Corkscrew, was a red-letter day for Alton Towers and its ambitious chairman. It was Good Friday, and holidaymakers were ready to celebrate with a ride on the UK's newest roller coaster.

Les Davies, the former Alton Towers archivist, remembers: "People were trying to climb over the fences and demanding to be let in. One car left, and another one would be let in. It was unbelievable. There was something like a 6 to 9 hour queue just for the Corkscrew. The roads were completely blocked back to Derby and Stoke. The police were ringing up saying they had shut the M6 and the M1. We closed about 1 o'clock, we'd estimated 40,000 [visitors in the park] with people still outside."

The chaos continued throughout the Easter weekend. "On the Bank Holiday Monday we had to close the gates, because we had that many people trying to get here to see the Corkscrew," remembers Brown. "We just couldn't cope with them." The Corkscrew's popularity showed no signs of dwindling during its first season, when queues as long as five or six hours to ride it were commonplace.

The impact on attendance at the park was immediate. "We went from just over 500,000 a year in the 1970s to just over 1 million in 1980, so we'd more than doubled the numbers of people coming to the park just by putting the Corkscrew in," says Brown. "It brought the leisure industry to the forefront in the UK." [115] Of course, those people were now paying more to get into the park, under the new unlimited ride ticket scheme.

Awaiting this flood of guests was a roller coaster that would seem relatively tame by today's standards, but was completely new – and rather intimidating – for the UK public of 1980. After boarding the train and pulling down the over-the-shoulder restraints, riders were carried to the top of a 75-foot lift hill. As they rounded a bend at the top, they were treated to stunning views of Alton village and beyond. Most, though, were pre-occupied with anticipation of the 68-foot first drop that awaited them. Plunging to the bottom of this, the train reached a top speed of 44 miles per hour, before racing around a helix and into the signature double corkscrew element. The remainder of the course was nondescript, with several further turns and helices before it pulled back into the station.

Riding the Corkscrew became a point of pride for thrill-seekers, who wore the experience like a badge of honour. Among the crowds on the opening day was Andy Hine, then aged 13, who went on to found the Roller Coaster Club of Great Britain and to receive an MBE for services to tourism. He recalls: "I was absolutely desperate to be there when it opened because I'd never been upside down before."[116] Broome himself was relieved: "We're very lucky to be able to open it as they are very much in demand now." Indeed, an identical ride would open at Yorkshire's Flamingo Land three years later, though it would never carry the same cachet.

Many riders recall the Corkscrew's loud chain-lift, which could be heard from some distance away due to the motor being located at the top of the lift hill. Even children who were too small to ride it would watch in awe as the train raced through the corkscrew. Phil Steadman remembers: "We used to be taken to Alton Towers as kids if we hadn't been good enough to go to Blackpool. Imagine my parent's shock when we turned up in 1980 to find the Corkscrew installed. A mild punishment suddenly became an absolute treat."

"It's difficult to explain to people now just how incredible the Corkscrew was back then. There were very few coasters actually around in the UK, and most of them had been around for a long time sitting in seaside resorts. Compared to everything else, Corkscrew was enormous, it was intimidating - it was a metal monstrosity needing to be conquered. We'd never seen anything like it, and certainly never ridden on anything which could come close to comparison."

"I still remember the feelings from that first ride - for many years I would tell the tale. The drop was surely vertical (as vertical to me as a seven-year-old as Oblivion actually is today), the loops made you feel like an astronaut and the twists pinned you into your seat like a racing driver. The ride was over before my stomach had caught up with me off the first drop."

"Coming into the station, both of us cried out wanting to go again - my Dad was struggling to stand. He'd gone a funny kind of grey/green colour and couldn't stop shaking. It was the last coaster he ever rode. He was proud to have got his certificate for riding (everyone coming off the ride was issued a certificate), but happy to leave it at that."

Humans weren't the only creatures to enjoy riding the Corkscrew. One ride operator from its later years recalls regularly strapping in the large cuddly toys that could be won from nearby games stalls, and sending them around for a spin.[117]

The image of the Corkscrew became part of popular culture, with a digitally rotoscoped version featuring in the opening title sequence for ITV's *Top of the Pops* rival, *The Chart Show*. An image of a train midway through the double corkscrew was used as the cover art for dance act The Prodigy's *Everybody in the Place*.

The Corkscrew remained in place for some 28 years, with the only minor change being a slight "retheme" to fit in with the surrounding prehistoric Ug Land area when it was introduced in 1999. In total, it carried over 43 million guests around its circuit before finally being shuttered in 2008.

By then, it had gained a reputation for being extremely rough, with guests banging their heads against its uncomfortable restraints. John Wardley, who helped design its replacement, recalls: "When the Corkscrew was first put in by John Broome, it was seen as the ultimate terror machine, a real challenge to ride. It no longer was that. Research indicated that although there was a lot of nostalgic value to the old Corkscrew, it was not up there with the top rides any longer. It was still in excellent condition, but it was time for the ride to go into retirement." [118]

Not everybody agreed. A day before the Corkscrew's final day of operation, roller coaster enthusiast Simon Rogers, a painter and decorator from Brighton, used handcuffs and chains to attach himself to the ride. The 26-year-old told staff that he first rode the coaster when he was 10-years-old, and had since been on it more than 200 times. Bolt cutters were used to remove him from the area, although staff decided not to call the police as they "felt sorry for him". He was adorned with a "Save the Corkscrew" t-shirt, but the plea was in vain.[119]

Some parts of the coaster were sold, with a carriage from one of its trains fetching £7,300 on the auction website eBay.[120] The buyer, John Taylor, intended to display it as a garden feature. The remainder of the trains were moved to Heide Park in Germany, which shared an owner with Alton Towers by this time. They are still in use on the Big Loop, the park's own version of the Corkscrew.

Alton Towers, though, did keep hold of one piece of its first major ride. The famous corkscrew element – repainted purple on the orders of local planning authorities – was installed as a monument in front of the park's entrance, where some confused guests initially mistook it for a new ride as they arrived on the monorail.

The Corkscrew was the big draw for Alton Towers' debut season as a theme park. The park, though, needed more rides and attractions to entertain the flood of new visitors, and several other additions were made alongside the roller coaster.

The most enduring of these was the Pirate Ship, which remains at the park today, where it is now known as the Blade. The attraction was manufactured by HUSS in Germany, and like the Corkscrew, was designed for travelling funfairs. Despite occupying a footprint of 275 square metres, it is capable of being packed onto two 40 foot trailers and shipped from place-to-place. Up to 45 riders can pack into its ship-themed gondola, which swings from end-to-end, reaching a maximum height of 57 feet.

HUSS Pirate Boat rides are commonplace at theme parks these days, with the company having sold more than 90 of them. However, while other manufacturers had produced similar rides, HUSS had only introduced its own in 1978. Like the Corkscrew, then, it had considerable novelty value when it arrived at Alton Towers. The site of the swinging ship close to the park's then-entrance was an impressive one.

Nearby was Cine 2000, one of the dome-shaped "immersive" cinemas that were popular at amusement parks during the 1980s. Standing up, guests would watch 12 minutes of first-person footage of roller coasters, motor vehicles, helicopters and other fast-paced action being projected onto the dome's interior. Designed to make viewers feel as though they were "part of the action", it also had the unfortunate side effect of causing many of them to lose their balance and fall over. They'd have to be careful not to land in a puddle of vomit, as nausea was also not uncommon.

Next to the Alpine Bobsleigh, guests could step back in time by entering Dinosaur Land (which had opened in 1979).[121] Here, they would come face-to-face with models of prehistoric creatures, including woolly mammoths and triceratops, ready – as the park put it – "to frighten the life out of you".[122] Also housed inside the area, which resembled a wooden fort, was a man dressed in a T-Rex suit who would jump out and surprise unsuspecting guests.

If they survived their encounter with the fearsome T-Rex, visitors could next put their putting skills to the test on the miniature golf course. Featuring the usual array of crazy golf elements such as windmills and tunnels, it could keep parents occupied while their kids joined the lengthy Corkscrew queue for another turn.

Live animals were also part of the burgeoning theme park's line-up. Housed inside a yellow, circus-style tent, the Parrot Show featured the feathered performers riding bicycles, squawking out words and counting to ten.

Having achieved stunning success in 1980, Alton Towers could not afford to rest on its laurels. Broome and his management team recognised the need to maintain the momentum with another big addition in 1981. They also desperately needed to increase capacity, so that frustrated guests wouldn't simply spend most of their day waiting in line for the Corkscrew or the handful of other rides that were on offer. Their solution was to add three major rides, each of which could handle significant numbers of guests, along with a new show.

The park had spent £1.25 million on the Corkscrew. It splurged almost double that - £2.25 million – on its next headline attraction. Like the Corkscrew, The Log Flume would use a standard ride system, in this case from German firm Mack Rides. However, it would feature a custom circuit that would become the longest in the world at 886 metres (2,907 feet), providing Alton Towers with a perfect tagline for its advertising. Construction, though, was much more complicated than it was for the Corkscrew, as reflected in the much higher price tag.

The record was achieved by winding the log flume's circuit through woodland close to the gardens, meaning that for much of the trip guests would have little to look at (this was rectified in 1984, when the dinosaurs relocated from their existing home and took up residence alongside the flume). Floating along in 5-seater boats, they would already have plummeted down one short drop before entering the woods. A second drop was housed inside a pitch-black tunnel, while the final 85 foot drop was designed to leave them soaked.

Despite the frequently cold and damp weather in the UK, the Log Flume proved to be enduringly popular and is still in place today, albeit with a "bath tub" theme that was added as part of a sponsorship deal with Imperial Leather in 2004.

In those early days, the park looked very different to how it does now. It was divided into "Centres" – Ingestre Centre,

Springfield Centre, the Talbot Centre, the Towers Complex and the Gardens. Guests arriving by car could enter via roads passing the Pirate Ship or the sea lions and park in one of several car parks that are much closer to the attractions than today's sprawling lots.

In Ingestre Centre, they would find the new Log Flume, along with the Aquarium that had been in place since the seventies. After viewing the Parrot Show, they could hop onto the Miniature Railway or the Cable Cars to take a trip over to the Gothic Prospect Tower in the Gardens. There, they could take a look at the resident craftsmen in action in the Pottery, or grab a bite at the Swiss Cottage restaurant.

Headlining the Springfield Centre area (located where X-Sector currently stands) was the towering Pirate Ship, which sat in front of the domed Cine 2000. After battling with the ineffective hand-brakes on the Alpine Bobsleigh sleds, they could wander through Dinosaur Land and play a round of Miniature Golf. Before dining at the Springfield Restaurant, they could pay 10 pence to propel a football around a maze using a water cannon.

The Towers Complex itself was home to the Planetarium, the Astroglide slides and the Model Railway in the chapel. The Towers Express land train, which had been operating since the seventies, took guests on a tour from the coach park, around the Towers and alongside the lake. When they returned, they could take a look around the new Victorian Dolls Museum, which housed "England's largest private collection of antique dolls and toys".[123]

On the main boating lake, rowing boats were still operating just as they had been for most of the last hundred years. On the nearby Ingestre Lake the motor boats - now known as the "Splash Cats" - could be taken for a spin. After a quick splash around in the paddling pool, kids could see (and smell) the sea lions in their enclosure.

The Talbot Centre, close to the Towers on the site of the current Dark Forest, was home to the mighty Corkscrew. In 1981, the pressure on the coaster was alleviated by the addition of no fewer than three new attractions including the Doom and Sons haunted house, the Around the World in 80 Days boat ride and the Fantastic Fountains show. Completing the line-up were the fairground's old Penny Arcade and adventure playground.

Like the Log Flume, Around the World in 80 Days was a custom-built creation. Clearly inspired by Walt Disney's It's a Small World (which had been built for the 1964 New York World's Fair and then shipped to Disneyland), it saw riders boarding boats before floating through scenes depicting various different countries. Mercifully, it didn't include the Disney ride's notorious cutesy soundtrack, but each country did have its own backing song. Among the locations included in the line-up - designed by Keith Sparks' Sparks Creative Services - were Burma, Egypt, New York, Venice, Greenland, Las Vegas, Vienna, Holland, Rio, Paris and London. One of the London scenes was set in Battersea – a place that, strangely, would play a key role in the long-term future of Alton Towers.

While it was somewhat derivative, Around the World in 80 Days' detailed scenes were impressive to a UK audience that had mostly yet to be exposed to Disney's creations. Its popularity was helped two years later, when the cartoon series *Around the World with Willy Fog* made its television debut, exposing a new generation to the Jules Verne story. Among the ride's most memorable effects were waterfalls that turned off just before the boat passed underneath them (again borrowed from a Disney ride, this time the Jungle Cruise), a menacing monster that terrified smaller children and set of can-can dancers. Kids who were tempted to splash the models with water could look forward to being marched through the backstage areas and reprimanded.

The rides and attractions at Alton Towers were now grouped into areas, but none of these featured any significant theming. That was to change in 1982, when the park introduced Talbot Street, a Victorian-style street where guests could enjoy "a relaxed Dickensian atmosphere". Incorporating several of the attractions from the Talbot Centre (though not the Corkscrew, which would hardly have fitted with the Victoriana theme), it boasted a cheerful soundtrack piped from a traditional organ located underneath the Towers.[124]

At the end of Talbot Street sat Adventureland 4-11, an area dedicated to the park's younger guests. There, they could take a trip past cardboard cut-outs of cartoon characters on the Adventure Railway, take a spin on a motorbike or truck on the Blue Carousel, slide down the Astroglide or try out the not-too-scary Mini Apple roller coaster.

By April 1982, The Times was reporting on "a race to seize a newly-emerging market in Britain for Disneyland-style theme parks", with "John Broome, a teacher from Chester turned property tycoon, as the forerunner". Broome was proudly boasting that the £12.5 million splurged on the park so far was paying off, with a 30 percent return on capital employed.[125]

Alton Towers attracted 1.6 million visitors in 1983, and Broome hoped to boost that figure to 2 million in 1984 by spending a further £5 million on no fewer than six new rides. Five of these would be off-the-shelf flat rides, but one was designed to have a similar impact to the Corkscrew four years earlier.

During the winter of 1983/84, the prehistoric inhabitants of Dinosaur Land were cleared off their hill in Springfield Centre and moved into the woodland surrounding the Log Flume. Construction crews moved into the site, excavating a quarter of a million tons of soil and creating an enormous hole that covered an area the size of a football pitch. They were paving the way for the introduction of the Black Hole, a £2 million roller coaster that would dominate Alton Towers' marketing campaign for the following season.

The roller coaster itself was installed on the site first, while the park was closed to the public. It was then enclosed in an enormous green and yellow tent, lending it an air of mystery. Most people arriving for its debut in April 1984 had little idea of what lay in store for them.

Keen to build on the growing excitement about its latest addition, Alton Towers began to market it as the UK's equivalent of Space Mountain at Walt Disney World's Magic Kingdom, which it would resemble both in its space travel theme and its enclosed location. Some of the reporting ahead of its opening day was wildly inaccurate, with the Staffordshire Sentinel claiming that it would be "the biggest ride of its kind in the world" (it wasn't) and that it would "cater for an extra 8,000 people an hour, reducing the high season queues" (in reality, the Black Hole had a capacity of around 900 riders per hour, leading to lengthy queues and long wait times).[126] Adverts for the ride showed a train looping upside down as it passed through an asteroid field, and publicity materials promised that riders would "ride a laser beam while beset by asteroids and other space phenomena", plunging down a 70 foot drop in the process.[127]

The reality was somewhat less spectacular. Disney's Space Mountain had been a custom "wild mouse"-style coaster packed with high-tech special effects, built at a cost of $15-20 million in 1975. The Black Hole, meanwhile, was an off-the-shelf Jet Star II model designed by Anton Schwarzkopf, identical to existing coasters at several other parks (the first was built in 1974). Again, Broome had saved money by buying a standard design, although its enclosure in the tent undoubtedly transformed the ride experience.

After queuing through the tent's darkened interior, riders boarded single-car trains in the loading station. Those with "fragile health" were warned not to ride (Disney had been plagued by lawsuits from injured riders who claimed not to have understood the nature of Space Mountain), while there was a discreet exit for those who changed their minds at the last minute.

The trains were pulled up a spiralling lift hill towards a model of a spaceman, before plunging down the 27 foot first drop (70 foot having been another spurious marketing claim – but who could tell in the dark?). They then raced through a series of short drops, tight corners and helices before hitting the final brake run. What would have been a relatively tame roller coaster mutated in the pitch black surroundings to become something much more menacing, with guests unable to anticipate the twists and turns. The only lighting came from the few stars and nebulae that comprised the "special effects". The "laser beam" actually consisted of some red strip lights mounted in line with the track.

Brian T. Jones recalls: "I don't think any coaster after the Black Hole created the same sense of buzz around the school-yard - you were nobody until you rode the Black Hole and proudly showed off your on-ride photo at school. In 1984 it was the Nemesis/Oblivion of its day, but back then, steel coasters were still new so it had a far greater impact on visitors than the later grand rides. And the fact that it was all hidden in the dark only added to its sense of menace."

"The first ride on Black Hole as a youth was like nothing else I'd ever experienced and those few seconds as the darkness turned pitch, the spiral lift flattened out and you waited for the drop were equal to the pre-drop moment on Oblivion back then." [128]

Another rider remembers: "It was a big deal at the time. The only rides in the area were the Pirate Ship, Cine 2000 and the fantastic Alpine Bobsleigh. So to walk into the area and see this massive tent appear, hear the deep low rumble of the ride and listen to the riders muffled screams was just so exciting!"

"The first thing you saw was a large sign warning of the dangers to those with heart conditions, weak backs etc. These were probably the first major warning signs for any ride on the park and made the upcoming experience seem even more scary. There were no real special effects, just a single spaceman within the spiral lift hill who seemed to be impossibly high up. We climbed the spiral watching the spaceman get closer and closer until we were actually above it. This gave you a sense that you were very high and you knew the drop hill was approaching. The smell at the top of the hill was also something I remember - stale, clean and cold." [129]

The result was exactly what Broome had hoped for – more than 2 million people visited Alton Towers during the 1984 season, leaving it ranked second only to the Tower of London in the UK leisure industry.[130] It also turned a £3 million profit – money that could be ploughed back into further investments aimed at doubling attendance over the following five years.

At the end of the 1987 season, The Black Hole was completely dismantled, subsequently returning as The Black Hole II. Though there was now an "exciting pre-show of stunning special effects", the ride layout was identical and the on-ride effects were similar.[131] However, the coaster was now capable of carrying two-car trains to improve its capacity - though this would remain woefully limited. The striking green and yellow exterior – a strange fit for a space-themed ride – was converted to a more fitting black and silver when the X-Sector area was created in 1998.

By 2004, the Black Hole had reached the end of the line. It was shuttered for the 2005 season, and the track was eventually dismantled and removed in 2007. The tent remained in place until 2012, seeing occasional use as a home for Halloween "horror mazes".

Nostalgic coaster fans can still ride the Black Hole in its new guise as "The Rocket" at Sweden's Furuvik. They'll have to imagine the special effects, though – the newly-repainted red-and-blue track is now located outdoors.

The years surrounding the opening of the Black Hole saw a rapid expansion of Alton Towers' ride line-up, with Broome investing millions to shore up the park's position at the top of the UK theme park industry. Most of the new arrivals were standard flat rides, which could be purchased and installed with a minimum of effort.

With the debut of the space-themed roller coaster in 1984, the park saw fit to rename its existing areas with exotic monikers that were more in keeping with a modern-day theme park. The Talbot Centre was renamed as Festival Park, the Springfield Centre became Fantasy World, while the Ingestre Centre and the lakes were absorbed into Aqualand. Only Talbot Street and the Towers themselves retained their previous titles.

Festival Park, which incorporated the Corkscrew, became the focal point for thrill-seekers. Much like the fairground of years gone by, its line-up changed frequently, with the park able to swap out the flat rides that dominated the area quickly and easily. With the Cable Cars and Miniature Railway only running as far as the gardens, new land trains – the Sunliners – were introduced to carry guests to the far-flung corner of the property from the entrance.

The Dragon roller coaster was the first to arrive, providing a tamer alternative for kids who were too small to ride the Corkscrew. It was followed in 1984 by Enterprise, the Wave Swinger and the Magic Carpet, with the Ferris Wheel and

1001 Nights arriving a year later. Two of these rides – Enterprise and the Wave Swinger – remain at the park today, albeit in new locations. The Wave Swinger is now named Twirling Toadstool and sits in Cloud Cuckoo Land, offering a classic "chair-o-plane" experience. Enterprise, meanwhile, retains its original name and sits alongside Oblivion in X-Sector.

The National Fairground Archive records that Enterprise was a ride born out of the intense rivalry between German manufacturers Schwarzkopf (who had designed the Black Hole) and HUSS (who had produced the Pirate Ship).[132] During the late seventies, this rivalry reached its peak, with the two firms trying to outdo each other by producing increasingly enormous rides that were too unwieldy to be used on the UK's travelling funfair circuit. They were, however, viable options for "static" theme parks such as Alton Towers.

The Enterprise had its roots in the Skylab ride that was developed by Dutch firm Bakker in the 1960s. Riders on this contraption sat in one of fourteen cars, arranged in a circular fashion like a merry-go-round. These span rapidly as the carousel was slowly raised into a vertical position. Though they were spinning upside down, riders were held in place by a powerful centrifugal force.

Anton Schwarzkopf produced his own, much larger version of the ride in 1973, standing at some 18 metres tall. The Enterprise name was derived from its appearance, with the cars being designed to resemble the Starship Enterprise of *Star Trek* fame. Seeing its growing popularity, HUSS launched its version of the Enterprise in 1975, featuring 20 two-seater cars with the now-familiar sliding door mechanism. Alton Towers acquired one of these, and not the much larger Skylab model that stood at an incredible 30 metres tall.

An example of the rapid, almost chaotic fashion of the expansion of Festival Park's roster of attractions is the addition of the Magic Carpet in 1984. A common fixture at travelling funfairs, the ride saw guests boarding a carpet-themed gondola which was lifted into the air by four arms with weights on each end.

The following season, the park installed 1001 Nights close to the Magic Carpet. The exciting new addition was...a magic carpet ride. Granted, it was larger than the existing one, but it still offered almost exactly the same ride experience. Perhaps realising its mistake, Alton Towers removed the Magic Carpet at the end of the 1985 season, leaving 1001 Nights to whisk guests above the treeline (in a rare break with planning regulations) until 1994.

The Festival Park line-up was rounded-out by the addition of Spider, a classic spinning flat ride, in 1986. Alongside its array of thrill rides, the area also hosted the Rupert Bear Magic Show (an ill-fitting carry-over from the former Talbot Centre) and, bizarrely, a wildlife museum.

Despite it lacking any real theming, many visitors from its heyday remember Festival Park fondly. One recalls: "Festival Park is THE area to beat all at Alton Towers. From Talbot Centre the area developed into Festival Park, and this is something that to this day I judge Alton Towers on. I'm not getting into the whole mathematics of it all, but I recall you could easily spend a few hours there." [133] The park's relative lack of flat rides these days is in stark contrast to the mid-1980s, when it was packed full of them.

Next to Festival Park, Talbot Street continued to host Doom and Sons, Around the World in 80 Days and Adventureland 4-11, along with a museum dedicated to British science-fiction series *Space 1999* and the puppets and models of *Thunderbirds*. The emphasis, though, was on dining and shopping at "authentic" Dickensian outlets such as the Talbot

Ice Cream Parlour, the Talbot Tea Shoppe, a photographic studio, Talbot Street Toyland and the Maison Talbot clothes store.

The Black Hole dominated Fantasy World, with the Pirate Ship, the Alpine Bobsleigh and Cine 2000 helping to consume the crowds. Strangely, after riding the futuristic Black Hole, guests could hop into a mock Model T Ford and trundle around the Vintage Car circuit that was built adjacent to it in 1983. A better fit was the Turbo Star, a dizzying triple-armed spinning flat ride that opened in the same year as the Black Hole.

The sprawling Aqualand was home to a variety of watery attractions, including the Log Flume, the aquarium, the Splash Cats, the rowing boats, the paddling pool and the sea lions. It also incorporated the Miniature Railway and Cable Car stations, the pottery studio, Cine 360 (a second dome-shaped theatre that one-upped Cine 2000 by displaying images around its entire interior) and the Circus Hassani (which replaced the parrots in their Big Top-style tent after they moved across the lake in 1983). These were joined by the rotating Octopus flat ride in 1984, and the fun house-style Mississippi Showboat the following year.

Guests would have to pay extra to enjoy all these new attractions. By 1985, the park's entrance fee had doubled to £5. Grumbling customers at today's theme park will be pleased to hear that parking was free.

Hidden Secret: See if you can spot the sign for the former Aqualand area that is still in place near the Congo River Rapids queue line.

Broome's spending spree showed no sign of abating. 1986 was to be another banner year for Alton Towers, with the opening of a second major water ride, the Grand Canyon

Rapids, along with two new "lands" in Towers Street and Kiddies Kingdom.

Just as it had with the Log Flume, Alton Towers took an existing ride system and blew it up to a scale never seen before in the UK when it constructed the Grand Canyon Rapids. This was to be the biggest project yet undertaken by Broome and his team. The park's car parks were moved in order to make room for it, with a total of 40,000 tons of earth and rock being excavated to create its 725-metre circuit. The rocks had to be blasted out of the ground, with the exposed ones that were visible to riders dating back to the Triassic Period some 220 million years ago.[134] The work also involved the installation of an electricity substation and an enormous reservoir capable of holding more than a million gallons of water.

River rapids rides are commonplace at modern theme parks, but in 1986 the concept was only six years old. Swiss firm Intamin had developed the first one for Houston's AstroWorld, acting on the instructions of the park's general manager, Bill Crandall. The result proved to be extremely popular, with the Six Flags chain opening a string of rapids rides at its US parks during the early part of the decade.

In contrast to today's Congo River Rapids (a rethemed version of the original attraction), most of the Grand Canyon Rapids' circuit was hidden from view. Guests had little idea what to expect when they boarded one of its circular rafts, although adverts promised that "You'll love our all new ride. It's sensational fun, just like shooting the real Grand Canyon Rapids. It's the world's longest and most spectacular water ride; the most exciting thing the country's ever seen."[135] The surroundings, though, were extremely bare – in contrast to the updated version, the original rapids ride was simply surrounded by mounds of earth and bare rocks.

The ride's six-seater boats (later updated to eight-seaters to increase capacity) were equipped with rubber rings, providing both buoyancy and the ability to cope with the many collisions with obstacles as they raced around its circuit. Logs were installed underneath the surface to create turbulence, while waterfalls, jets and fountains were added to soak riders. A large part of the thrill came from guests not knowing exactly how wet they would get, with every ride being slightly different due to the spinning movement of the boats.

As with the log flume, the Grand Canyon Rapids proved to be very popular and was capable of processing large numbers of guests per hour (around 1,350). Rival Thorpe Park introduced its own rapids ride, Thunder River, in 1987, but it couldn't match the Alton Towers ride for scale and ambition.

Alongside Aqualand, on the site of today's Adventure Land and Storybook Land, a sprawling new adventure playground was installed as headline addition in the new Kiddies Kingdom area. Featuring attractions such as the terrifying Freefall Slide and the delectable Cookie Mountain, it ate up another quarter of a million pounds of Broome's budget.

The biggest transformation, though, was to the park's entrance area, which had been moved to its current location in 1985. Again raiding Disney's stockpile of ideas, the park installed a "street" boasting turn-of-the-century architecture and lined with shops and dining outlets. As they walked down Towers Street past attractive leap-frog fountains, guests would be drawn towards the Towers themselves, standing magnificently on the opposite side of the main lake.

While the barking sea lions remained in place at the end of the street, there were no rides or attractions in the Towers Street area. Instead, the focus was on shopping. High-end clothes, glass, ceramics, toys and novelty foods were among the items on offer - a far cry from today's souvenirs. The presence of a bank ensured that guests wouldn't run out of money to spend.

By 1987, Alton Towers boasted no fewer than six themed lands, as well as the Towers and gardens. While there were dozens of attractions to keep visitors entertained, there was one major issue: tired legs. All those attractions were spread across a massive 800-acre site. By comparison, Disneyland covers just 85 acres. The Sunliner Trains had been brought in to transport guests from the entrance to Festival Park, but their capacity was limited. To compound matters, the car parks had been moved to make way for the Grand Canyon Rapids and guests now faced a mile-long walk or bus ride just to get to the park itself.

The solution was to build not just one, but two multi-million pound transportation systems for the 1987 season. The first, the Monorail, would bring guests to the park. The second, the Skyride, would replace and extend the existing Cable Cars.

When Walt Disney opened the first daily-operating monorail system in the western hemisphere at Disneyland in 1959, he hoped it would lead to the installation of similar systems at cities across the globe. It didn't, but it did result in the concept being copied by several other theme parks, Alton Towers among them. Planning had begun before the construction of Towers Street in 1986, with the buildings that would host its station already being in place.

Alton Towers' monorail wasn't built specifically for the park. In fact, it was acquired second-hand, having operated at the Expo '86 World's Fair in Vancouver, Canada from May 2 until October 13, 1986. Manufactured by Swiss specialist Von Roll, it was built at a cost of $10.5 million and featured ten trains of nine cars, with each train capable of holding a hundred passengers. Sponsored by Canadian Tire, it had stations in the Purple, Red, Blue, Pink, Green and Yellow Zones of the Expo, and carried an estimated total of 10.2 million people.[136] Riders could look forward to taking in scenes such as the International Traffic Jam (a collection of vehicles from across the globe that were intentionally displayed in chaos), a giant wooden elephant and the robotic mascot, "Expo Ernie". After the Expo closed there were suggestions that the monorail could be reused to provide local transit in the West End of Vancouver, but it was instead shipped over to England to be installed at Alton Towers. Most of the Expo's exhibition buildings were also torn down, but some segments of monorail track did remain in place where it was too expensive or difficult to remove them.

Once the track had been installed on-site, linking the car parks to the grand entrance, the monorail was ready to open in August 1987. The park claimed that the total cost came to a staggering £15 million, although this seems questionable given that this is higher than the cost of its original construction in Canada. Broome was delighted, billing it as "the greatest high-tech monorail system in the world".[137]

In keeping with its futuristic nature, the monorail was opened by *Star Trek* stars William Shatner (Captain Kirk) and George Takei (Commander Sulu). *Star Trek* fans turned out in huge numbers, many of them in costume. Despite being capable of acting as helmsman on the Starship Enterprise, Takei unfortunately lost his way in fog at Heathrow airport and arrived late. After a countdown, the first train burst out of the station, tearing through a sheet of paper and accompanied by smoke effects. Shatner was at the helm, quipping: "Of course we're breaking the sound barrier. We're going at warp 2.5."

The old Cable Car system had played an important role at Alton Towers since its introduction in 1963, but by 1987 it was showing its age. The ride's capacity was far too limited to cope with the volume of people that were now visiting the park. In addition, it had been designed to carry them to and from the gardens, which were now almost completely ignored by most guests.

Still, the Cable Cars had some advantages. They offered a much more pleasant ride experience than the Sunliner Trains and the Towers Express, and they could also travel across areas where road-bound transport systems couldn't. The decision was made to tear down the existing system and replace it with a modern one, which would be capable of carrying much larger numbers of passengers.

The Cable Cars' replacement, the Skyride, was manufactured by Poma, a French company that specialises in building lift systems and tramways for ski resorts. Installed by the McAlpine construction group at a cost of £6 million, it was capable of carrying almost 3,000 passengers per hour – three times as many as its predecessor. Its 12-seater gondolas travelled at 240 metres per minute, compared to 150 for the previous system. They could also accommodate wheelchairs and pushchairs, which was not an option on the old-style system.

Most importantly, the Skyride wouldn't just deposit guests in the gardens, away from the park's rides. Instead, in addition to the 466-metre stretch between the entrance and the Gothic Prospect Tower, a new 488-metre link was added from the gardens to a third station close to Festival Park. This enabled the Sunliner Trains to be retired.

Alton Towers promised that the panoramic views on offer from the Skyride would "really give a lift to your day".[138] The attraction has since saved millions of guests from traipsing up and down the valleys of the gardens, although it has also played a role in helping to ensure that even fewer guests view them from ground-level.

John Broome was determined to pitch Alton Towers as a destination for families. By the late eighties, though, it was increasingly gaining a reputation as being predominantly a teenage thrill-seeker's paradise. This perception was enhanced by the 1988 debut of "Coaster Corner", located close to the historic Flag Tower at the end of Talbot Street. In this relatively small area, the park managed to pack in no fewer than three roller coasters. Officially, it was part of Talbot Street, but it soon came to be known by its "Coaster Corner" nickname.

The first coaster to take up residence in the area was the 4 Man Bob, which debuted in 1985. The second ride at the park to feature a bobsleigh theme, it saw riders boarding sled-style cars in groups of four, and was reminiscent of the Matterhorn Bobsleds at Disneyland. Every car had to be filled to capacity before it was dispatched, which could hold things up somewhat if crowds were light.[139] The ride's circuit was packed into a small footprint, with very tight corners. "My over-riding memory of this little coaster was how long it seemed to last," says one reviewer on the Towers Almanac website. "The track was so narrow and tightly-wound that you just didn't know when it was going to end."

In 1988, two new roller coasters were crammed into Coaster Corner. The first of these was the Alton Mouse, the only steel "wild mouse" coaster ever to be manufactured by Vekoma. In common with other rides of its type, it featured lots of sharp corners and small dips, designed to throw guests from one side of the small cars to the other. It also boasted a strange tilted lift hill, a carry-over from its previous incarnation as Speeedy Gonzales at Vienna's Wiener Prater, where the hill was enclosed in a rotating tunnel.[140] The reason for its unique, one-of-a-kind status may have been the uncomfortable experience that it offered riders. One thrill-seeker recalls "I've never experienced anything quite like it", and they never would again as it was doomed to leave the park once it suffered a minor accident in 1991.[141] Sid the Mouse, its friendly mascot, would continue to appear in the park's parade, however.

The final addition, the Alton Beast, was a curious one. Billed as having "the steepest drop in Britain", it may have caused feelings of déjà vu for visitors who had already experienced the Black Hole. That's because it featured a near-identical track layout, being a Schwarzkopf Jetstar III model, the successor to the Black Hole's Jetstar II. The only small differences were a taller lift hill and an extra drop, and the Black Hole's old trains were even moved to The Beast following its upgrade to the Black Hole II in 1988. The additional height did enable it to go a little faster than the Black Hole, hitting a top speed of 44 miles per hour. The outdoor location offered one other advantage, too, as one rider recalls: "When you were at the top of the spiral lift-hill, the view was incredible".[142]

Coaster Corner was very popular, but its presence at the park was short-lived. Broome had installed the rides and then applied for retrospective planning consent. The application for the Alton Mouse was rejected in March 1989 as the rides were generating too much noise in a location not far from local villages, and Broome was given six months to remove the coasters, though this was later extended.[143] The 4 Man Bob was taken out in 1990, being sold on to Pleasure Island in Cleethorpes. The Alton Mouse, meanwhile, was removed a year later and packed off to the historic Idlewild park in Pennsylvania. The Beast stayed in place until the end of the 1991 season, when it was moved to the new Thunder Valley area and renamed as The New Beast. Coaster Corner was no more, and is still closed off to guests today.

Alton Towers had evolved out of a combination of a stately home and an old-style fairground into one of the UK's leading visitor attractions. It was inevitable that during this change some attractions would be installed that seem a little strange by today's standards, and would look very out of-place at the modern day park.

One unusual attraction that is fondly remembered by many 1980s visitors is Doom & Sons, the "haunted house" that was installed alongside Around the World in 80 Days. Despite being billed by the park as "more fun than scary", many children begged to differ.[144] Housed inside a building designed to resemble a Victorian-style undertakers, the walkthrough attraction made extensive use of ultraviolet lighting and physical special effects – including smells. One sign carried the ominous warning "Don't Look Up". A dead librarian hung from the ceiling above. Other areas saw guests sinking into the spongy floor, or opening a door (against the "Do Not Open" instruction) to be confronted by a screaming zombie. In another scene, a pair of feet protruded from a burning fireplace. "First time through you didn't really know what to expect," recalls one visitor. Many parents of terrified children probably wished that they had explored the attraction by themselves first.

Another quirky addition was the Mississippi Showboat, which arrived at the park in 1985. Designed to resemble an old steamboat, it sat in its own dry dock close to the current site of the Battle Galleons attraction. It was similar in style to the Fun House that had been removed from the fairground several years earlier, with its narrow corridors hosting moving walkways, spinning barrels, trick mirrors and other traditional effects. As they navigated its tight corridors and deck, guests would often be accompanied by the sound of live performers the Mississippi Jazz Band.

The iconic Swan Boats ride arrived in 1987, taking up residence in the Ingestre Lake. It was billed as "the only ride of its kind in the world...glides you round the lake in style".[145] Due to the glacial pace at which they moved, it took some six minutes for the swans to make their way around the course, directed by a series of pulleys. Predictably, this made it a popular make-out spot for teenage couples. Despite being one of the most recognisable rides at the park, it was removed in 2003 and eventually replaced by the Battle Galleons.

Some of the attractions opened in the 1980s were designed to inform as well as entertain. One of these was the Motor Museum, which charted the history and development of the motor industry. This was inspired by the activities of the twentieth Earl of Shrewsbury, who had introduced the Grand Fetes to Alton Towers. In 1903 he partnered with French carmaker M. Clement to open the Clement Talbot Motor Works in Paris. A second factory opened in England a year later, with both churning out Talbot-branded motor cars. In 1913, one of these was the first automobile to cover 100 miles in an hour. The park boasted that its museum hosted "one of the finest collections [of old cars] in the country".[146]

The Britannia Building Society Farm, opened in 1989 by the Duke of Edinburgh as part of the National Food and Farming Year, aimed to teach kids about how food was produced. There were live displays of traditional skills including sheep shearing, weaving and dry stone walling, and a canal boat ride took guests past live goats and fields of arable crops. Perhaps the most intriguing element was the milking parlour, where modern-day milk maids showed how technological advances had helped ease the passage of pints "from the cow to your breakfast table".[147]

Animals in the Towers weren't always safe from marauding children. Sally Carter accompanied a school party to the park during the 1980s, with a great time being had by all. The bus had to make a u-turn on the return journey, though, when it was discovered that one of the children had smuggled a goose onto the bus under his jacket.

There was a heavier emphasis on live entertainment in the eighties than at today's Alton Towers. This was exemplified by the parade that ran around the park's grounds every day. Kicking off at 3pm from a location behind the Towers, it proceeded around the lake, past Kiddies Kingdom and Fantasy World, back past the Towers and on into Talbot Street, giving guests in almost every area of the park a chance to view it.[148] Park mascots Henry and Henrietta Hound were prominently featured, and there were also floats dedicated to the Pirate Ship, the gardens, the swan boats, the farm, Aqualand, the Circus, the park's open air theatre and a birthday cake (to celebrate the park's jubilee in 1988). The demise of Henry in 1993 brought an end to the parades.

Over in Aqualand, the Circus Hassani continued to perform in the Big Top until 1988 before being replaced by an ice skating show. The parrots, by now performing in the Pirate Parrot Show in Kiddies Kingdom, left in the same year. The sea lions remained in place until 1990.

In Festival Park, the park's Open Air Theatre opened in 1987, before transforming into the Festival Park Dome with the addition of a rainproof cover two years later. This hosted live performances from bands, as well as the Henry's Celebration musical show.

Perhaps the star performers, though, weren't human at all. Installed in the Talbot Theatre (formerly the Fun House) in 1981, the Fantastic Fountains remained in place for more than a decade. The park boasted that the "spectacular display of colourful dancing fountains" employed 500 water jets, with shows running at 20-minute intervals. It was possible to watch the show multiple times on the same day, as the fountains performed six different sets.[149]

Cine 360 was modified in 1988 to take advantage of the latest craze in 3D movies. Guests were equipped with a pair of 3D glasses, before watching a sequence of clips from famous films. Though pretty basic by today's standards, the effects could be convincing – one guest remembers asking to switch seats with his mum because "the things were hitting me".[150]

While it was unmistakably British, the fingerprints of Walt Disney were all over Alton Towers. The park had stated its ambition to "take Alton Towers into the Disney league", with its executives visiting Disney parks in the US to learn about strategies that they employed. Like Disney, John Broome was unimpressed by traditional fairgrounds, which were often dirty and staffed by gruff employees. Dennis Bagshaw said in 1980 that "a full scale fairground was established in the early 1960s. This is now being removed from the Estate, as this type of thing is unacceptable to our new way of thinking". He was critical of Disneyland, though, saying that Alton Towers' approach would avoid the "intensive plastic and concrete approach of Disneyland".[151] Despite this, the park began to promote itself as "the Disneyland of the UK".

Disney influences could be seen all over the park. Guests arrived on a monorail, just as they do at Disneyland and Walt Disney World. They then walked down Towers Street towards the mansion, in a clear homage to Disneyland's Main Street, USA, which leads towards the mock Sleeping Beauty Castle. Period shops lined both Main Street, USA and Towers Street. Around the World in 80 Days was "inspired" by It's a Small World, while the Black Hole was openly marketed as the UK's answer to Space Mountain. Henry Hound's Parade was a transparent copy of similar parades starring Mickey Mouse at Disney's parks.

Whatever his influences, Broome's conversion of Alton Towers into a theme park had been a spectacular success. As early as 1982, he was boasting that he was developing a second theme park, and was looking around for a third site.[152] He forecast that the market would support only three to four fully developed theme parks – a prophecy that wasn't completely inaccurate, given the dominance of Merlin's four theme parks (Alton Towers, Thorpe Park, Chessington World of Adventures and LEGOLAND Windsor) in today's market.

"The inland leisure park is here to stay, and it's only now being realised that there is a tremendous market in this field. I think we've proved at Alton Towers that this market is ripe for tapping into further," boasted Broome.[153] Even as Alton Towers continued to add ride after ride, Broome was already planning to develop a sister park just eighteen miles away.

Located on the southern fringe of Stoke-on-Trent, the Trentham Estate's history is not dissimilar to that of Alton Towers. From the 1630s onwards, an imposing mansion stood on the site, and this was modified in the early 18th century to make it "both larger, higher and handsomer than it was before." [154] Between 1759 and 1780 the famous landscape designer Lancelot "Capability" Brown was commissioned to overhaul the estate's grounds. He enlarged the existing lake and created a beautiful park. The house itself was remodelled during the same period. In 1833, the second Duke of Sutherland hired the celebrated architect Charles Barry to once again redesign the house, transforming its appearance such that in 1851: "The present mansion [Trentham Hall] is on a larger and more magnificent plan and the gardens rank amongst the finest in England".[155]

Like Alton Towers, the estate went into decline in the early 20th century. Pollution from the rapidly-expanding Potteries had diminished its appeal, with sewage spewing into the lake. In 1905, it was abandoned by the Duke and Duchess, who were unable even to give it away. The Staffordshire County

Council declined the Duke's offer to hand it over for free. Instead, he sold it to local building firm Young & Son, which immediately demolished the house and sold the contents for a mere £500. The north-west corner of the estate was subsequently turned into a golf club.[156]

In 1931, Trentham Gardens Limited was formed to transform the estate into a tourist attraction along the same lines as Alton Towers. The gardens were opened to the public, but the major attractions were the ballroom and outdoor swimming pool (lido) that were installed by the new owners.

The Trentham Ballroom opened in 1931, gaining a reputation as one of the finest dancing venues in the country. An 18,000 square foot maple wood floor could host up to 3,500 dancers, and during the post-war era it was frequently packed. The 1960s saw its use evolve, as it began to host concerts from bands including the Beatles, Led Zeppelin, Gerry and the Pacemakers, Pink Floyd and The Who.[157]

The lido was opened in 1935, taking advantage of natural spring water from gravel beds that was reputed to have medicinal qualities. Constructed using reinforced concrete, the 132x60 foot pool boasted a stainless steel slide, as well as springboards and a 15 foot diving board. A special sound system piped music into the area (with the speakers hidden in nearby trees), while an upper terrace hosted a cafeteria. At night, the pool could be illuminated, with former General Manager Philip Bradbeer recalling in Graham Bebbington's *Trentham Reflections* that "the magic of the place left a lasting impression…it was wonderful, just like part of a Hollywood film set. I can't imagine another pool that came anywhere near it." [158]

In 1938, a miniature railway was installed. As well as offering views of the lake, this made the trip to the lido much easier. By this time, the estate was pulling in 20,000-30,000 guests on holiday weekends – comparable to attendances at

Alton Towers during the same period. The two grand estates shared some commercial interests, with Anthony Bagshaw, a leading shareholder in Alton Towers, opening a short-lived cable car system at Trentham in 1969.[159] This carried guests up to a monument of the first Duke of Sutherland, gazing down on the estate just as the statue of the fifteenth Earl of Shrewsbury looks over Alton Towers' gardens.

By the 1960s, as at Alton Towers, a fairground had been installed at the Trentham Estate. This boasted a similar array of temporary rides, including dodgems, a merry-go-round, a Speedway attraction (which saw riders racing around on motorbikes on an undulating platform) and a Peter Pan Railway similar to the one at the Towers. As it evolved, many adult-oriented rides were removed and replaced by children's rides such as a Helter Skelter and a small roller coaster.[160]

In the late 1970s, the Trentham Estate was in a seemingly terminal spiral of decline. The pool had been shut in 1975, with evidence that it had been damaged by subsidence caused by coal mining activities.[161] Trentham Gardens Ltd was struggling financially, and in 1979 the Countess of Sutherland announced that the estate would be sold.[162]

John Broome must have noticed the parallels between Alton Towers and Trentham, and had already proven that it was possible to transform a former stately home into a leading tourist attraction. On September 30, 1981, he purchased the site for around £3 million.[163] Improvement work started immediately, with Broome spending half a million pounds on the restoration of buildings and a replanting scheme in the gardens.[164]

On July 15, 1982, Broome announced his grand plans for Trentham. He promised to invest £20 million over the course of two-and-a-half years, creating an "American-style development with sporting, recreation and conference facilities, including a hotel".[165] Broome promised that

Trentham would be transformed into "Europe's finest leisure centre", creating more than 1,500 jobs. The estate would be developed "on the pattern of Florida's Wet 'n' Wild water park, with the emphasis on sporting facilities, park and lakeside living and with a 4,000 capacity conference facility and hotel running in tandem." The hotel alone was forecast to cost £5 million, with Broome admitting that the path to profitability might be longer than it was at Alton Towers.[166] Still, he expected annual income to eventually reach £10 million.

Broome published his plans in a booklet entitled *Project Trentham*, and applied for planning permission. This was granted on November 23, 1982, paving the way for work to commence.

A major part of the revamped Trentham estate would be aquatic attractions based around the enormous, 1.5-mile-long lake. This would include rowing boats, miniature stern-wheelers, fishing and even a floating restaurant made up of several small, connected islands with a Polynesian theme. The famous lido would be refurbished, adding a wave machine and several Wet 'n Wild-style water slides to become the "Spring Valley Wild Water Lido". There were proposals to construct a retractable roof over the pool, capable of withstanding two feet of snow.[167] A jacuzzi, sauna, solarium, gymnasium, bar and restaurant would round out the area.

The ballroom, too, would be rescued from its state of decay. Sitting at the heart of the 18,000-square-foot Trentham Centre, it would once again host concerts, as well as conferences and exhibitions. The surviving conservatory of the long-since-demolished Trentham Hall would host a high-end restaurant. Businesses would be able to take advantage of cutting-edge conferencing facilities, including satellite communications for international links. The conferencing centre would accommodate 1,600 conference attendees, 3,000 diners for banqueting events and audiences of 2,000 for indoor sporting events.

In the gardens, floodlights would bring the area to life in the evening. The "biggest pair of decorative fountains in the world" would jet half a million gallons of water every hour, with computers controlling the show just as in the Fantastic Fountains display at Alton Towers.[168] Eventually, a "people moving system" would connect the different areas of the estate, but in the meantime a Towers Express-style land train would fulfil that role. Guests would be transported from an enormous new car park by tram cars to the admission booths.

The estate's Italian-style laundry houses would be refurbished, forming part of an "Italian Village" that would host a restaurant, a bistro, a tea shop, a country life museum, craft shops, a nursery and 50 holiday apartments, all surrounding a main square. A central "piazza" would host craft workshops, a flea market, bistros, cafes, museums and galleries. The planning authorities were not happy with the "Disneyland scene" proposed for the Italian area by Broome, describing it as "inappropriate" and demanding "careful reconsideration".

Further accommodation would be available in a 150-room hotel in Trentham Centre, with a second, 200-bedroom hotel and sports club opening during a later phase close to the lake. Guests would be able to take advantage of riding trails, horse riding facilities and floodlit tennis courts. Two golf courses were included in the plan – an 18-hole course to complement the conference centre, and a 9-hole course for day visitors and beginners.

To fund all these changes, existing houses on the land would be refurbished and sold, while new, "low-density" housing would be built in small estates. In addition to the hotel, guests would be able to rent one of 100 self-catering lodges on the west side of the lake, along with 49 holiday cottages and apartments elsewhere on the estate.[169]

The fairground, by now almost derelict and partly overgrown with weeds, would be converted into the small-scale "Adventureland", and would be aimed primarily at children. Broome immediately began to install new rides, including a bobsled-style roller coaster, a Ferris Wheel and a spinning, polyp-style flat ride. A vintage car circuit, a carousel and donkey rides were also on offer. Future additions would include a "Mini Dragon" roller coaster, and a Wild West Adventure Playground boasting ropes, catwalks and a stockade fort. Qualified play leaders and supervisors would be on hand so that parents could leave their children while they explored the rest of the estate.

Given its location just five minutes away from the M6, Trentham was easier to reach than Alton Towers. Broome hoped that the two properties would complement each other, with the major thrill rides being located at Alton Towers, and accommodation and water attractions being on offer at Trentham. He boasted that his plans for the estate were so prestigious that they had led to him dining with Margaret Thatcher and being asked to attend a major leisure forum in the USA attended by Ronald Reagan. "Without my takeover," he said, "the situation here would have been a considerable disaster." [170]

Unfortunately for Broome, his plans were literally undermined by the subsidence problems that had already forced the closure of the open air swimming pool. The lake had to be drained to carry out repairs, while areas of the gardens also required major work. Eventually, Broome decided to cut his losses and sold the estate to the National Coal Board for £3 million in 1984, with the NCB promising to make good the damage caused by activity at the Hem Heath Colliery. By this point, according to the Trentham

Estate's own historical timeline, the estate was "in serious decline and had lost virtually all of its dignity".[171]

Broome continued to run the gardens and fairground under a leaseback agreement, but invested little. The 4 Man Bob roller coaster and the Ferris Wheel were moved to Alton Towers in 1984, with the polyp ride following two years later (becoming The Spider). The trains from Trentham's miniature railway were moved to Alton Towers in 1988 after it closed, with the Trentham Flyer eventually being employed on the Towers' own railway. By this time Broome had sold the Trentham lease to Country Sports International.[172]

Trentham's swimming pool was demolished in 1986 by the NCB, which had deemed it beyond repair. The ballroom survived until 2003, when it was also demolished as part of a £120 million regeneration scheme that has seen Trentham Gardens once again developed into a successful attraction. While there are only one or two children's rides remaining, the lure of the gardens and an enormous "monkey forest" populated by 140 Barbary Macaque monkeys continue to pull in the crowds.

With his success at Alton Towers, Broome had almost single-handedly created the UK theme park industry. Even as he was trying (and failing) to develop a second park at Trentham, though, competitors were circling, determined to grab a slice of the pie. Some of Broome's contemporaries had big ideas, but could they pull them off?

Among the first to try was KLF, a Kent-based company fronted by chairman and managing director Peter Kellard. In 1979 – before the debut of the Corkscrew – the firm had signed a deal with Derbyshire County Council to redevelop a 350-acre former opencast mining site into a major theme park that would celebrate Britain's past, present and future. The initial plan was for Britannia Park to open in 1982, with £5 million being invested by KLF on the park itself and the council chipping in £750,000 to cover the cost of access roads, car parks and toilets.[173]

Announcing the project at Hyde Park in London, Kellard was in a confident mood. "There was never any doubt that this joint venture could be successful given a potential market of 17 million people within a 70-mile radius and the fine site we had," he said. He went on to predict that Britannia Park would eventually replace the Tower of London as the UK's most popular tourist attraction, with more than 5 million visitors per year.[174] "This is literally the bull's eye of the country," he said. "We can provide every member of the family with something new and exciting to see and do." Councillor Norman Wilson, meanwhile, said: "Certainly Derbyshire County Council expects a healthy return for its money."

Kellard was sure that the park would open on time: "There is no question that we shall open in the spring of 1982 – Disneyland was built in one year and one day. We can at least do as well as that." [175] Almost immediately, though, local residents objected to the project on the basis that it would generate a huge volume of traffic, as well as being overly noisy. They took the council to court, and the agreement between it and KLF was found to be invalid. Worse was to come. The Conservative council was swept out in the 1981 election, and the victors – Labour – had pledged to scrap the Britannia Park development.

KLF were determined to proceed anyway, and took the council to court for violating the agreement. After a series of legal battles, they were victorious over the Friends of Shipley Park residents group, paving the way for construction to begin in 1983 – some three-and-a-half years after the project was announced.

The company's pedigree wasn't exactly world-class. It had built Tucktonia Park in Bournemouth, which featured small-scale models of well-known landmarks (similar in style to the Miniland attractions at today's Legoland theme parks). Still, it had ambitious plans for Britannia Park. These were largely based on the model established by Epcot at Walt Disney World, which combined educational exhibits with high-tech rides. Involvement in test promotions in the US had convinced KLF that the theme park industry was moving away from thrill rides: "People want to be informed in a nice, entertaining way," explained Kellard.[176]

Epcot had cost upwards of $800 million to build. The budget for Britannia Park was a tiny fraction of this. KLF, though, hoped that – as with the Disney park – sponsors would cover some of the expense. "To participate in Britannia Park is to contribute to the success and share in the benefits of a major national tourist centre," was the promise in the park's brochure.

The initial plans were for "an exhibition of British genius in industry, science, social reform and invention", based around an enormous lake.[177] Guests would enter via a "classic colonnade", lined by shops and cafes. The lake would host water sports activities, while a Wonderland exhibition would portray characters from British children's literature in indoor and outdoor areas. Adventureland would be a "high-quality", family-friendly amusement park featuring "spectacular catapult rides" and an assault course. Festival Village would host demonstrations of blacksmiths and other craftspeople in a period setting. As at Tucktonia Park, 1/24 scale models would be employed (supported by animation and audio systems), in this case to tell the history of the Commonwealth in Small World. An amphitheatre would host concerts, military displays, sporting events and exhibitions. The centrepiece, though, would be the British Genius area, boasting eight Epcot-style pavilions sponsored by private sector companies, which would show off major industries. A second phase of construction would add centres for sports, horse riding, golf, sailing, plus a motel, hotel and a 100-unit caravan park.[178] Guests would also be able to stay in rustic log cabins, complete with a "frontier post" shop.

By June 1985, £20 million had been raised, with KLF promising that this would eventually rise to £50 million. The park's opening day was scheduled for June 27, and Kellard was already boasting of plans for a second theme park elsewhere in the country.[179] However, Britannia Park would take another five years to complete. "We have been making it clear we are there to stay," said Kellard. "There is a 125 year lease on the land. All the buildings are to full constructional standard so we can gain the value appreciation once the operation gets going." [180] His company expected to break even during the park's first year of operations, attracting more than 1 million guests. "This country is always growing, this project will always grow," he promised.

"Rule Britannia, Britannia Park is great" was the catchy jingle that accompanied the park's advertising. Heavyweight boxer Henry Cooper was on hand to open the park, while a Concorde performed a flypast. Kellard promised that guests would "see a whole representation of the country in one day".[181] For this privilege, adults would pay £3, and children £1.50.

Unfortunately, the park was far from finished. The entrance area was in place, along with five of the pavilions in the British Genius area and a miniature railway line. The Bass brewing firm sponsored one pavilion, as well as a pub called the Britannia set around a "village green". The National Coal Board sponsored another, while the Royal Mint was also on-board. Much of the rest of the site hadn't even been landscaped by this point, and resembled a construction site.[182]

The 1985 season proved to be a disaster, with wet weather keeping visitors away and hindering construction efforts. Mere weeks after the grand opening, KLF was selling shares in its business in order to pay off creditors, and some staff were laid off after just a month. It was a futile effort, and Britannia Park was placed into receivership on September 9. The park shut its gates after just 12 weeks in operation at the end of November 1985.

With no private sector rescuer stepping up, Derbyshire County Council was forced to buy back the park for £2.5 million with the aid of a bank loan. It would eventually reopen two years later as the American Adventure, a park that Broome would cross paths with later in his career.

The Fraud Squad subsequently launched an investigation into the running of the park, resulting in one of the longest criminal trials in UK history. Lasting fourteen months, this revealed that KLF was in £8.7 million of debt. Bass Breweries was owed £130,000, while even Henry Cooper's appearance fee of £10,000 was unpaid. Kellard was eventually sentenced to four years in prison for his part in the fraud (he served just one, for health reasons), with the chairman of Britannia Park, John Wright, receiving a six-month sentence.

One potential competitor had fallen by the wayside, but an even greater threat to Alton Towers' dominance was brewing in an unlikely location. Corby, a former steel town in Northamptonshire, had been in the doldrums since the closure of a British Steel plant in 1980, leading to a total loss of around 20,000 jobs. "It was almost a one horse town," recalled instrument mechanic Steve Purcell, and the local authorities were determined to revive it.[183]

Two men, Gerald Baptist and Ian Quicke, felt they had the answer. They wanted to build an enormous, Epcot-style educational theme park and resort dubbed Wonderworld. In Baptist's words, the park would "create a completely new industry in Corby", one based around tourism and leisure. The local council were sold on the idea, and the pair formed Group Five Holdings and began to seek funding. 1,000 acres of derelict open cast land owned by the British Steel Corporation were set aside, ready to be transformed into a park that would "out-Disney Disney".[184]

The plans may have been along the same lines as Britannia Park, but the budget was much more realistic. The first phase was projected to cost £143 million, with the park opening in 1985. Within a decade of the park opening, Group Five expected to have spent some £376 million in total.[185] About £15 million of the initial round of funding was expected to come from the City of London, with leading Wall Street Broker The Ohio Company talking of putting in £25 million.[186] Grants from the European Economic Community were expected to amount to as much as £23 million, given that this was a regeneration project.

Group Five were keen to stress that Wonderworld would "not be an amusement park". Instead, it would encourage "maximum participation" by visitors, in a "British version of Disneyland" that would be "unusual in Britain, if not the world".[187] Minister of State for Industry Norman Lamont was on hand to unveil the plans at the Design Centre in London on September 7, 1982, and Prime Minister Margaret Thatcher had "commended to the country" this "ambitious, imaginative and high-risk" project.[188] Corby was billed as a suitable site due to research which showed that 22 million people lived within a two hour drive of the town.

Derek Walker, the chief architect for the new town of Milton Keynes, was brought in to design the resort. At the heart of Wonderworld was to be an enormous, 450-metre-long glass dome "the size of five football pitches", reminiscent of the Crystal Palace that housed the Great Exhibition of 1851. This would host areas dedicated to land, safety, the "Lost Village", air and space, communications, the body and the world. As with Britannia Park and Epcot, sponsors would be sought to help fund these exhibits and lend them credibility.

In the area dedicated to the body, guests would ride on a "sausage-style" canoe past "surrealistic" scenes depicting the human interior designed by Monty Python's Terry Gilliam. Following this tour, they would arrive at a presentation by Dr Jonathan Miller on the "mysteries of the anatomy", based on his television series *The Body in Question*.

The communications area would be housed inside a separate structure contained in a transparent bubble, linked to the other areas by a monorail system. Here, school parties and drama groups would be able to make their own television programmes and musical recordings. This kind of "education through participation" would make Wonderworld "superior to Disneyland".[189]

The headline attraction in the air and space area would be an observatory designed by astrologer Patrick Moore. Nearby would be a section dedicated to science-fiction hero Dan Dare (expected to generate a fortune in merchandise sales), and much of the area had been designed by Arthur C. Clarke, author of *2001, A Space Odyssey*. A Second World War-themed flight simulator would round out the line-up.

In the land area, guests would be able to go on a mock "safari" designed by botanist David Bellamy, which would whisk them past scenes of giant plants, trees and shrubs.

In the Lost Village, meanwhile, characters from famous nursery rhymes would be brought to life. A range of merchandise aimed at children and babies was designed, including Bo Peep furniture, a Boy Blue range of games and Jack Spratt fast food. In 1984, Quicke promised that the first products would go on sale in 1985, ahead of the opening of the park, including a range of learning books produced by the

Ladybird organisation. Companies contracted to produce merchandise were to be obliged to move production to Corby.[190]

Outdoor activities would be concentrated on the outskirts of the sprawling site. This would include an 18-hole golf course designed by Jack Nicklaus, as well as a 10,000-seater sports stadium boasting restaurants and facilities for tuition by leading sports personalities. A huge concert arena, capable of seating 30,000 people, would be designed to resemble a Martian "tripod" fighting machine from *War of the Worlds*.

Negotiations were held with British Rail around installing a new railway station close to the park, with special trains in Wonderworld livery bringing in visitors from London's St Pancras. The possibility of British Rail taking over the operation of the monorail system was also discussed, and there were even plans to develop a nearby airstrip.[191]

Wonderworld was expected to be such a big draw that it would pull in guests for entire holidays rather than just day-visits. To accommodate this, 1,000 lodges would be constructed, along with as many as seven hotels. As at Britannia Park, the aim was to celebrate everything British. The resort's restaurants would serve fast food, but the designers hoped to move away from American dishes and produce English fare instead. Group Five predicted that it would attract 4 million visitors per year initially, but that this could rise to as many as 13 million – Walt Disney World levels – eventually.[192]

Having been conceived in the late seventies, by 1982 Wonderworld was being described as "the main opposition" to Alton Towers by The Times.[193] The first attractions were scheduled to open by the middle of 1985, and the resort would have posed a real threat to the dominance of Broome's park. Investors were not convinced, though. By 1985, the opening window had been pushed back to early 1988.[194]

When 1988 actually rolled around, the date had been shunted to 1992 "to coincide with the opening of the Channel Tunnel".[195]

By that stage, at least some funds had been pledged. Former heavyweight boxer and entrepreneur George Walker stumped up £5 million via his Brent Walker leisure group, saying that he was "really optimistic that this will now move forward and come into being." Walker was a controversial figure, having served a 15-month prison sentence for theft earlier in his life.[196]

As at Britannia Park, there were suspicions of fraud, perhaps driven by the involvement of Walker. Former Northampton Police Commander Bob Thorogood revealed in his autobiography: "I could not see Corby competing with Paris, Los Angeles, Florida or other such exotic locations. Indeed, I believed that we might be witnessing a major fraud even though I could not see how it was to be perpetrated or who the beneficiaries would be. Certainly the land was worth many times the price paid for it [just £1 million] as it was in a prime commercial location, but the vendors (indirectly British Steel and their associated companies) had an option to repurchase the land for the sale price if the project failed to materialise. I resolved that one of my CID officers would maintain an interest and a file on the project to at least give the Fraud Squad a head start if it did all end in tears." [197]

Ultimately, no fraud was disclosed but Walker lost his £5 million pounds. The only thing built on the site was a large Wonderworld sign, along with a small cabin. Financing was never forthcoming, and the project was finally abandoned some fifteen years after it was initially proposed when the council ran out of patience. The only reminder is a scale model, now installed in the Corby Cube, the £47.5m building that opened as part of yet another regeneration scheme for the town in 2010.

While two potential threats had come to nothing, some competing theme parks were more successful. Thorpe Park opened in 1979 on the site of a former gravel pit in Surrey owned by Ready Mix Concrete Ltd, which was partially flooded to create an aquatic theme. It was less ambitious than Alton Towers, with a greater focus on educational exhibits. By 1985, the owners had spent £14.5 million, with the main attractions including a British heritage exhibition, an aircraft museum and a 1930s-style working farm. A single small roller coaster, Space Station Zero (now known as the Flying Fish) was in place, but the park still pulled in more than 1 million visitors in 1984.[198] Elsewhere, Chessington Zoo was converted into Chessington World of Adventures in 1987, and regional theme parks such as Pleasurewood Hills in Suffolk found a niche.

The magnificent Wonderworld had not become a reality, then, but it was the fate of two other "phantom" theme parks that would result in a major change of direction for Alton Towers as it reached the end of its first decade as a theme park.

The iconic Corkscrew, viewed from ground level.

The mighty Pirate Ship in its original location.
Image: Glen Fairweather

The Skyride, pictured in 2009.
Image: Natalie Sim

The lake at Trentham Gardens, minus John Broome's
planned Polynesian restaurant. Image: Natalie Sim

For more images, visit
http://www.themeparktourist.com/tales-from-the-towers/

4. The house of wax takes over

John Broome's plans for a sister park for Alton Towers at Trentham Gardens may have failed, but this had little effect on the success of his primary business. However, Broome's next attempt to develop a second theme park elsewhere in the UK was to have a dramatic impact on the future of Alton Towers – ultimately, contributing to its eventual sale to Tussauds and the radical change of direction that this brought.

Just as with his first park, Broome planned to base his next attraction around a listed building. However, the location was even more unusual and potentially problematic than Alton Towers. The entrepreneur hoped to build a massive leisure complex in and around Battersea Power Station, an iconic London landmark situated next to the River Thames in Wandsworth. The hugely ambitious scheme caught the imagination of leading figures including Prime Minister Margaret Thatcher, but eventually led to the fall of Broome's empire and a losing streak that left his reputation in tatters and his finances in dire straits.

Construction work on Battersea Power Station commenced in 1929, with electricity production beginning four years later. It became the largest power station in Britain, and was housed inside an extraordinary structure that was quickly dubbed a "cathedral of power".[199] Boasting four enormous chimneys (the last of which was not completed until 1955), it was the largest brick building in the world. Incredibly, it was capable of holding five hundred jumbo jets, or swallowing up Madame Tussauds' waxworks museum one hundred and thirty times over.[200] While the construction of such a large facility in London had been controversial (it was opposed by the boroughs of Westminster and Chelsea, on the grounds that it would generate too much pollution[201]), it was widely praised, being lauded as the second best modern building in Britain by an *Architects Journal* celebrity panel in 1938.[202]

To appease the opponents of the power station project, the London Power Company brought in the renowned architect Sir Giles Scott, who was largely responsible for its stunning external appearance. He was not involved, though, in the development of its equally impressive interior. This included a control room with an illuminated ceiling and walls of black marble, and an enormous turbine hall lined by giant fluted pilasters. The art deco-style marble floor in the building's entrance hall was swept every morning by a female cleaner – one of very few women working on the site.[203]

Despite the very permanent appearance of the building, Battersea Power Station was only expected to have a working life of around thirty years. In the end, it operated for fifty, with Battersea A closing in 1975 and Battersea B following three years later.[204] In August 1980, the Firestone Factory elsewhere in London was demolished, with its owners having reportedly been tipped off that it was about to be awarded listed status. In order to rescue it from the same fate, Secretary of State for the Environment Michael Heseltine quickly made Battersea Power Station a Grade II listed building.[205]

The Central Electricity Generating Board (CEGR)'s initial hopes of selling the site to a housing developer were thwarted due to a mandate from the Department of the Environment that no listed buildings could be demolished until every possible alternative use had been explored.[206] Responsible for finding a new role for the power station, it was encouraged by a 1981 feasibility study commissioned by Save Britain's Heritage, which suggested that the structure could be converted into a combination of an indoor sports arena and an engineering museum, with the surrounding land being used to host shops and housing.[207]

With a number of ideas being put forward, the board decided that the best approach was to run a competition. It launched this with an advertisement in The Times on October 19, 1983, which invited interested parties to send in their proposals for the "re-use and rehabilitation of Battersea Power Station" (remembering, of course, to enclose a cheque for £25 Sterling). Construction giant Taylor Woodrow was brought in to run the competition, which offered a prize of £100,000 to the winner.[208]

The competition drew eleven entries, seven of which were shortlisted as finalists. This included proposals to convert the power station into a giant rubbish incinerator, an enormous sports complex, a theatre, a shopping mall and, predictably, shops and housing.[209] The most unusual, though, was a scheme to build a huge theme park dedicated to Britain's industrial heritage, put forward by a consortium led by Sir David Roche. A notable participant in the consortium was Alton Towers, which lent credibility to the ambitious plan due to its success following the opening of the Corkscrew.

The notion of a theme park in the Battersea area was not entirely unusual. In 1951, Battersea Fun Fair had opened at nearby Battersea Park, part of a huge investment linked to the "Festival of Britain" celebrations. It was a major attraction until a tragic accident in May 1972, which saw five children killed and thirteen injured when two trains collided on the Big Dipper roller coaster. The fun fair never recovered from the bad publicity surrounding the incident and the lack of a major attraction following the Big Dipper's closure, and shut for good in 1974. Later that year, a plan was put forward to convert the site into a theme park "along the lines of America's Disneyland" at a cost of £5 million, but this ultimately came to nothing.[210]

The judging panel for the Battersea Power Station competition looked favourably on the Roche consortium's theme park plans. Eventually, the other proposals were whittled away until only two remained: the theme park and the refuse burning plant. The panel decided that the theme park concept had greater potential to create jobs, and thus it was announced the winner.[211]

While the consortium was ostensibly led by Roche, it was John Broome who had claimed most of the column inches surrounding the project. By 1985, the consortium had evolved into Battersea Leisure, with Broome at the helm. It submitted a full planning application for the conversion of the site, which was approved by Wandsworth Council in February 1986.[212] Broome eventually acquired the site for just £1.5 million in 1987.

Broome, who had been exploring options beyond Alton Towers for some years, was delighted. "We started looking for a site in the South East six years ago, when Alton Towers in its present form was four years old," he said in a promotional brochure. "I had often seen this monster of a building from Southern Region trains, but never really dreamt we could start a brand new leisure park in the centre of London."

"When I first walked inside, its magnificence overwhelmed me. Unlike most immense buildings, the more you looked at it, the larger it grew. Only private enterprise could raise the money to take on a challenge like this, to restore it and give it a rebirth. We're putting the fun back into London. London is one of very few capital cities in Europe without its own major entertainment complex. Now, Londoners will have a fabulous £200 million up-market centre, in an area where they have traditionally taken their leisure, beside the Thames, with standards of presentation and quality among the finest in the world." [213]

Asked by ITN whether he was afraid that the Battersea Power Station would become "an enormous white elephant", Broome exuded confidence. "I most certainly am not. I think it is going to be quite something for London, quite something for the nation," was his assured response.[214] He boasted that the theme park would become "London's Tivoli Gardens", creating four-and-a-half-thousand jobs in the process and sprawling across a total area of thirty million cubic feet. Broome was intent on creating "the jewel in London's pleasure industry crown".

Not everybody was pleased about Wandsworth Council and the CEGR's backing for Broome's dream. Leader of the Greater London Council (and future Mayor of London) Ken Livingstone was sceptical about the job numbers that were put forward, warning that many of them would be "Mickey Mouse" roles in food preparation and cleaning. Indeed, Broome himself admitted that a third of the jobs would be in catering.[215] Local amenity groups were up in arms, claiming that the theme park would provide a tourist attraction "of only the shallowest kind, with very little of value to the local community".

The competition judges though, including the former National Coal Board chairman Lord Ezra and Sir Hugh Casson, president of the Royal Academy, were sold. They claimed that the plan offered the greatest number of jobs and the best chance of retaining the landmark building.[216]

So just what exactly would be on offer at "The Battersea" (the name selected ahead of "Alton Towers II", "Tower Inferno", "The Battersea Powerhouse" and "The South Chelsea Fun Palace" [217])? Well, for an entry fee of £4.50 for both adults and children, guests would gain access to five floors of attractions inside the building, as well as a handful of outdoor rides. The indoor attractions would operate from 10am until 2am, and the park's array of themed shops would be "not like Tesco's or anything like that". The overall effect would be "a little bit Disneyland but in a far more English way", and it was expected that visitors would be drawn from all over the UK, as well as Europe and the United States.[218]

The Battersea was forecast to pull in visitors at a rate of seven thousand per hour during peak periods.[219] Many of these guests would reach the park via a special £4 million "Battersea Bullet" rail link from Victoria station, featuring futuristic windowless trains. For those travelling by car, 2,730 car parking spaces would be provided.[220]

As with the doomed Britannia Park and the never-built Wonderworld in Corby, plans for The Battersea drew heavy inspiration from Walt Disney World's Epcot, which opened in 1982. The goal was to combine education with entertainment, with less of the emphasis on thrill rides that was a feature of Alton Towers at the time.

Visitors would enter the Battersea via a spectacular entrance colonnade, surrounded by fountains and terraced gardens. Escalators and glass-walled elevators would transport guests between the floors, with a total of forty rides and two hundred attractions being on offer across the immense main gallery and the two turbine halls. An enormous wall of water would cascade down one side of the building's interior.

The ground floor of the main gallery would be dominated by a huge ice rink dotted with islands and spectacular dancing fountains (seemingly one of Broome's favourite attractions). Battersea Leisure promised that the area would combine "English nostalgia" with futuristic shows, rides and theatres. Indeed, the ground level would also host attractions as diverse as a craft village, "entertainment simulators", a shooting gallery, a mirror maze, an aquarium and a traditional carousel. The simulators would be themed as a "Journey into Tomorrow", with concept art closely resembling Disney's *Star Wars*-themed Star Tours rides (which didn't open until December 1986). The stand-out element, though, was Charles Dickens' Street, an "authentic actual village" populated with craft shops and restaurants, clearly based on the model established by Talbot Street at Alton Towers.[221]

A mezzanine level would host a Disney-style dark ride, featuring three-seater cabins that would pass through sixty animated tableaux populated by seventeen thousand animated figures telling the story of the history of the British Empire.[222] Elsewhere on the same level were "electronic entertainment exhibits", restaurants and twin cinemas.

On the second floor would reside a version of Alton Towers' Gravitron ride. A "Haunted Theatre", meanwhile, would be designed to spook guests, and a "Puppet Magic Theatre" would entertain little ones.

The third level would accommodate the Epcot-style Imagination Pavilion, as well as a "Computer Golf" attraction, a *Pinocchio*-themed toy shop and a pub, the Yellow Sub. The fourth level would host a movie memorabilia museum, the London Legends exhibit and large Thai and German restaurants. Live bands would play in a gazebo to add to the atmosphere.

Up on the fifth level, Broome planned to install one of The Battersea's signature rides. This was a balloon ride, which would see riders boarding mock balloons that would swoop around a circuit overlooking the Main Arena.

Down on the basement level would be a gigantic children's play area dubbed "The Magic Castle", boasting a cargo net climb, a "ball crawl" pit, slides, mazes and "educational electronic equipment". An animated puppet theatre would enterain kids, while the lower floor would also host a health and fitness club, squash courts, a gymnasium and an indoor jogging track.

One end of Turbine Hall A would be dominated by an enormous theatre. The other would host the traditionally-themed Battersea Pub, complete with beer garden. Fountains would surround the Gazebo Bar in the centre, while shops and a World Food Fair would line the sides of the hall. Up on a mezzanine level would be the Henry VIII restaurant and a set of bumper cars. The basement would host a medieval-style, "Dungeons and Dragons"-themed dark ride.

In Turbine Hall B, meanwhile, the Super Train roller coaster would provide mild thrills. A freefall ride and a 360-degree "omni-theater" would also be on offer.

The outdoor area surrounding the power station, previously used as a coal store, would be put to dual use. Firstly, taking a leaf out of Alton Towers' book, it would be home to "beautifully landscaped gardens" stretching along six hundred and eighty feet of river frontage. These would be open for free to the public, and would be brought to life at night with "twinkling Tivoli lights". As usual, Broome included dancing fountains in the design, along with Japanese, Asian and European gardens, topiary animal sculptures and a hedge maze. In a nod to Alton Towers' Pagoda Fountain, one of the snack stands would feature a pagoda theme.

Alongside the gardens, four major rides would be accessible only to ticket holders. The headline thrill ride of The Battersea was to be the Jumbo Jet Coaster, a custom-designed Schwarzkopf creation that would hit a top speed of fifty miles per hour, exerting forces of up to 3G on riders as they passed through lighting, laser, music and fog effects. Although located outside of the power station, it would be enclosed in a ride building, much like The Black Hole.

A second roller coaster, The Runaway Train, would be similar in style to the Runaway Mine Train that was eventually installed at Alton Towers by Tussauds in 1992. Its circuit would wind around the garden area, with caves, tunnels and waterfalls adding to the visual spectacle.

With the Grand Canyon Rapids having proven to be hugely popular at Alton Towers, Broome planned to bring a version to The Battersea. This would sprawl across a huge outdoor site, offering the usual array of waterfalls and jets to soak riders. Nearby, a Flying Island ride would see guests entering a glass-walled circular cabin, which would rotate as it rose to a height of 150 feet, offering impressive views of the surrounding area.

Broome had friends in high places, and one of the chief backers of the Battersea project was Margaret Thatcher herself. The "Iron Lady" attended the naming ceremony for the complex on June 8, 1988, hailing Broome as a man of "enterprise and vision".[223] Thatcher fired the largest laser gun in Britain during the ceremony, which detonated two mid-air maroons and dropped a white curtain to unveil the power station's new name, spelled out in flame. Purple smoke billowed out of the building's iconic chimneys. The stunt was a little too effective, though – four fire engines, a fire boat, an emergency rescue tender and several ambulances raced to the scene after local residents dialled 999.

Thatcher later enjoyed a hard-hat tour of the Battersea site, providing a clear glimpse at the scale of the task facing Broome. Seemingly unconcerned, she proclaimed: "We have seen the past today. We will be back again in two years' time to see the future."

Broome was in his element. He loudly declared that The Battersea would open to the public at precisely 2.30pm on May 21, 1990. "Don't come at 2.35pm or you'll miss it" he promised. Later that month, he offered to host the Thyssen art collection at The Battersea, in the knowledge that Thatcher had earmarked £100 million to bring the works to Britain.[224]

Construction work finally began in November 1988, leaving Broome with a huge challenge to meet his self-imposed deadline.[225] In reality, there was no chance of The Battersea opening on time. The initial cost estimate from Broome for the project was just £34 million – ludicrously low, given that the CEGB had in 1983 estimated that it would cost up to £20 million simply to keep the building structurally sound.[226] The budget subsequently leapt to £45 million, then to £170 million. By 1988, the price tag had soared to £240 million.[227]

It quickly became clear that just getting the basics in place would cost a fortune. Tons of toxic asbestos were found on the site, and there were huge problems with the building's foundations, which were "virtually non-existent".[228] On top of this, the UK was in the grip of a recession and the property market was depressed. Work ground to a halt after just four months, but not before the power station's roof and west wall had been demolished to remove the giant turbines. This left parts of the building exposed to the elements for years, accelerating its decay. Rather than building a theme park, Broome recalls ruefully, "I had to spend 4 months just putting in 300 piles 600 feet deep to pin up the building".

While Broome was struggling, Thatcher was embarrassed. An Early Day Motion proposed by Tooting MP Tom Cox and backed by a host of other London MPs in June 1990 reminded the Prime Minister that she had referred to the project as a "wonderful example of private enterprise and local government working hand in hand for the benefit of Britain", saying that "this colossal undertaking has that touch of pure genius that has always made Britain great". Broome had even been awarded a CBE. Now, though, the power station was a "desolate, empty hulk". Cox demanded an urgent investigation into this "major scandal".[229] Thatcher was making a habit of backing doomed theme park projects, having already thrown her weight behind Wonderworld.

Broome hadn't given up altogether. In 1990 he submitted a second, less ambitious proposal put together by architects RHWL. The new plan focused primarily on offices (covering 1.5 million square feet), retail outlets (covering 100,000 square feet) and a one thousand room hotel, with the leisure elements deprioritised.[230] Significantly, this was to be part-financed by the sale of Alton Towers. While the plans were approved by Wandsworth Council in August 1990, no work was ever carried out.[231]

As it fell apart around him, controversy continued to dog Broome and his Battersea project. He found himself embroiled in a legal dispute with McAlpine, the lead contractor, which issued a writ seeking the return of £16 million pounds that was transferred from Battersea Leisure to Alton Towers.[232] Wandsworth Council, meanwhile, was trying to claw back £200,000 in outstanding building and legal fees owed by Broome's firm.[233]

While the legal issues were eventually resolved, Battersea Leisure had reached the end of the line. The firm collapsed into receivership, and the theme park plans were permanently shelved. Taiwanese brothers George and Victor Hwang bought up the firm's debts, paying just fifteen pence in the pound to the Bank of America, which had lent Broome some £70 million.[234] The Hwangs were declared the new owners of Battersea Power Station in February 1993, and put forward a proposal to convert it into a combined hotel, office and leisure complex. Again, the plans were approved, but construction never commenced.

Finally, after another round of proposals, the latest plan for the power station's redevelopment was approved in 2013. It will be converted into a mix of shops, restaurants, leisure facilities, flats and town houses. A rival plan from Chelsea Football Club to convert the site into a new stadium was rejected. By May 2013, more than eight hundred flats had been pre-sold at a cost of £675 million.[235]

For his part, Broome later claimed that the Battersea debacle had personally cost him some £85 million, deflecting claims that he had lost other people's money.[236] "Nobody, not even a government agency or department, has ever spent as much money on a historic building as I have on Battersea," he claimed. "It is still up, it looks safe."

It may have failed miserably, but John Broome's wild dream to convert a derelict power station into an urban theme park was to have a huge influence on the future of Alton Towers.

While Broome's Battersea project was collapsing around him, the first credible challenger to Alton Towers' dominance of the UK theme park market had begun to emerge. Unlike Britannia Park and Wonderworld, this time the threat came from a company with vast experience in the UK tourism market, and the financial resources to follow through on its ideas.

The Tussauds Group had built its reputation on the back of its hugely popular waxworks museum in London, which was one of the few paid-for tourist attractions in the UK that could match Alton Towers in terms of attendance. It owed its success to Marie Tussaud, the French daughter of a housekeeper for Dr. Philippe Curtius, a physician who also dabbled in wax modelling. After learning the art from her mother's master, Tussaud inherited his collection on his death in 1794, and began to tour Europe under the banner of "Madame Tussaud's". Eventually, trapped in London due to the Napoleonic Wars, she set up shop in Baker Street, and established her first permanent museum in 1835. The Chamber of Horrors – still one of Madame Tussauds London's leading attractions – helped establish it as a major draw for tourists. Following his grandmother's death in 1850, Joseph Randall moved the museum to a larger site on Marylebone Road in 1884. The cost of this move, though, eventually forced the sale of the museum to a consortium of businessmen.

An upswing in fortunes began in the 1960s, when improved marketing and a pick-up in tourism as Britain exited its post-war slump led to increased revenues.[237] In 1970, Tussauds opened an exhibition in Amsterdam, and quickly realised the potential to expand far beyond its London roots. It bought the Wookey Hole Caves attraction in Somerset, before setting its sights on Chessington Zoo in south-west London in 1978.

The owner of Chessington Zoo was Pearson, a multinational conglomerate based in Britain that was best known for its publishing businesses, which included the Financial Times. By the late 1980s, it had diversified into industries as eclectic as book publishing (via its Penguin Books and Ladybird Books arms), satellite television (via a stake in the British Satellite Broadcasting Company), fine china (it owned the Royal Doulton brand) and even oil production and banking. Rather than selling Chessington Zoo to Tussauds, it turned the deal on its head and instead bought Tussauds.

Backed by its wealthy new owner, Tussauds continued its expansion with the purchase of the 13th-century Warwick Castle for $2.7 million. It quickly installed a waxworks exhibit representing a 19th century royal weekend. Plans were made to open a major new waxwork exhibit in London. Based near Windsor Castle and dubbed "Royalty and Empire", it would recreate Queen Victoria's Diamond Jubilee celebrations of 1897.

Tussauds' waxwork figures, which cost an average of $18,000 apiece, could still pull in a crowd.[238] However, Disney's invention of audio-animatronic figures – ones that could move as part of an animated scene – was beginning to make them look outdated. Tussauds' hunt for an equivalent technology to use in its new exhibits would bring it into contact with the man who would ultimately – and unexpectedly – lead the company into the burgeoning theme park industry.

John Wardley's career didn't pan out quite as his father had hoped. The owner of a prestigious print business in London, Wardley Sr. had hoped that his son would follow in his footsteps and take charge of the family business. The younger, Wardley, though, had other ideas.[239]

Inspired by his great aunt and uncle, who together performed as "Russian" illusionists Vadir and Dorinova, Wardley set his heart on forging a career in showbusiness. Using miniature versions of the pair's illusions, he became "the star of the show" at his friend's birthday parties. Hoping to prove to his son that this wasn't such a glamorous vocation after all, his father sent him to Great Yarmouth to work for Jack Jay, who owned a chain of entertainment establishments in the seaside resort.

The plan backfired. The 15-year-old Wardley, who was employed in a variety of "rough jobs" during his time with Jay, was hooked.[240] Rather than "knocking all this starstuck nonsense out of his head", the summer in Great Yarmouth had further convinced him that his future lay in entertaining people. Jay reported back to his friend that his son was "not cut out for your business". Conceding defeat, Wardley Sr. sent his son back to Great Yarmouth to undertake a "serious apprenticeship", which included working as a doorman at a nightclub, as a projectionist in a cinema and even as an under-aged croupier in a casino. "I got a real insight into what makes the British public tick," Wardley recalls.

"If you're going to go into showbusiness, do it right – get some qualifications," was the instruction from father to son.[241] So Wardley applied to the London Academy of Music and Dramatic Art in the late 1960s, learning how to perform backstage tasks for the big-budget musical productions that were running on Broadway and in the West End at the time. This led to a career as a Stage Manager at the Theatre Royal in Windsor.

The theatre was located close to Pinewood Studios (where the *James Bond* movies were produced) and Bray Studios (where the *Hammer Horror* movies were filmed). Wardley quickly developed a side-business developing props and special effects for the two studios' productions, with his earnings from this eventually outstripping his meagre wages from the theatre. This prompted a full-time move into the movie effects industry, although Wardley recalls: "I missed the live audience. I like contact with the people I'm entertaining. We were creating some amazing effects, and whenever we had any visitors come to the sets it blew their minds. I thought it such a shame that we couldn't bring a live audience here to the movie studios to see what we're doing. This must be what Disneyland, and theme parks, are all about." [242]

Wardley had plenty of downtime during his career as a special effects technician, and used this to develop a sideline producing model skeletons (based, incredibly, on a mould of a *real* human skeleton).[243] The operators of fairgrounds and amusement parks quickly became his main customers, using the skeletons to frighten riders on ghost train rides.

The skeleton business brought Wardley into contact with John Collins, the co-owner of the Barry Island amusement park in Wales. Impressed with Wardley's work, Collins invited him to perform a complete makeover of the park's ghost train. The result – Uncle Frankenstein's Scream Machine – was a huge success, and further work on the park's Jungle Boat Ride and Wacky Goldmine enhanced Wardley's growing reputation.[244]

During a tour of America, Wardley met companies such as Arrow Developments that were at the forefront of ride production, and learned about the basic transit systems that could be employed by theme park operators. However, he could not persuade Disney to show him how their audio-animatronic creations worked. With no other companies producing similar, life-like animation systems, and believing them to be an essential part of a theme park experience, Wardley decided that he would go it alone. He began designing an ingenious pneumatic system, keeping its workings strictly under-wraps. The result was a singing, moving character named Charlie Pluckett, who shot to stardom following an appearance on the BBC's popular *Tomorrow's World* programme.

The day after the programme was aired, Wardley says, "my phone didn't stop ringing". One company even wanted to employ an animated dummy to test out its range of incontinence wear. A more serious interest, though, came from a delegation of visitors from London. Eventually, they revealed that they were from Madame Tussauds, and that they were looking to enhance their exhibits with moving figures – in strict secrecy.

Ian Hanson, the head of Madame Tussauds Studios at the time, compared seeing Wardley's moving figure to seeing a Wright Brothers aeroplane in action for the first time.[245] After engaging an engineering firm to "industrialise" the crude model, animated figures began to be produced at a cost of around £30,000-60,000 each, and installed in the Royalty and Empire exhibit over a two-year period. When it opened in 1984, it was a major success. More of the animated figures were subsequently used in the music-themed Rock Circus, which was opened by pop star Jason Donovan in 1989. "Static wax figures are something we've been famous for for more than 180 years," said spokeswoman Juliet Simpkins. "What we're doing [with animation] is enhancing the illusion." [246]

While working on the Royalty and Empire project, Wardley was engaged by Tussauds director Graham Jackson, who was responsible for turning around the struggling Chessington Zoo's fortunes. At the time, the zoo – which also featured a circus and a funfair not dissimilar to the one that had operated at Alton Towers in the 1960s and 1970s - was "not doing so well", and Wardley was asked to provide advice on "how we can sort out the carnival rides". After looking around the site, Wardley quickly came to the conclusion that updating the funfair and circus would be a futile gesture. "There is precious little point in people travelling long distances for permanent facilities if, what they could see when they got there, arrived at their local village green six weeks later," Wardley says. "In order to develop an attraction that had a future, it had to provide something special, which meant custom-built rides on a permanent site." [247]

Wardley reported back to Jackson that a much bigger project was needed to revive Chessington Zoo. It wasn't until around six months later that Jackson's replacement, Ray Barratt, followed up on Wardley's suggestions. He invited him to come up with a plan to convert the site into a theme park, and – backed by Pearson's funds - provided him with a team and resources to make it a reality.

Whereas many of Alton Towers' early attractions, such as the Grand Canyon Rapids, featured minimal theming, Wardley was determined to take guests "on an adventure". He believed that the ride systems themselves should be secondary to telling a story, a philosophy that Disney had pioneered with huge success. The revamped Chessington Zoo's new name reflected this when it debuted in 1987 – it became Chessington World of Adventures.

The grand plans to create Britannia Park and Wonderworld from scratch had failed, but Wardley's conversion of the existing Chessington attraction was a huge success. Pearson stumped up £10 million, with Wardley installing rides including the Runaway Train roller coaster, the quirky Fifth Dimension dark ride and the oriental-themed log flume Dragon Falls. The park pulled in 850,000 guests during its first year of operations, and this jumped to 1.15 million in 1988, placing it firmly in the top ten paid-for attractions in the UK.[248] For his role in this success, Wardley was made a non-executive director at Tussauds.

By 1989, work had started on installing the new Transylvania area, boasting an inverted roller coaster (Vampire) and a new dark ride (Professor Burp's Bubbleworks). It was hoped that this would attract a further 200,000 visitors in 1990. A hefty £1.5 million advertising budget would be used to achieve this goal.

Tussauds was still a relatively small company, with an annual turnover of around £30 million.[249] Pearson, though, was a multi-billion pound company. It wasn't interested in settling for second-place in the UK theme park market behind Alton Towers – in Wardley's words, it wanted to "become the brand leader".[250]

After discussions with local planning authorities, it soon became clear that the company couldn't achieve that goal at Chessington. The restrictions on the number and size of attractions that could be installed on the site were simply too severe. Instead, the company began to hunt for a second site, where it hoped to build the UK's number one theme park.

Tussauds set three criteria for the site of its next park. Firstly, it would need to be attractively landscaped. Secondly, it would need to be within reasonable driving distance of a large section of the UK population. Finally, it would need to be subject to less restrictive planning policies than Chessington.[251]

One of the first sites that came under consideration was the 1,000-acre plot that had been set aside for Wonderworld in Corby. With that project floundering, the local authorities were desperate to attract a major player such as Tussauds to the area. Red-tape would not be a problem, and studies had already shown that the required transport links would be in place to make the park reachable by vast numbers of people. However, the task of converting the former open-cast mining site into a visually-appealing theme park was viewed as too much for Tussauds to take on.[252]

Next on the radar was Woburn Abbey – like Trentham, a site with a number of parallels to Alton Towers. Owned by the Duke of Bedford, it had developed from its roots as Cistercian abbey that was founded in 1145. Rebuilt in 1744, the Abbey stood in one piece for more than two centuries before the discovery of dry rot after the Second World War led to half of its being demolished. Determined to keep the property in his family's hands, the thirteenth Duke of Bedford followed an Alton Towers-style approach and turned it into a tourist attraction. By 1970, a safari park had been installed on the site and it quickly became very popular.

Ray Barratt, the Tussauds director, was a former General Manager at Woburn and well-acquainted with the Duke's son, Henry Robin Ian Russell, who was by now running the estate. Wardley recalls that on a return trip from Corby to London, Barratt suggested calling in at Woburn.[253] Following several further meetings, Tussauds and the Duke's family agreed to work on plans to convert the site into a "mega park" that would attract 2.25 million visitors per year – on a par with Alton Towers. The closer proximity of the Woburn site to London – the UK's biggest urban centre, and its wealthiest – meant that, if it came to fruition, the new park could potentially topple Alton Towers from its position at the top of the UK's theme park leader board.

Armed with Pearson's millions, Tussauds developed ambitious plans for the Woburn site. As at Chessington, some animal attractions would remain, but major new rides would be added alongside them. Just as he had for Tussauds' first theme park, John Wardley drew up a masterplan for the Woburn site, which was to be dubbed "Woburn Festival Park". It would sprawl across a total site of 525 acres, although only 131 of these would house the theme park itself. The park was expected to attract upwards of 20,000 visitors on peak days – significantly more than the existing safari park. Seven themed areas would be included, each designed to cater for the entire family. Tussauds promised that the park would enable visitors to "escape for one day into a different world that is clean, safe and has adventure, wildlife and some tranquility."

Wardley's outline plan for the park offers an insight into what would have been on offer. Arriving by car, guests would have time to "forget the world outside" as they drove along the approach roads to Festival Park's entrance. After buying their tickets, they would pass through a leafy square onto a "village street" beyond. This would be lined on either side by shops, visitor facilities and a restaurant. Bunting would hang everywhere, and the street would have the "atmosphere of a carnival", with street-theatre, clowns, jugglers and "mad games" to entertain the crowds. Covered arcades on either side would allow movement in wet weather.

Reaching the end of the street, visitors would walk through a grove of tall oak trees with thick rhododendrons to block out the views on either side. Within this woodland, they would see an enormous adventure playground stretching out in front of them, with people climbing on platforms, crossing rope bridges and plummeting down slides. Further on, they would hear the sounds of riders on a wooden roller coaster, although this would be concealed by dense vegetation until they were much nearer. Even up close, the majority of the coaster would be hidden by two steep valleys and dense vegetation. "For those brave enough to ride it," Tussauds promised, "[the coaster] will be an unforgettable experience."

Moving down into the valley, guests would come across another village overlooked by a "sinister house", which would accommodate a dark ride. While this sounds conceptually similar to the Haunted House that was subsequently built at Alton Towers, Wardley describes it as "nothing more than a name on a plan". Outside, a runaway train based on that at Chessington would leave the village for a "hair-raising" trip across the wooded valley and back.

Next, visitors would come to the Safari Area, which would feature lakes and waterfalls at its centre populated by flamingos and other waterfowl. A family restaurant, decorated with creepers on round poles, would look out over the "generously planted" lakes, offering an intimate dining experience.

From the main lake, "Jungle Queen" boats would take riders on a trip past a number of animals, with paths allowing a closer look. For younger guests, there would be a "Safari Jeep" ride and an African Village display of juvenile and domestic animals. There would also be an indoor wildlife presentation and a new tropical house.

Much of the former safari park would remain in place, with guests touring it in land trains that left from the outskirts of the Safari Area. A monorail would give an overview of the animal enclosures as well as providing transportation back to the entrance and other attractions.

Also overlooked by the monorail would be a rapids ride, occupying the position of the former safari park car park. This would flow through a series of densely-planted rocky gorges, with overlooks and bridges allowing people to enjoy the area whether they wanted to ride or not.

Returning to the valley, a log flume ride would draw its water from newly-made ponds. The flume's circuit would climb up the contours of the valley through pine plantations, before splashing back down into the ponds. Once again, paths and overlooks would make this "a spectacle to enjoy both on and off the ride". A Pirate Ship-style flat ride would take off from the water level and swing through the trees.

After exhausting themselves in the theme park, guests could take advantage of large areas of previously off-limits parkland that would be set aside for nature trails and a picnic area.

The park, as described above, would be built in five stages over the course of five years at a cost of around £50 million. Phase 1 would see existing areas refurbished and replanted and the removal of the safari park's cable car system. Visitors would still drive around the animal enclosures themselves before parking.

Phase 2 would see a new entrance constructed, linking to the valley area where the log flume would be built. The monorail would provide a further wet weather transportation link, while the safari park's lion and wolf enclosures would be returned to parkland. Guests would now tour the remaining enclosures on a land train.

Phase 3 would see the addition of the wooden coaster and adventure playground, Phase 4 would add the Runaway Train and village, and Phase 5 would involve the installation of the rapids ride.

Two further phases were also planned to bring the park up to full capacity, although the rides that would be included in these had not yet been finalised. Phase 6, though, would have included "moderately-sized dark ride structures".

Legendary American designer Curtis D. Summers was working with Wardley on the design of the wooden roller coaster, which would have featured dual, "racing" tracks. Wardley was also collaborating with Arrow on the design of a steel roller coaster, presumably to be added to the park during one of the later stages. Other attractions referred to in the plans include a tea cup ride, a "Big Apple Coaster" and an old-fashioned carousel. With Tussauds aiming for outline planning consent, though, Wardley says that "all the plans for Woburn were just outline concepts, and none were worked up in any detail."

Tussauds submitted its initial application for outline planning consent on June 6, 1989. It faced intense opposition, with dozens of letters of objection being received by Mid-Bedfordshire District Council. One, from the Ampthill and Distict Preservation Society, said: "The concept of theme parks is a fairly new one and it is quite likely that this fashion will only last a decade, in the same way as the Safari Park has done. Consequently, the infrastructure will probably be left as a blot in a rural area, while the Tussauds scheme has long been forgotten."

Alton Towers was frequently cited as an example of a theme park development in a conservation area that had been allowed to grow out of control. Tussauds' solicitors reacted to this comparison by writing: "It is abundantly clear that Tussauds are approaching Woburn in a manner quite dissimilar to Alton Towers, which, I must stress, was developed without either Tussauds' or their professional teams' involvement." In its noise assessment, Tussauds noted that rides such as the Runaway Train at Chessington were far quieter and better concealed than the Alton Beast and Alton Mouse at the Towers. Pleasurewood Hills, Drayton Manor and Camelot were all cited by the firm as examples of permitted theme park developments in Green Belt areas.

The response from the council was emphatic. The theme park, it said, would "conflict with the intentions of the Local Planning Authority to conserve areas of attractive landscape and prevent development that would adversely affect their character." Not only that, but it would "detract from the amenities and quiet enjoyment of residents living within the vicinity of the site", would create too much traffic around Junction 13 of the M1, would increase local traffic to "unacceptable levels" and generate too much noise. "The proposed theme park would have a seriously adverse affect upon historic parkland of outstanding importance," was the council's summary. Seemingly, there was no chance of

Tussauds ever gaining planning consent to build its "mega park" at Woburn Abbey.

Frustrated by its inability to find a site that met the three criteria, Pearson and Tussauds set their sights on acquiring an existing operation – one that could be developed and expanded into the kind of major theme park that had been designed for Woburn Abbey. Already established as the market leader, Alton Towers was an obvious target.

Just as he had with Chessington Zoo, John Wardley paid an anonymous visit to the park. While he felt that there were significant flaws in the way the park's rides had been designed and were laid out, he believed that it still represented a major opportunity for Tussauds, if it could be acquired at the right price.

Wardley spoke with Barratt and suggested that Tussauds make a move for Alton Towers. Barratt responded that this was a "daft idea", given that Broome's park was already very successful and was therefore likely to be priced at a premium, if it was available at all.[254]

Inevitably, though, the massive losses at the Battersea had to have an impact on Broome's primary business. Wardley spoke to his contacts at the park, who "bemoaned the fact that John Broome's Battersea project was drawing valuable resources from Alton Towers…numbers were decreasing, and new attraction developments were being put on hold."[255] He passed this information onto Barratt, who asked one of Pearson's merchant banks to look into a potential deal.[256]

In March 1990, Pearson placed 11 million shares at 655 pence, using the funds to purchase Alton Towers for £60 million. The park had made a profit of just £3 million the previous year, but it had assets totalling £60 million, as well as permission to build a hotel and chalet complex worth £8-

10 million.[257] While Broome said at the time that the sale was unconnected to the Battersea project, it was later claimed that the funds would be put towards the power station's redevelopment.[258]

So what became of John Broome, the man who had started the theme park era at Alton Towers, after the Battersea debacle? Typically, given his entrepreneurial streak, he had not given up on grand, ambitious projects – or the theme park industry. But he was never again to achieve the same level of success that he managed at the Towers.

First up was a plan to convert Carden Park, a 750-acre estate near Chester, into a "corporate playground" boasting an 83-suite hotel, a golf course and clay pigeon and archery ranges. Just as he had planned to turn Trentham into a successful conferencing centre, he hoped that the £20 million he invested during the late 1980s and early 1990s ("mainly of other people's money", according to the Daily Express, although Broome claimed it was all his own[259]) would help Carden Park fulfil its potential.

Broome had acquired the 1,200-acre Carden Park site for an undisclosed sum in 1988, immediately repairing 14 miles of dry-stone walling, planting 17,000 trees, re-establishing a herd of 400 red deer, remodelling the estate's lake and stocking it with trout, renovating ten cottages and setting up a ten-acre vineyard. There were plans to build an ice rink for curling. The year-round resort would provide "five-star plus activities for families, diplomats, executives and sportsmen and women at three-star prices."[260] A thousand staff would serve a thousand people every day. The luxury suites at the hotel would each feature a butler's pantry, with butlers available to hire for a small fee.

Just as with the Battersea project, problems soon began to emerge. By October 1993, Broome had been forced to sell his

153

Stretton Hall home in Cheshire for £3 million, as well as his prized Rolls Royce and boat, to raise money for work at Carden Park.[261] Broome assured The Independent that the resort would open its gates on November 1 that year, and that he would build a new home for himself on the estate. His aides dismissed rumours that the project was in dire straits due to the failure of Manchester to win its bid to host the 2000 Olympics, with the estate having been due to host seven events (Broome was on the Manchester 2000 organising committee). "This is the most exciting project I have ever undertaken," said a bullish Broome. "There is huge demand for a sports resort like Carden, so not surprisingly I am looking forward to proving the gloom and doom merchants wrong again."

The gloom and doom merchants were right, though. The Bank of Scotland called in receivers in 1994, and Broome sold his overseas home to raise more funds – although creditors accused him of putting assets out of their reach (a claim he always denied).[262] Forced to work with receivers Grant Thornton to save the project, Broome was unable to do so. Carden Park did eventually become a successful conferencing venture, but Broome had lost ownership by that stage.

Seemingly undaunted by the successive failures of two expensive projects, Broome took the helm at Ventureworld, a new company that acquired the American Adventure theme park in Derbyshire (on the site of the failed Britannia Park) in 1997. The park's name was changed to American Adventure World immediately, although signs within it still read "The American Adventure". Despite plans to introduce new attractions (including a Nemesis-style Bolliger & Mabillard inverted roller coaster and a wooden coaster) and to rename the park once again to "Adventure World", dropping the all-American theme, little came of them – although a Flying Island attraction similar to the one planned for The Battersea did open in 1998. Broome left his role in 1999 and the park was sold on to the THG Group, the owner of Pontins holiday parks. It would eventually close for good at the end of the 2006 season.

Broome's involvement with the theme park industry was over. Never likely to retire, he resurfaced in December 2000 as the Chairman of London Launch, an events company founded by his son William, which continues to operate today.

Most accounts of Tussauds' dalliance with the Duke of Bedford suggest that plans for a theme park at Woburn Abbey were dropped immediately after the Alton Towers acquisition. In reality, Tussauds submitted a renewed planning application for the Woburn site on July 17, 1990 – some four months after acquiring Broome's park, although it had probably been working on this for some time in case the Towers deal fell through. This time, to address the issues raised about traffic levels, the proposals included plans to build a new link road to bypass local villages (at Tussauds' expense) and the funding of a new roundabout for Junction 13 of the M1. The development would now take place over seven years, building up from 300,000 visitors in 1991-92 to 2.25 million in 1999. The size of the theme park would be reduced, so that it did not encroach on 18th century parkland of historic importance, helping to alleviate concerns from English Heritage, which had objected to the original application. Funds would also be set aside to pay for refurbishment projects within the site, while more than 750,000 trees would be planted. These changes were largely welcomed, but opposition from local residents and environmental groups remained vociferous.

It was a lost cause. On September 11, 1990, the plan was again rejected on the basis that it would "be detrimental to the quiet rural character of the area". Residents, supported by the Campaign to Protect Rural England, had won the day.[263]

The Woburn theme park rumours wouldn't die. In late 1993, Tussauds was reported to be in discussions with the BBC about establishing a £100 million theme park on the site based on the broadcaster's most popular programmes. The aim was to emulate the success of Granada's Studio Tour in Manchester, which attracted 780,000 guests to the set of *Coronation Street* in 1994.

The park, dubbed "Beeb World" by the Mail on Sunday, would have included themed restaurants, a quiz show studio, stunt shows and replicas of sets from BBC shows. Cybermen and Daleks would fight on the set of *Doctor Who*, and guests would be able to enjoy a pint in a recreation of the Queen Vic pub in *Eastenders'* Albert Square. An *Only Fools and Horses* ride would see guests boarding Reliant Robins chauffeured by an animatronic Del Boy for a tour around his London haunts, while a Universal Studios Hollywood-style tram tour would take them past sets from *Dad's Army*, *Birds of a Feather*, *Casualty* and *Noel's House Party* (featuring Mr Blobby).[264]

"Anything's possible at this stage," commented Michael Jolly, Tussauds' chief of operations. "A fairly high proportion of the park would be covered and it won't be a small-scale attraction."

Pearson conducted a feasibility study, which also considered the BBC's Elstree Studios in Hertfordshire as a potential location (in reality, this was a more likely choice than Woburn, which was speculatively suggested as the host site by the Daily Mail). The project was quietly dropped after the study was completed in 1995, with Wardley revealing that: "The project failed to go ahead because of complications in negotiating the intellectual property rights of the various programmes which were to be featured as rides and shows within the park, and which the BBC did not actually own themselves."

Just as he had been at Chessington, John Wardley was tasked with enhancing and adding to the existing attractions at Alton Towers. His first impressions were mixed. Alton Towers "probably had the best rides in Europe," he said, but they were not very heavily themed.[265] Indeed, Wardley did not consider the park to be a true theme park at all: "John Broome had added some large semi-demountable continental fairground equipment, implemented a pay-one-price admission policy, and called the place a 'theme park'. The British public believed that they needn't travel to America any longer to experience mega theme park rides and attractions." [266]

"The definition of a theme park is a much-abused thing and a lot of people think a theme park is any kind of amusement park with a pay-one-price policy, preferably in land," said Wardley in a 2012 interview.[267] "People were calling themselves theme parks, when they had no right to call themselves a theme park." [268]

The real definition, accordingly to Wardley, was a place "where you provide a series of adventures and attractions on a theme and tell a story in the process." [269] Theme park attractions should not simply be relabelled travelling fairground rides. Instead, they should employ fairground-style transit systems (such as roller coaster and dark ride technology) and use these to create an "adventure". The adventure, not the ride itself, should be the focus. This would turn a basic ride into a "special experience".[270]

Attractions such as the Grand Canyon Rapids and the Corkscrew were not meeting Wardley's expectations – the focus was very much on the ride itself, rather than telling a story. Indeed, most of the rapids attraction was not even visible to those queuing to ride it – the complete opposite of Wardley's approach to the proposed rapids ride at Woburn. It would be two years, though, before Wardley would really stamp his mark on Alton Towers.

The first major attraction to be added to Alton Towers' line-up following the Tussauds takeover was very much in the Broome mould of off-the-shelf rides with minimal theming (and, indeed, had likely been acquired prior to the takeover). The Thunder Looper roller coaster was added close to the Skyride's garden station, giving thrill-seeking guests a compelling reason to disembark rather than simply carrying on to Festival Park or Towers Street.

The ride was actually some thirteen years old, having debuted in 1977 as "King Kobra" at Kings Dominion in the US state of Virginia. It was the first Schwarzkopf Shuttle Loop coaster, and used a weight-drop mechanism to launch riders to a top speed of 53 miles per hour. A 40-tonne weight was dropped down a shaft, pulling a catch car which pushed the train up to its maximum speed. The train then raced through an enormous vertical loop, before climbing up a 138 foot hill. Having come to a halt, it plummeted backwards, once again navigating the loop, before returning to the station. It had a brief stint at the Jolly Rodger Amusement Park in Maryland before moving on to Alton Towers.

Despite its age and the minimal theming, the Thunder Looper was a hit with the park's guests. Opened by boxer Frank Bruno, accompanied by Henry Hound in a boxing gown, it offered a fast-paced experience that left some guests stunned. "For the people who experienced the ride, it really was special," remembers one early rider. "We went for the front seat every time. Seeing the long take-off track stretching out in front of you with that massive loop, waiting for the countdown, was the most fantastic experience. The trip back through the loop was made even greater as you couldn't see it coming, then backwards through the station at an incredible speed, watching the people in the station fly past in a blur, then up the small de-acceleration hill, still climbing quite high and down into the station where the air brakes tried to force your head from your shoulders." [271]

On disembarking the Skyride, Natalie Sim – then 12-years-old – remembers: "We were met by the towering Thunder Looper. My jaw dropped with excitement and my dad's jaw dropped with fear. We joined the queue and away we went. I remember on that first ride being totally aware of going upside down – it seemed as if it was in slow motion. Without even a chance to catch our breath it was time for another go, but this time backwards! I think that was the killer for my dad. We alighted and I saw a rather pale face in front of me. When I put my glasses back on, the true colour of my dad's face became clear – it was a nasty shade of green. Dad went to the first bench he saw to sit down, and my mum was ordered to fetch a cup of tea. He didn't move from the bench for the rest of the morning and didn't ride anything else all day. I still don't think he's forgiven me, but I *loved* the Thunder Looper."

By the time Tussauds acquired Alton Towers, the park had begun to gain a reputation as a haven for teenage thrill-seekers – an image that was further reinforced by the addition of the Thunder Looper, and flat ride the Tri-Star a year later. The park's marketing director in the early 1990s, Nick Varney, said that people had it "fixed in their minds that Alton Towers is a big funfair in the woods." [272]

This was a major issue for the park's new owners. "We wanted it to be a family park with something for everybody," said Varney. There were sound business reasons behind this ambition – a population forecast had indicated that there would be a significant drop (1.7 million) in the 15-24-year-old demographic during the 1990s.[273] To continue growing its profits, Alton Towers would have to appeal to the family market. Tussauds planned to do this by following the same model it had at Chessington, allowing Wardley to create themed adventures that would provide fun for all age groups – not just teenagers.

The first big changes arrived in 1992, and started right at the entrance to the park. Towers Street had been envisaged by John Broome as a high-class shopping area, much as Disneyland's Main Street, USA had been during the early years of the park. As with later Disney management, Tussauds didn't see the value in running expensive shops selling specialist products in a theme park environment. Many of the shops were closed, becoming office space for the park's staff.

Wardley was handed a relatively modest budget of around £6.5 million to transform two areas of the park, as part of a masterplan that was designed to "look as though we had done a mega hit on the park, but without involving a huge amount of capital." [274] This would involve the complete redesign of a large area of Aqualand, as well as the addition of two new rides. Market research had led Tussauds to settle on these being a family roller coaster and a dark ride. [275]

During his first trip to the Towers, Wardley had noted that the Grand Canyon Rapids, while an excellent ride, was "sadly underexposed". He believed that people should be able to enjoy watching the ride, even if they were too afraid to experience it. A new queue line was constructed through the centre of the attraction, while the barren surroundings were remodelled into an African Village setting. From now on, the area would be known as Katanga Canyon - and would bear a strong resemblance to the African-themed areas that had been planned for Woburn's Festival Park

Weaved around the rapids' circuit was the new roller coaster. Just as at Chessington, Wardley opted for a powered mine train coaster manufactured by Mack, naming it as the Runaway Mine Train. The two attractions were designed to interact, most notably in an iconic new tunnel section where the coaster's train would race past the rapids' rafts in close proximity. Unlike the Corkscrew and the Thunder Looper, the Runaway Mine Train was designed to be a "pink knuckle" ride – one that grandmas and granddads could ride, but on which teenagers would still have fun.[276]

Alton Towers pulled out all the stops to ensure that Katanga Canyon would feature authentic African theming. This included engaging the Royal Botanic Gardens at Kew in London, who provided a list of suitable plant life, aiming to "create a sense of theatre" with plants that would represent "broadly themed vegetation types" and that would flower during the peak summer season. A "wadi" or river bed was recommended to run in parallel to the water channel, with thickets of reed and rush crowding and overhanging the visitors. The village square area would contain elements of spectacular Victorian colonial planting, the forest would emphasise "lushness, vigour, exuberant growth and shade", while the savannah would consist of low grass and herbaceous plantings.

With the forced closure of Coaster Corner, The Beast was relocated to a site next to the Thunder Looper, creating a new land dubbed Thunder Valley. The two coasters were somewhat isolated, and required an extensive walk to reach on foot on days when the Skyride was busy. The solution was to create a new through-route to Thunder Valley from Katanga Canyon, and to open another new themed land – Gloomy Wood – between the two.

Next to the monorail depot on the Gloomy Wood site was a large spot that was perfectly suited to the installation of the new dark ride. An enormous building the size of a football pitch was constructed here, hidden from the view of guests by a Haunted House façade. Inside, Wardley hoped to create a "good, old-fashioned, laugh-in-the-dark-type pretzel dark ride", along the same lines as his legendary Uncle Frankenstein's Scream Machine at Barry Island.[277]

The main problem with replicating the experience of his earlier ride was capacity. On ghost train-style rides, individual cars were dispatched every 20 seconds, meaning that they could cope with around 300-400 people per hour – a number that was completely insufficient for a major theme park such as Alton Towers. Traditionally, most theme park dark rides had used long, continuous trains of ride vehicles in order to maximise capacity. This, though, would remove the feeling of intimacy that comes from riding in individual cars.

Mack, the German firm that was manufacturing the Runaway Mine Train, had earlier worked with Wardley to create the innovative rotating cars on the Fifth Dimension dark ride at Chessington. The company was again called upon by Wardley, who asked for an alternative to "endless transit systems", which removed the element of surprise by enabling guests to see what was happening to those in front of them. He wanted riders to "feel as though they were on their own".[278] The solution was a custom system that loaded continuously (enabling a high throughput), but with individual, six-seater cars that accelerated as they left the station to leave them ten seconds apart. This, says Wardley, was a "nightmare" to produce, with a sophisticated computer system being used to control the distance between the cars, which cost some £18,000 each.[279]

Wardley himself designed the basic Haunted House circuit, and employed Sparks Creative Services to produce the special effects (the company had earlier produced the scenery and animations for the Bubbleworks attraction at Chessington). Given that the ride was designed to process some 1,800 people per hour, this was a major challenge. A different group of riders would pass by each effect at 10 second intervals – so all the effects had to be displayed and reset within that time.[280]

Guests would queue through an eerie graveyard populated by tombstones with comical engravings. Once inside the building, they would encounter ghostly apparitions designed to tie in with the history of the Towers. One, a miniaturised "Emily Alton" figure, roamed around in a doll's house. Another, "Sir Henry Alton", spoke to them from a burning fireplace. Keith Sparks, the director of Sparks Creative Services, played Sir Henry himself.

After an eighteen-month construction period, the Haunted House debuted on March 31, 1992, being opened by Phillip Schofield, then the presenter of Saturday morning kids' show *Going Live!* on the BBC, and wildlife presenter Michaela Strachan. The high-tech computer system controlling the cars broke down just in advance of the opening ceremony, requiring Alton Towers staff dressed as undertakers to ride alongside guests and VIPs and manually reset them.[281]

A huge number of effects were packed into the ride building, including a rotating "Tunnel of Doom" that gave riders the sensation of turning upside down, an enormous spider and a ghost that took riders by surprise by whizzing over their heads from behind. The ride's circuit encompassed the interior of the house itself, as well as scenes in the garden and a swamp.

The Haunted House proved to be another major hit for Wardley, and still has a sizeable cult following today. "I can remember riding the Haunted House during its opening year, and finding it maybe the most bone-chilling experience of my life," remembers one young rider. "This is probably because I didn't dare open my eyes from the front doors to the shop."[282]

"It used to be such a unique experience back when it opened," recalls another. "I remember being fascinated by everything, confused by the tunnel and scared of the spider. The holograms flying above were also amazing."[283] Many fans regret the 2003 conversion of the ride into the interactive Duel: The Haunted House Strikes Back, bemoaning the fact that most riders now ignore the effects as they are too busy wielding a laser gun.

The impact of Wardley's makeover of Alton Towers was immediate. 1991 was a disappointing year for the park, during which only the basic flat rides Tri-Star and Gallopers Carousel were introduced. Attendance plummeted to 2,070,000. The following year, after the introduction of Katanga Canyon, Gloomy Wood and Thunder Valley, it leapt to more than 2.5 million. At the time, the UK was gripped by a recession that appeared to have a disproportionate effect on attractions in the south. Chessington suffered a 15 percent fall in visitor numbers during the same year, while Alton Towers finally overtook Madame Tussauds London to become Britain's most popular paid-for attraction.[284] During a difficult year for Pearson, the Tussauds Group was one of the star performers.

The focus on attracting families and upgrading existing areas of the park continued into the 1993 season, when the Land of Make Believe was introduced. This replaced the former Talbot Street area, another relic of Broome's focus on retail establishments. In place of the Dickensian theme came dazzling colours reminiscent of a children's cartoon, while the Motor Museum – a poor fit with Tussaud's plans for the park – was replaced by the indoor playground Children's World. The Vintage Car Ride was moved from its unlikely location next to the Black Hole to form part of the new land's line-up. Sweet-toothed children would be well served by Bertie Bassett's Corner Shop, the Haagen Dazs World of Ice Cream and the Cadbury's Chocolate House.

The retheme of the area spelled the end for one of Broome's signature attractions, the Fantastic Fountains. These were replaced by the Magic Theatre, which hosted a magic show featuring Henry Hound and friends. Attendance at the park continued to creep up, hitting 2.6 million for the year.[285]

Initially, the Land of Make Believe simply incorporated attractions from the former Talbot Street area. In 1994, though, it received a new headline ride, as Around the World in 80 Days was extensively rethemed to become Toyland Tours.

Replacing the globe-trotting scenes of the original were ones depicting the inside of a toy factory, in a whimsical ride reminiscent of Professor Burp's Bubbleworks at Chessington. While old-fashioned toys were well represented, there was also a room dedicated to videogaming giant Sega, featuring a foot-tapping model of Sonic the Hedgehog. An erotic-looking hippopotamus, complete with an enormous bust and balanced on a cupcake, became something of a cult figure.

Toyland Tours was another popular addition, and is firmly etched into the memory of many young visitors. "Toyland Tours was my favourite ride as a child," says Alex Machin. "It really summed-up what the Alton Towers magic really was. Everything about it was funny and colourful and well-presented. It didn't rely on a high-tech simulator and it didn't have to either." [286]

It wasn't just suitable for children, though. "It had something for everyone really," recalls Adam James. "The kids had the colourful characters and toys to look at, the teenagers had a 'tunnel of love'-esque experience, and adults could have a giggle at the puns and the hippo." [287]

The soundtrack was a particular hit. "You just couldn't get it out of your head," remembers Natalie Sim. "Luckily, it was on sale in the gift shop – so you didn't have to."

Further evidence of Tussauds' focus on Disney-style themed areas came with the conversion of the farm area into Old MacDonald's Farmyard in 1995. The emphasis on education was reduced, with the Tractor Ride taking over part of the paddocks, the noisy Doodle Doo Derby carousel being introduced and the Pottery finally being removed from the park to make way for the musical animatronics of Old MacDonald's Singing Barn.

More radical changes were to come to the neighbouring area of the park, Kiddie's Kingdom, the following year. This was split in two to become Adventure Land and Storybook Land. Adventure Land incorporated many of Kiddie's Kingdom's existing adventure playground attractions, which had been expanded since Tussauds' takeover. Storybook Land, meanwhile, absorbed the Peter Rabbit on Ice show that had debuted in 1994. It featured some very intricate theming, and was headlined by the new Squirrel Nutty Ride, a monorail with "acorn" vehicles that circled the area.

In the meantime, many of the off-the-shelf rides that were left over from the Broome era began to be removed from the park. The 4 Man Bob and the Gravitron (a spinning ride introduced shortly before Broome's departure) were sold to Pleasure Island in Cleethorpes. Cine 2000 was finally shuttered in 1993, with 1001 Nights following it out of the park two years later. Quaint attractions from the estate's pre-theme park years, including the rowing boats and the Splash Cats, were also doomed, along with the Miniature Golf course. Some flat rides were still introduced (if only to maintain capacity), such as the Astro Dancer (a HUSS

Breakdance ride) in 1993 and Energizer (a gondola that rotated unpredictably) in 1995.

Tussauds couldn't focus exclusively on the family market – it still needed teenagers and adrenaline junkies to prop up Alton Towers' attendance figures. The park may have done little to attract them during its first three seasons under its new management – but it had a secret weapon up its sleeve.

Battersea Power Station in its early years, long before John Broome tried to convert it into a theme park.

Woburn Safari Park could look very different had Tussauds' plans gone ahead. Image: Natalie Sim

John Wardley's Runaway Mine Train.
Image: Matthew Wells

The spooky façade of the Haunted House.
Image: Brian Negus

For more images, visit
http://www.themeparktourist.com/tales-from-the-towers/

5. The Secret Weapons

The creation of a path through to Thunder Valley from Katanga Canyon had helped establish the Thunder Looper as Alton Towers' most popular attraction. There was a major problem, though: the coaster only had temporary planning permission. It was big, it was noisy, and – unless management could somehow persuade the planners to let them keep it – the park would have to remove it at the end of the 1994 season. "We'd created a pathway to nowhere, unless we could find something to replace Thunder Looper," recalls John Wardley.[288]

Tussauds had opted to focus on the family market following its acquisition of Alton Towers, seeking to soften its image as a haven for young thrill-seekers. However, it could not afford to alienate the teenage market altogether – and the removal (without replacement) of the Thunder Looper would certainly do that. Aware of the issue, almost immediately after purchasing the park, the company began to plan for the construction of a major roller coaster - one that would ultimately be four years in the making.

The installation of the Thunder Looper in 1990 had bought Tussauds valuable time while it sought to add a truly world-class roller coaster to the park's roster. One that would firmly establish Alton Towers as the leading theme park in the UK, and cement its position as one of Europe's leading tourist attractions. The result was one of the most successful theme park attraction development projects ever undertaken, combining cutting-edge engineering, theming on an unprecedented scale and an ambitious marketing plan to ensure that its end-product transcended its status as a mere theme park ride and become a cultural icon. That end-product, of course, was Nemesis.

As it had done with Katanga Canyon and the Haunted House, Tussauds turned to Wardley to take the reins on the coaster project. In common with his previous creations, Wardley was determined to create a unique, custom experience that could not be easily replicated elsewhere. This was a major departure for Alton Towers, where John Broome had built the park's early success on the practice of buying off-the-shelf models.

The Thunder Looper was an off-the-shelf coaster of the type that Wardley frowned upon. Nevertheless, it had opened up Thunder Valley as a new home for thrill rides at the park. A flat, unremarkable site close to it was earmarked as the location for the new roller coaster, which was allocated a multi-million pound budget.

Wardley's biggest issue was how to design a ride that would satisfy Tussauds' management's need for something that was original, remarkable and easily marketable, within the strict planning constraints placed on the park by local authorities. Even the relatively modest Thunder Looper was on the way out, so building a skyscraping monster was out of the question.

"We probably have the most trouble of any park in the world when it comes to getting planning consent",Wardley explained during a presentation to mark Nemesis' tenth anniversary.[289] "It's dead easy to build a high roller coaster. We had a huge problem. Our site here at Alton Towers does not allow us to build big, high rides. We couldn't build anything that went above the trees. We couldn't build anything that could be seen from outside the park. How on earth could we build a sensational, world-class roller coaster when we had to keep the thing no higher than the tallest tree on site?"

Wardley and his team floated helium balloons above the site, in order to establish the maximum height of the coaster. It rapidly became clear that there simply wasn't enough height available to create the fast-paced experience that Alton Towers needed. The solution was simple: build *downwards*, into the ground. The team proposed excavating an enormous pit, an unusual approach that would cost a fortune. Management were receptive, though, and so were the local authorities. Outline planning permission was secured, but work could not begin until detailed plans were in place.

The design, and even the actual type of coaster to be used for the park's new headliner, had yet to be decided. While it had engaged with leading coaster manufacturers to understand the new technologies that they were developing, nothing had quite hit the mark. Until, that is, Wardley heard rumours of a new, never-seen-before coaster model that was being developed by Swiss firm Bolliger & Mabillard for Six Flags Great America near Chicago.

Based in Monthey, a small Swiss town with a castle at its center, B&M had by 1994 established a growing reputation as a coaster design firm of international standing. The company was founded by Walter Bolliger and Claude Mabillard, two former employees of Giovanola, which manufactured rides for B&M's now-rival Intamin. While working there, the pair had been involved in the design of Intamin's first stand-up roller coaster, Six Flags Magic Mountain's Shockwave. With Giovanola undergoing a change of management, Bolliger and Mabillard left to start-up their own consultancy. They continued to specialise in stand-up coasters, selling their first, Iron Wolf, to Six Flags Great America in 1990.

B&M's next project for the Chicago park was shrouded in secrecy. Wardley called his friend at Six Flags, Harold Hudson, then the American company's Vice President of Engineering. Hudson initially refused to share any information on its mysterious B&M coaster, but cracked after Wardley flew to Six Flags Over Texas (where Hudson was based) and convinced him that Tussauds was not in competition with Six Flags and that it would return the favour in future (and it appears it did, with flying coaster Superman: Ultimate Flight opening at Six Flags Over Georgia not long after Air debuted the concept at Alton Towers).[290]

Wardley was staggered by Hudson's description of the new attraction. Like Vampire at Alton Towers, the "inverted coaster" would see riders sitting in trains that dangled beneath the track. Unlike existing suspended coasters, though, the ride's trains would be "floorless", with riders' legs dangling freely beneath them. Not only that, but it would be capable of including loops and other inversions in its circuit – something that Vampire, with its swinging trains, could not do. "That's impossible," was Wardley's reply, "you can't turn an inverted coaster through loops." [291] B&M, though, had found a way.

"It was like nothing that ever had been built before", said Wardley. It was also exactly what Alton Towers was looking for, and this was confirmed when Wardley was among the first people to ride the yet-to-open first version, Batman: The Ride, at Six Flags Great America. Agreeing to maintain complete secrecy, Alton Towers engaged with B&M and began the process of designing its own, custom inverted coaster. Two earlier plans for the site had been based around a high-security military installation, and had been given the codenames of "Secret Weapon 1" and "Secret Weapon 2". The inverted coaster project became known as "Secret Weapon 3".

The next challenge was to design a track layout that squeezed as much excitement as possible into the limited footprint imposed by the pit. "Although we curse the various statutory bodies that control Alton Towers' heritage, they do force us to be creative", Wardley concedes.[292] "It would be so easy and so much cheaper if we could just throw steel up into the air way above the trees." [293] Between them, Wardley and B&M were able to come up with a design that worked, packing four inversions (two corkscrews, a zero-g roll and a vertical loop) into the circuit.

The final inversion, a corkscrew, was added at Wardley's insistence having been left out of B&M's original layout. He was determined that the circuit would not be "front-loaded" with thrills, as was often the case with roller coasters. Instead, he wanted the fun to continue right through to the end of the circuit. He was also concerned with those who might be too scared of coasters to ride Nemesis: "The whole idea of the layout of Nemesis was that you could enjoy it even if you couldn't ride it. Roller coasters were traditionally put behind a barbed wire fence. I wanted Nemesis to be enjoyed by everybody. You could get in and amongst it." [294] The corkscrew was deliberately placed at spectators' eye level.

A large extended team was working on the coaster project, including – for the first time at Alton Towers – Tussauds' own studios. To ensure that everybody involved had a clear view on the theme and styling of the coaster, Wardley developed an elaborate backstory. He accepted that it would be lost on most riders, but this was seen as a positive. "We want the visitors scratching their heads in disbelief. What they see must be an enigma to them." [295]

There was another motive for developing the alien backstory for the ride. While inverted coasters were a new concept, it was inevitable that they would eventually spring up at other parks, perhaps including Alton Towers' UK competitors. "The hardware is available to anyone with sufficient cash," said Wardley in a memo in November 1992. "We are therefore determined to conceive its theme so as to make it the most sensational in the world and one which cannot be copied." The unique location would aid the park in this goal.

Wardley's backstory was that yellow slime had been oozing to the surface in the Alton Towers' grounds, while loud rumbling sounds had led to rumours that a huge creature was living under the ground. A team of investigators from the Ministry of Defence had been sent to look into this, with excavations taking place under a cloud of secrecy. These had unearthed a massive alien organism, which acted as a central host. This beast sent out tentacles through cracks in the rock, with "exploratory organs" leaving its body and moving out along these to gather nutrients and procreate. Support structures were added by the MoD to pin these tentacles to the ground.

Few guests riding Nemesis today will realise that the station represents the alien itself, the "tentacles" make up the track and the trains are the "exploratory organs". Nonetheless, the backstory – and concept art produced by Tussauds Studios' John Knowles to bring it to life - helped to ensure consistency in the project's design, from the visual look through to the music played in the queue. In the early years of the ride's operation, a version of the story was narrated by former *Doctor Who* Tom Baker and played out to waiting riders.

With construction progressing and a marketing plan being drawn up, the coaster still had no name. Wardley and Nick Varney, the park's marketing director, locked themselves into Varney's office, vowing not to leave until the name had been decided. Aided by a bottle of Southern Comfort, they debated potential options for several hours. "I don't care what you call it," declared Varney, "but it's got to end in '-is'. It sounds mystical." "What about 'Nemesis'?" asked Wardley.[296] The suggestion was put to a development meeting, and the naming issue was settled.

The construction of Nemesis was not straightforward. In 1991, the site was still part of Alton Towers' car park. The grassy surface hid a huge amount of solid rock under the ground. This was positive in one sense – the walls of the pit would be self-supporting. However, it would be hugely expensive to excavate a hole large enough to house a roller coaster. "They were probably the most complicated foundations ever built for a roller coaster," said Wardley.[297] Ultimately, creating the pit would cost some £5 million – as much as the coaster itself.

The surrounding area, which still hosted the Thunder Looper until its removal in 1996, was transformed from Thunder Valley into Forbidden Valley. Breaking with the Broome-era tradition of housing rides in largely-unthemed locations, the new area was littered with small details, as well as larger elements such as the Nemesis Nosh dining outlet, housed in a decrepit bus (later removed as its condition deteriorated).

Alton Towers was determined to make a huge splash with its new addition, building Nemesis into a recognisable brand that would pull in visitors for years to come. Having spent around £5 million on the ride and the same amount on the pit, it allocated a further £5 million for an extensive advertising campaign. Declaring the coaster to be "the world's most intense ride experience", it plastered the Nemesis name across national newspapers and prime-time television. A public relations campaign was just as successful, securing considerable media coverage including a slot on the BBC's *Blue Peter* that is still remembered by many then-young viewers of the children's show today.

The marketing spend was necessary, given that Nemesis faced competition from two other major roller coasters introduced in 1994. One was the Intamin-designed Shockwave at Drayton Manor, located just an hour's drive away. This was the first stand-up roller coaster in Europe, and the only ride of its kind to feature a zero-g roll in the world. The biggest threat, though, came from something gargantuan that was being constructed at the historic Blackpool Pleasure Beach amusement park.

The owners of Pleasure Beach had taken a more traditional approach to gaining attention for their coaster than Alton Towers, opting for sheer height and speed. The Big One dominated the skyline at the seaside resort when it opened, with its lift hill topping out at some 213 feet. At the time, it was the tallest and steepest roller coaster in the world, and it still holds the title of being the tallest coaster in the UK.

Other than its sheer scale, its design was a fairly traditional steel creation manufactured by the now-defunct Arrow Dynamics. However, its top speed of 74 miles per hour and a sponsorship deal with Pepsi ensured that it generated a similar amount of media interest and public awareness to Nemesis.

Speaking in 1997, Wardley was clearly disdainful of the approach taken by Blackpool Pleasure Beach. "I'm not interested in the industry's blinkered view that the only way forward is through statistics of height, speed and g-force. If people get off one of my rides and say, 'that was terrifying, I wish I hadn't done it', then I consider that I've failed. I'm not out to terrify people. I'm an entertainer. I want to exhilarate them. Rides should provide surprise, mystery, laughter, amazement." [298] The Big One lacked the kind of subtlety that Wardley was referring to.

In March 1994, Tussauds and Alton Towers' staff held their breath as Nemesis was opened by TV's *Gladiators* (one of whom was reputedly made somewhat ill by a couple of trips around the circuit). After an enormous financial outlay, would the ride prove to be a hit with the British public?

From a distance, Nemesis didn't appear to be anything spectacular, with those arriving on the park's monorail only capturing the briefest glimpse. Once they had entered the queue line, though, cleverly designed to wind around the major elements of the ride, they were quickly exposed to the screams of passing riders. The queue area was visually stunning, with waterfalls of "blood" crashing down the rocky sides of the pit. The ride itself proved to be a smash hit.

The impact on Alton Towers' performance was immediate. The park welcomed 3,011,000 visitors in 1994, up fifteen percent from the previous year.[299] The Nemesis brand was also rapidly established, with Wardley later quoting a report that claimed that the word "Nemesis" was used four times as often in common parlance in the English language in 1994 as it had been in 1993.[300] Wardley's own reputation grew still further, with Nemesis cementing his position as a worldwide celebrity in roller coaster enthusiast circles.

Wardley is in no doubt that the difficult process of gaining planning approval for Nemesis benefitted the ride in the long run: "The restrictions force us to be much more creative, which gives the rides greater appeal both in the short and, most importantly, in the long term." [301] In his view, this has given the Alton Towers headliner a longer shelf-life than either Shockwave or The Big One: "Nemesis is still way up there and when the American Coaster Enthusiasts and the various roller coaster societies around the world come to Britain they make a bee-line for Nemesis and both the Big One and Shockwave just don't get a mention."

Along with Batman: The Ride, Nemesis also helped to establish the inverted coaster as a theme park favourite and to further establish B&M as world-leader in coaster design. Alton Towers' (and Wardley's) unique relationship with the company resulted in two further collaborations in the following decade.

Nemesis even inspired two "sister" rides – the Nemesis Inferno roller coaster at Thorpe Park and Nemesis Sub-Terra, an enclosed drop tower ride that debuted at Alton Towers in 2012. Neither has established the same reputation as their more famous sibling, which remains one of the most popular rides at Alton Towers almost two decades after its introduction.

Hidden secret: Take a look at the enormous tree that stands next to Nemesis' station. It once stood in the middle of the flat field that acted as Alton Towers' car park, and was carefully preserved during the construction process.

The debuts of Gloomy Wood, Katanga Canyon and the Land of Make Believe had helped to ensure that Tussauds was successful in moving away from Alton Towers' previous "thrill-seekers only" image and had drawn families to the park. By the late nineties, though, the balance had swung too far the other way, and the park was in danger of losing its appeal to teenagers – still an important sector of the market. The "Nemesis effect" had kept them coming through the gates since 1994, but this would inevitably wear off over time.[302] Another major roller coaster was needed, and development work on "Secret Weapon 4" was soon underway, with Wardley once again at the helm.

Having built a solid relationship with B&M while working on Nemesis , Wardley once more turned to the Swiss firm. The focus, as with the previous Secret Weapons projects, was on building something unique and original that could not be found anywhere else. Ideas for a "flying roller coaster" – one in which riders would lay face-down under the track – were discussed, but deemed too complex to be delivered within the required timescale. Instead, the group settled on the idea of a coaster with a vertical drop, knowing that if they could pull it off they would achieve a "world's first".

The project was shrouded in secrecy, and even the most avid roller coaster fans were unable to extract any information from Alton Towers about the nature of its new ride. Instead, they watched as a site in Fantasy World – close to the Black Hole – became a hive of activity. The Pirate Ship and AstroDancer were closed at the end of the 1996 season, ready to be moved to Forbidden Valley and Festival Park respectively. Huge earth-moving machines were brought in. Something big was happening – but what? The only hint was a sign reading "World first ride opens March 1998".

B&M had produced early designs of the vertical drop coaster concept. These showed a steep lift hill, followed by an enormous, 90-degree drop down into a watery "splashdown" area below. They had also given the model a name – the Dive Machine.

While the designs were exciting – and indeed closely match the layout of B&M Dive Machines subsequently built at other theme parks around the world – everyone involved knew that they would not work at Alton Towers. The height of the drop (180 feet) would place the ride's track well above the treeline, while the splashdown would be unpopular on the frequent days when the weather was cold. As with Nemesis, the obvious – and expensive – solution was to build an enormous hole in the ground.

Whereas Nemesis had simply been placed, almost in its entirety, into an enormous pit, the hole for SW4 would be in the form of a u-shaped tunnel. The vertical drop would plunge directly into this, with the trains emerging out of the other side.

Hidden Secret: Get your protractor out and align it with the "vertical" drop on Oblivion. You'll find that it's actually a little shy of being truly vertical, at around 87 degrees.[303] SheiKra at Busch Gardens Tampa – another B&M Dive Machine – holds the distinction of having the first truly vertical drop. Other coasters have since surpassed this with "beyond vertical" drops.

Constructing the tunnel was a lengthy process. Observers had few clues as to the end result, with a deep hole being dug out first before later being covered over to create the tunnel. Of the £12 million budget for SW4, a staggering £6 million was spent on the tunnel alone. "The few people in the industry that heard what we were doing said 'you must be mad'," remembers Wardley. "The hole cost us as much as the rest of the ride put together. In our industry, certainly in America, you spend 95 percent of your budget on some big great machine. The idea of actually spending 50 percent of your budget on just digging a hole seemed crazy to people." [304]

Recalling the scale of the task, he later said: "This was probably the most audacious piece of civil engineering that anyone had ever done in a theme park ever." [305]

As with the Haunted House, the next major problem was capacity. For a major roller coaster, this would have to be high – at least 1,500 riders per hour. The issue, though, was that standard roller coaster trains simply couldn't be used on a vertical drop roller coaster. Wardley explains: "The first car of the train would hang over it [the drop], but then as the train started to accelerate the rear car would be flipped with enormous force so that people would be subjected to a 'forward-flipping' g-force that was completely unacceptable."[306]

The obvious solution was to have single-car trains, as on wild mouse-style coasters. Traditionally, though, these only held two to four riders – which would result in a pathetically low capacity. Wardley and B&M decided that if the Dive Machine was to have an acceptable throughput, the trains would have to be *very* short *and very* wide. The result was unlike anything ever seen before on a roller coaster – trains that were eight seats wide, by two rows deep. To ensure that everyone got a "front row seat", the second row of seats was raised above the first. "Nobody had ever built a vehicle that was more than four people wide," says Wardley, "the idea of 6 or 8 was unheard of".[307] To accommodate the wide trains, which were very heavy, the track would have to be much wider than that of B&M's other models. The ploy worked – the resulting ride has a capacity of some 1,900 people per hour.

There was one final innovation, added at Wardley's insistence. Rather than simply plunging straight down the vertical drop, riders would instead dangle "on the brink" for a few seconds, staring down into the abyss below. At a cost of £350,000, a second chain conveyor was added to this section of the circuit, along with reverse-acting chain dogs fitted to the coaster's trains to achieve the desired effect.[308] To increase the tension, a recorded voice would boom out "Don't look down!" via a loudspeaker system. Once out of the tunnel, the trains would glide around a simple curve and back into the station.

Unlike Nemesis, the name for the new ride wasn't difficult to devise. Riders would be staring down into a black pit – on the edge of oblivion. "Oblivion" it was. The loose backstory would be based around the mysterious disappearance of the ride cars, with warning videos being on view in different areas of the queue.

The Fantasy World area, which had until now featured an eclectic mix of rides ranging from the space-themed Black Hole through to a swinging ship (and in previous years, even vintage cars and miniature golf), was to be completely updated to welcome the new addition. It would now be known as X-Sector, and would boast a futuristic theme, with a colour palette dominated by black and silver (though orange would also feature prominently on Oblivion itself). The coaster would be joined by Enterprise and Energizer, both relocated from Festival Park, creating an area that would appeal almost exclusively to thrill seekers.

Wardley, always conscious that many people do not enjoy roller coasters or other fast-paced attractions, again designed Oblivion so that it would be almost as much fun to watch as it was to ride. Guests could stand right at the opening of the tunnel, enabling them to stare up at terrified riders before they plummeted into it. This also provided an ideal photo-taking spot for relatives. "It used to really sadden me when I would go to a park and see people that were scared to ride a coaster, and all they could do was look through a chain-link fence at a ride in the distance. I believe I have an obligation to entertain those people as well," says Wardley.[309]

Matching the marketing budget for Nemesis, £5 million was set aside to promote Oblivion. Hoping to "rebuild its credibility with the youth market", the park positioned the new ride as a "challenge" to competitive teenagers. It aimed to ensure that 80-85% of 16-24 year olds in the UK would see its television adverts, which featured the "don't look down" slogan. With the coaster unfinished, the ads were actually mocked up using a ride car in a studio.[310]

Secrecy over the precise nature of the ride was maintained until two weeks prior to the start of the 1998 season, in order to create a maximum impact. When the cat was let out of the bag, the world's first vertical drop coaster featured heavily in newspapers, television broadcasts (a *Blue Peter* feature was again seen by millions of children) and even on packets of Kellogg's breakfast cereals. 2.7 million people visited Alton Towers in 1998 – not quite matching the levels seen in 1994 for the debut of Nemesis and Toyland Tours, but still a healthy figure.

Wardley had tried out the ride for himself a few weeks prior to its opening day, during the testing phase. He was impressed: "For the first time riding a roller coaster I was genuinely scared, nobody had ever dropped vertical into a small hole in the ground like this before. It's an extraordinary ride. The only place in the world that you can experience dropping from that height down into a hole in the ground, which never looks big enough to contain you." [311]

The anticipation created by the ride's steep lift hill was almost as important as the drop itself. Natalie Sim, an early rider, remembers: "The car stopped halfway up the lift hill for several minutes due to a technical fault. A staff member came out to reassure us by making idle chat about the weather, but I was absolutely terrified. I couldn't wait to go over the drop in the end. It was a relief just to be back on the ground! There's nothing else like Oblivion in the world – it's probably still my favourite ride at Alton Towers."

Oblivion was the first B&M Dive Machine, but it was not the last. Taller, faster models featuring splashdowns, multiple drops and inversions would be built elsewhere during the following years, but none featured the signature tunnel of the Alton Towers version. Wardley is in no doubt that this gives his creation a unique distinction: "B&M have built Dive Machine coasters on the ground and they have had to be two or three times the size. That's all very exciting, but the idea of dropping into that hole and not knowing how deep it is and whether you're ever going to come out again, that was how the whole project came about." [312]

Hidden Secret: Hidden under the O2 Arena in London (the former Millenium Dome) is a time capsule containing an overview of Oblivion. It was written by Matt Davies, a 13-year-old theme park fan at the time of ride's opening, who won a *Blue Peter* contest to suggest items representative of 1998 to be included. Oblivion merchandise is buried alongside a Tamagotchi, a Spice Girls CD and photographs of Princess Diana. The capsule is due to be dug up and opened in 2050.

Work on Secret Weapon 5 began not long after Oblivion opened, but Alton Towers was busy planning something very different to celebrate the new millennium. This time, the park's new attraction would make use of the very structure that lends it its name.

The once-grand mansion that sits at the heart of the park was in need of significant repairs, which would cost a vast sum of money. John Wardley recalls: "We sat down with English Heritage and said 'look, there's this gigantic structure in the middle of the park which we can't use, we can't do anything with it. It's not safe to let people in it, we can't put a ride in it – we can't do anything. But yet you want us to spend millions of pounds just literally saving it from falling down. What can we do?'" [313]

Taking a constructive approach, the heritage body asked the park to come back with some ideas. The options were limited. The park could not knock down any walls, or add emergency exits. Installing a dark ride inside the Towers was therefore impossible. Running a roller coaster around its exterior would be inappropriate and would never gain planning consent.

The Towers, though, could potentially be used to house the *queue* for an attraction, as well as a pre-show. This would provide a solid business reason for restoring ruined areas. The ride itself, meanwhile, could be hidden in a concealed building at the back of the Towers - one that could later be removed if needed without damaging the building or leaving a permanent imprint.

It was decided at an early stage that the attraction's theme should tie in with the history of the Towers, given that it would be housed within them. Wardley and his team held a brainstorm with Les Davies, the park's archivist. Davies shared some of the myths and folklore surrounding the Towers, and one in particular stood out: the legend of the Chained Oak.

The legend tells that in the 1840s, the sixteenth Earl of Shrewsbury, John Talbot, was travelling past the site of the oak tree en route to Alton Towers. An old woman blocked the passage of his carriage, begging him for some spare change. The earl cruelly dismissed her, commanding her to leave his property. The woman, scorned, screamed a curse at him: "For every branch that falls from the old oak tree, a member of your family will die." Later, during a violent storm, a single branch from the tree fell to the ground. True to the beggar's word, the earl's son suddenly – and unexpectedly – died. Shocked and determined to avoid a repeat of the tragedy, the earl ordered that every branch of the tree be chained up to prevent further incidents.

Wardley remembers: "When Les told us this story, it was all very appealing and we chuckled and thought it was a good story. When he said he'd take us to see the oak, the smiles left our faces. He led us through the woods, and there was this gigantic oak tree, completely tied up in gigantic iron chains. We had got ourselves a real gem here - we could tell this story in the new attraction. It was just asking to be told." [314] The project would be referred to as "Project Les", in honour of the archivist.

Seeking an appropriate ride to fit with the theme, the development team looked at "Madhouse" attractions, which create the illusion that riders are spinning upside down. They visited The Haunting at Drayton Manor, which had opened in 1996, and decided that it was a good fit with the Towers, given its mysterious nature and limited footprint. Alton Towers acquired a Vekoma Madhouse, the same model employed by its fellow Staffordshire theme park.

The queue line for the attraction would run through the Armoury and Picture Gallery, with a pre-show taking place in the Octagon. Just as guests during the nineteenth century had passed through these magnificent rooms as they entered the building, now modern day guests would do the same. The Armoury was already the site of a gift shop, but still required extensive repairs to its roof. Many of its stained-glass windows were replaced or restored by the company that had originally installed them more than a century ago, John Hardman Studios of Birmingham. The Octagon, meanwhile, was in terrible condition. The central column had collapsed, and had to be rebuilt. Just reinstalling the top section cost some £90,000, with some of the cost being funded by a grant.

While the restoration work was taking place, a large pit was dug behind the house, with an exit tunnel leading into Her

Ladyship's Garden via the House Conservatory. This would accommodate the Madhouse ride system. The total budget for the project was £4 million, with half of this being spent on the ride, and the other half being spent on the Towers.[315] The updates included restoring a fountain in Her Ladyship's Garden back to working order for the first time in over a century, for guests to gaze at as they exited the attraction.

Wardley and his team extended the mythology behind the Chained Oak in order to provide some context for the Madhouse experience, which was dubbed Hex – The Legend of the Towers. In the new version of the legend, the earl brings the fallen oak tree branch back to the Towers, where he performs a series of bizarre experiments on it to try and eliminate the curse.

Seated in rows on either side of the branch, riders on Hex watch in amazement as the room begins to rotate around them, creating the impression that they themselves are turning upside down. Fittingly, the ride is an update of a system that dates back to Victorian times, when rotating rooms would be used to confuse and disorient funfair visitors. The Vekoma version adds in a hydraulic system that enables the seats to tilt as much as 15 degrees in either direction. This is synchronised with the spinning room effect to create the sensation of being inverted.

"Is the legend really true?" is the question on many riders lips as they leave Hex. Well, the tree itself is real, and is located on the former grounds of the estate (though outside the boundaries of the current theme park, with the land having been sold off in 1918). Staring at its enormous branches, held in place by sturdy metal chains, it is very easy to believe the myth. It does indeed sit close to the route of an old carriageway that would have been used by the earl to visit nearby Cheadle, and he would have been the only person in the local area with the resources to put the chains in place.[316]

It is likely that the earl had the chains installed simply to keep the prized oak tree in good condition, given that it was so close to the carriageway. However, no documentation has survived to prove this, and so the actual reason behind the chaining of the tree is open to speculation. There is nothing to disprove, or indeed prove, the validity of the legend of the curse.

However, if there was actually a curse, it would appear to have lost its effect. On April 9, 2007, a huge bough of the oak tree fell to the ground, chains and all. Thankfully, no member of the current Earl of Shrewsbury's family died as a result.

The reaction of visitors to Hex in 2000 wasn't quite what Alton Towers had hoped. Wardley explains: "As soon as Alton Towers announces a big new ride, fans assume that it will be a very dynamic, new roller coaster." [317] As a result, in its first year the ride did not achieve the guest satisfaction scores that the park had hoped for. "It's very difficult to market a dark ride unless you have an intellectual property, and not overbuild people's expectations," laments Wardley. One teenager was heard to comment: "I'm here to go on rides, not to be lectured about history."

However, "as the years have gone by, the satisfaction scores for Hex are way up there with all the other big rides and attractions," says Wardley. Freed from the burden of being a new, headline attraction, Hex has attained something of a cult status.

Hidden Secret: It is still possible to visit the Chained Oak today. Close to the service entrance of Alton Towers sits the Chained Oak Bed & Breakfast. Through a gap in a stone wall, a path leads down from the hotel's driveway into the Barbary Gutter (following the route of the old carriageway). Walk down this for around five minutes, and you will come to the old oak tree, standing on the right at the top of a flight of time-worn steps. The fallen bough from 2007 still lies on the ground, covered in its chains.

In parallel to the Hex project, Wardley was already working on his next Secret Weapon creation. Having parked the "flying coaster" concept during the development of Oblivion, the designer and his contacts at B&M revived it, determined to somehow make it work.

They weren't alone in pursuing the idea of a flying coaster experience. Alton Towers' hopes of achieving building a second "world's first" roller coaster in succession were dashed when Vekoma (the firm that had supplied the Hex ride mechanism) launched its "Flying Dutchman" model in 2000. The first example was Stealth at Paramount's Great America (now California's Great America) in Santa Clara. Guests boarded the coaster in a seated position, with hydraulic pistons being used to lower the backwards seats towards the track. This left them lying on their backs, with a 180-degree twist in the track being used to put them in the correct position underneath the track before they "flew" around the rest of the circuit.

Wardley was unimpressed. "The restraint mechanism was the problem," he says, "they were very uncomfortable." [318] To achieve a satisfactory sensation of flying, he felt, B&M would have to develop something much better. The rest of the ride would use fairly standard coaster technology, so this became the major challenge for the project. Somehow, riders would have to be loaded into the flying position in a way that was fast (to maintain capacity) and comfortable.

The end result was ingenious, and achieved the desired effect. Riders would board in a seated position, with their legs dangling below them much as they do on Nemesis. They would then pull down a harness over their chest and waist, which would lock into place. Comfortable ankle restraints held their legs in position. Then came the fun part – mechanisms located in the station would rotate the seats so that riders were facing the ground. As an alternative to the convoluted method employed by the Vekoma flying coasters, it would generate much more excitement among riders. It would still be time-consuming, though, so dual loading stations were planned.

The site for the coaster – close to Nemesis in Forbidden Valley - had been vacant for some time, having previously been home to the New Beast. As with Nemesis and Oblivion, balloons were floated above the site to determine the maximum elevation that was allowed without rising above the tree line. On this occasion, no enormous pit would be necessary. The huge expense of developing the ride system, though, meant that the budget for the ride matched that of Oblivion, at £12 million.

Both Nemesis and Oblivion had been themed around "villains", but Wardley felt that this didn't fit with enabling guests to achieve their childhood dreams of flying like Superman. Despite its location in Forbidden Valley, the new ride – named Air – would be themed as a "hero". Riders would fly over a lush oasis, providing them with pleasant scenery to take in as they soared overhead. Light blue track would create a "softer" look, less threatening to those terrified of the previous two Secret Weapons. To match the theme, the layout of the circuit would be less thrill-packed than that of Nemesis. Instead, it would focus on providing riders with a pleasant experience of "flying", giving them time to watch the ground rushing past below.

In a departure from the marketing plans for Nemesis and Oblivion, the nature of Air was not kept a secret (perhaps because plans submitted to the local authorities had already led coaster enthusiasts to deduce that it was a flying coaster). It was openly promoted within the park during the 2001 season, with a model of the ride being installed in the Towers

Trading store. £4.5 million was invested in the associated advertising campaign, with the ride making the now-standard appearance on *Blue Peter*. In January 2002, the first successful test run was completed, and Air opened alongside the park for the start of the season.

Unfortunately, the huge cost of the ride itself had led to cutbacks in other areas. The oasis seen in early concept artwork, packed full of vegetation, rockwork and water features, was gone. Instead, riders passed over a fairly bland, grassy area, as well as a dull pavement towards the end of the ride.

Perhaps as a result, Air has never achieved quite the same lofty status among roller coaster enthusiasts as its predecessors – although it remains a very popular ride with the general public. Wardley had achieved his objective of producing a coaster that was not intimidating to non-thrill seekers. "I was terrified of Nemesis and Oblivion," says Kathryn Lummis, "but Air isn't scary at all. It's my favourite ride at the park by far."

"Put your arms up and relax and you will never come as close to the sensation of flying, I presume, without actually being on a plane!" says one rider. "Not fiction - this coaster actually makes you feel like you're flying," says another. "The near misses and easy inversions make the experience surreal – sure, the scenery is lacking but the fact that I could fall asleep on this coaster makes it different from the rest." [319]

Wardley was pleased with the result, believing it far superior to Vekoma's attempt.[320] "It gave a more satisfactory sensation of flying," he said. "It was terribly difficult [to achieve] and that's why it took a long time to get the technology perfected."

Nemesis has proven itself to be an enduring favourite.
Image: Natalie Sim

Skeletons greet plummeting Oblivion riders at Halloween.
Image: Natalie Sim

The legendary Chained Oak of Hex fame, seen in 2013.
Image: Natalie Sim

Air swoops overhead in Forbidden Valley.
Image: Natalie Sim

For more images, visit
http://www.themeparktourist.com/tales-from-the-towers/

6. Merlin's magic wand

More and more of our guests are choosing to spend more than one day at Britain's No. 1 theme park so that they can really make the most of our 125 rides and attractions. At Alton Towers we are always looking for new ways to extend the "magic" and make sure you are able to spend the longest possible time enjoying the fun - so we have decided to open our own very special hotel next March. – Alton Towers Hotel brochure, 1995

Alton Towers had dabbled in providing on-site accommodation for visitors as far back as the 1970s with the International Caravan Park. Walt Disney World in Florida had proven that a theme park could form the basis of a "destination resort", and the idea of transforming the park's offering from a simple day out to a multi-day short break was always on John Broome's agenda.

Despite local opposition, Broome had secured outline planning permission for a Center Parcs-style complex boasting 107 chalets, as well as a 56-room hotel in the valley on the site of the Alton Mill.[321] While work had not yet started on this when Tussauds took over Alton Towers in 1990, it is likely to have had an impact on the sale price of £60 million.

In the end, Tussauds opted not to pursue the chalet complex proposal. However, entering the short break market was very much part of its plans. A revised hotel proposal was put to the planning authorities in September 1993, and approved later that year. Alton Towers' transformation from theme park to resort had begun. The 183-room Alton Towers Hotel opened its doors in March 1996, set in a 7-acre plot close to the park's car parks.

Again taking inspiration from Disney, Tussauds opted to make the hotel a heavily themed experience. It devised a backstory based around the adventures of explorer Sir Algenon Alton, which was to influence every area of the hotel.

Walking into the lobby, guests were greeted by an enormous recreation of Sir Algenon's Jules Verne-style flying machine. The reception desk, appropriately, was created from a pile of "lost luggage". A quirky soundtrack accompanied guests as they rose in the "magical" lifts up to their rooms, all of which were themed in some way. Even the toilets were fitted with "magic mirrors".

Around half of the rooms were Explorer Rooms, themed around Sir Algenon's travels and packed with memorabilia brought back from his adventures. Fitting in with Alton Towers' heritage, Garden Rooms featured lamps designed to resemble watering cans. Those willing to pay extra could stay in the Disney-style Princess Suite, a Coca-Cola-themed room featuring its own soda fountain, or a Cadbury's-sponsored room in which they could devour as much chocolate as they could manage.

The Secret Garden Restaurant, complete with a talking tree, offered a more upmarket dining experience than could be found in the theme park itself. The menu featured an elaborate telling of Sir Algenon's story, detailing his "culinary discoveries". Just as the Swiss Cottage restaurant had in the past, it overlooked attractive landscaped gardens. Also in the hotel's original catering line-up was Time for Tea, a traditional tea shop that has long since closed.

Swimming pools were often the focal point of Disney's hotels, but the Alton Towers Hotel opened with the relatively small Pirate's Lagoon pool. Tussauds hadn't skimped on the theming, though - the pool, reception and changing rooms were also covered in detailed murals depicting swashbuckling pirate scenes, created by artist Steve De La Mere.[322]

Most hotels feature a television channel that offers nothing more than adverts for their own services. Alton Towers, though, rigged up a camera in an owl box and streamed the footage to its rooms. Merchandise, too, was somewhat out of the ordinary – particularly when compared to today's offerings. High-quality paintings of Sir Algenon's adventures were on offer, providing a pricy but unique memento of a stay at the hotel.

Tussauds continued its march to dominance of the UK theme park market in 1998, when it sold its stake in the Spanish PortAventura resort for £58 million to fund the acquisition of Thorpe Park. The Surrey park was located close to Chessington World of Adventures, and the two properties had been competing for the same audience. Under Tussauds, Thorpe Park would target thrill-seekers, with Chessington focusing on the family market.

The company now owned three of the top five parks in the UK, but Pearson was losing interest in theme parks. Chief executive Marjorie Scardino – who took the helm in 1997 - had developed a strategy which involved focusing on the conglomerate's media and publishing interests, and had begun to sell off non-core assets. Tussauds was one of the businesses that Scardino was looking to offload, although Pearson rejected an offer from leisure giant Rank to take it off their hands in March 1998, holding out for a sale price above £300 million.[323]

In October that same year, venture capital group Charterhouse Development Capital met Scardino's asking price, agreeing to acquire Tussauds for £350 million.[324] Tussauds had tripled in size since Pearson had originally bought it, and in 1997 had made a profit of £35 million on sales of £107 million. Scardino, though, was happy to use the sale as a means to reduce Pearson's debt, saying: "The Tussauds Group is a wonderful company full of creative and committed people and we wish them every success with their new owners. We've always said that someone would have to pay us a good price and provide Tussauds with a good home to convince us that a sale was worthwhile. Charterhouse has done both." [325]

John Wardley, then a non-executive director of four companies within the Tussauds Group, was forced to resign along with his fellow directors. In his autobiography, he says that he was "perfectly happy with the situation", and indeed little seemed to change in Tussauds' strategy in the years immediately following the takeover.[326] Wardley continued his work on Hex and Air as a freelance consultant. Other existing plans, such as the conversion of the ageing Festival Park into the prehistoric-themed Ug Land in 1999, were also implemented.

Less than a year after being acquired by Charterhouse, Tussauds revealed its intention to build a second on-site hotel. Not only that, but it would also construct an indoor water park – a second major attraction that would further encourage two or three day stays at the resort. The water park would be exclusive to hotel guests, providing a competitive advantage over other local accommodation providers. The hotel, water park and an associated conference centre would cost a combined £40 million to construct.

Head of hotel operations Phillip Baker explained: "The idea behind the water park is to encourage people to stay at Alton Towers for longer and to come in the winter months when the theme park is closed." [327] The new hotel would also provide extra capacity – the Alton Towers Hotel had been consistently fully-booked during the summer months since its 1996 debut.

Scheduled to open in time for the 2003 season, the Splash Landings Hotel and the Cariba Creek water park would share a "Caribbean paradise" theme. Public areas in the hotel would overlook the water park, at the heart of which would sit an enormous tipping bucket with a capacity of four tonnes. The backstory revolved around a sinking island that was rescued by the Paradise Plumbers, Crazy Bob and Mumblin' Pete, who would appear as walkabout characters in the hotel.

The 40,000 square-foot water park would span both indoor and outdoor areas, boasting a selection of water slides, several swimming pools, an enormous climbing structure and a large number of interactive water elements. To maintain a family atmosphere, a strict adult-to-child ratio would be enforced.

Inside, the main attraction would be the Master Blaster, a water slide with a 208-metre circuit. Unusually for a water slide, guests (sitting in rubber rings) would be propelled uphill in some sections by powerful jets, with the final section being a more traditional downhill plunge. Two other slides, Rush and Rampage, would also be on offer. The main pool, Lagoona Bay, would feature water cannons, geysers and a waterfall, with the Little Leak offering similar thrills for small children. Wacky Waterworks would be an enormous wooden structure boasting climbing nets, tunnels and bridges, plus seventy interactive features such as water cannons, tipping buckets and taps. After braving the slides, guests would be able to relax by floating around the leisurely Lazy River.

Outside, a total of five slides would plunge into the Flash Floods pools. The steamy Bubbly Wubbly Pool would allow guests to soak in its heated waters, while tired parents could take a break on a deckchair.

The attached 216-bedroom hotel would feature slightly more basic rooms than the Alton Towers Hotel, but each would have a "Beachcomber" theme. The Flambo's Feast restaurant and Ma Garrita's Bar would keep guests fed and watered.

The first customers arrived at the Splash Landings Hotel on June 1, 2003, ready to enter a tropical paradise. Unfortunately for Alton Towers, what they actually found resembled a building site.

The problems started right at the entrance to the hotel, where a themed water feature was meant to impress arriving guests. Instead, tools and parts surrounded it, and it was bone dry. Construction walls, scaffolding and building materials were highly visible around the building's exterior, while families had to skirt around unprotected holes in the ground to make it into the lobby. Once inside, they were greeted by the scene of a ladder and tins of paint, along with workmen painting the ceiling.

After the dazed guests had checked in, they could head up to their rooms – taking the stairs of course, since the lifts weren't yet operating. On their way, they could admire more ladders and tools, often being wielded by workmen (adding authenticity to the building site theme).[328] If they were hungry, they could head down to the restaurant, being careful not to touch the wet paint on the entrance desk or fall over the scaffolding piles on the floor.

From the hotel, they could gaze at the water park, which was in an even worse state. The Master Blaster wasn't operating, with equipment and materials clogging up its flume. Lucky guests *could* take a dip in the Lagoona Bay pool, but the entire outside area was unfinished. The other pools sat empty. Alton Towers blamed bad weather for the construction delays, but many were left wondering why even internal work such as painting had not been completed.

Despite warnings from the resort that the water park wasn't yet finished, hotel guests paying more than £200 per night were not happy with the situation. Within days, faced with a wave of negative publicity, Alton Towers offered unhappy customers compensation and shut both the hotel and the water park. Both would reopen some weeks later once work had been completed, ultimately proving to be just as popular as the Alton Towers Hotel. Within a year, though, the hotels had lost one of their distinctive perks, with day visitors being given the chance to visit the water park.

Hidden secret: Be careful not to end up with sunburn at the Alton Towers Water Park. The roof is designed to let in ultraviolet light.[329]

By 2002, Charterhouse had succeeded in doubling the size of Tussauds' business, aided by the acquisition of Heide Park in Germany and an estimated £300 million investment from the owners. The company's profits had grown from £31 million in 2000 to £65 million in 2003 under the new management team.[330] Marketing initiatives such as the installation of a statue of Brad Pitt at Madame Tussauds in London – complete with a squeezable backside – were credited with the turnaround.

In September 2002, though, Charterhouse announced that it was looking for an "exit strategy" from Tussauds within 12 to 18 months. By September 2003, the firm had appointed investment bank Lazard to advise it on "strategic options". This included the possibility of floating Tussauds on the stock market with a valuation of around £900 million, or selling it outright. Rumours suggested that Six Flags, the American theme park chain, could be among the bidders.[331]

While it studied its options, Charterhouse was making changes at Tussauds' theme parks. Tussauds Studios had played an increasingly heavy role in the design of new attractions since the creation of Nemesis in 1994. Now, with Air completed, the board of the Charterhouse-owned company decided that it no longer required the services of John Wardley. Instead, Senior Creative Director Candy Holland and her team would take the lead on the development of new rides at Alton Towers.[332]

With a new strategy in place, the Secret Weapon codename was dropped for Alton Towers' next two coaster projects, which would open in consecutive years in 2004 and 2005. Neither would feature the focus on uniqueness, heavy landscaping and extensive theming that had been the hallmark of the Wardley-led projects – largely as a result of significantly smaller budgets.

First up was Spinball Whizzer, opened in Adventure Land in 2004 at a cost of around £3.5 million. The ride was one of two custom Spinning Coasters purchased from manufacturer Maurer Söhne, with the other being Dragon's Fury at Chessington World of Adventures (which opened in the same year). Riders were seated in groups of two, back-to-back, in each of its small cars. These would race around a garishly-coloured track, spinning rapidly as they went.

The new coaster featured a pinball theme, with pinball-style games being located in the queue to entertain riders (and they would need them – the coaster often attracted long waits, partly due to its position near the front of the park). The theming, though, was relatively lightweight in comparison to many of the additions earlier in Tussauds' reign.

With its modest capacity of 950 riders per hour, Spinball Whizzer was clearly intended as a mid-level attraction, rather than being a Secret Weapon-style headliner. The same could not be said of Rita – Queen of Speed, which opened a year later and carried a heftier price tag of £8 million (still £4 million less than the budgets for Oblivion and Air). In a break

...lationship with B&M, rival Intamin's Accelerator
,ystem would be employed, enabling riders to be
...1 from 0 to 62 miles per hour in just 2.3 seconds.

As v.1th Spinball Whizzer, Tussauds acquired two similar
coasters in a relatively short time period - fellow Accelerator
Coaster Stealth would open in 2006 at Thorpe Park. Whereas
Stealth would launch riders to the top of a huge 205 foot
tower, the Alton Towers ride would stick much closer to the
ground in order to placate the planning authorities. Thrills
would instead be provided by a series of high-speed turns and
smaller drops.

The launch sequence for both rides is accomplished using a
cable and a catch-car that connects to the train. In preparation
for the launch, pumps push hydraulic fluid into a number of
accumulators, each of which is divided into two
compartments by a piston. With hydraulic fluid filling one
compartment, nitrogen gas in the other is compressed. The
pressure that this creates is released as part of the launch
process, and the hydraulic fluid is forced into several
turbines, which in turn drive a winch. This pulls in the launch
cables, dragging the catch car (and the train) up to its top
speed.

Naturally, advertising billed Rita as "your best Alton Towers
ride ever", and it has continued to attract long queues in the
years since its April 2005 debut. It has drawn criticism,
however, for the impact that it had on the Ug Land area.
Much of the prehistoric theming that had been in place was
removed to make room for the coaster, which was given a
drag racing theme. Whereas Festival Park had once been
home to a large number of flat rides, Ug Land now had room
for just Rita and the Corkscrew, along with the Ug Swingers
flat ride.

Despite the two additions, attendance at Alton Towers declined from nearly 2.5 million in 2003 to around 2.2 million in 2005.[333] Charterhouse had scrapped the idea of a stock market flotation or sale of Tussauds in December 2003, instead opting to borrow money to fund the expansion of the business.[334] In March 2005, though, a bid for the theme park group met Charterhouse's asking price of £800 million.[335] It came from Dubai International Capital (DIC), a new investment arm set up by Dubai Holding, a sovereign wealth fund of the government of Dubai. Tussauds' chief executive, Peter Phillipson, would remain in place after the takeover, and expected the firm's strategy of aggressive expansion to continue. "We would consider ourselves to be a candidate to lead the consolidation of the European theme-park industry in the coming years," he commented.

The first year following DIC's takeover, 2006, saw the minor addition of the Peugeot 207 Driving School children's attraction, as well as the loss of one of the biggest new additions of the early years of Tussauds' ownership of Alton Towers. Toyland Tours, which had been suffering from a lack of maintenance for several years, was shuttered. A reported £8 million – the same amount that had been spent on Rita – was invested in transforming it into Charlie and the Chocolate Factory: The Ride (though some sources claim the real cost was much lower, at around £5 million[336]). Based on Roald Dahl's classic book, the ride would take its visual inspiration from the illustrations of Quentin Blake.

The Toyland Tours boat ride system was retained, with the scenes being reworked to replace the former toy factory with the interior of Willy Wonka's chocolate factory. Rather than simply disembarking at the end of the ride, guests now entered a simulator that recreated the flight of the Great Glass Elevator. A combination of projectors, mirrors and semi-translucent walls were used to surround riders with images of the sky and the ground below. The floor trembled to give the impression of flight.

Considering the huge financial outlay, Charlie and the Chocolate Factory did not have the impact that its creators surely intended. When Toyland Tours opened in 1994, it had contributed – along with Nemesis – to a record-breaking attendance of over 3 million guests. In 2006, around 2.25 million visitors passed through Alton Towers' gates – only a minor increase on the previous year. [337]

The impact on the park was immediate, with budget cuts beginning to have an effect on the guest experience. In September 2006, operational hours for some rides were slashed. On weekdays, the Skyride and Monorail were closed entirely, The Flume, Congo River Rapids, Submission, Enterprise and the Corkscrew didn't open until lunch time, major coasters operated with fewer trains during the morning and late afternoon and Hex closed an hour before the rest of the park.[338]

Staff were affected as well as visitors. In the same month, Alton Towers announced that as many as 23 employees were likely to be made redundant as part of a "major restructuring programme". While the numbers were not huge for a park that had 700 permanent employees and 1,200 season staff, they were indicative of what general manager Russell Barnes said had been a "difficult year".[339]

Hopes were not high for a recovery in 2007, with DIC-owned Tussauds confirming that it would add no major new attractions to the park that year. A new walkthrough experience, Haunted Hollow, was added through the woodland close to Gloomy Wood, with the quirky There's Something in the Dung Heap play area opening in Old MacDonald's Farmyard. The Extraordinary Golf miniature golf course was added close to the car park's monorail station, expanding the resort's offerings and potentially extracting a few extra pounds from guests as they left the park. None of these minor additions were likely to entice back the customers that had deserted the park in the previous year, and indeed attendance declined slightly to 2.2 million.[340]

Hidden secret: Feeling nostalgic for an old attraction? Some of them can be relived via Extraordinary Golf, which currently still features a hole based around Ug Land despite it having been rethemed as the Dark Forest back in 2010.

DIC's reign as the owner of Alton Towers had not been a particularly auspicious one, although it had expanded Tussauds' line-up of attractions by completing a full takeover of the London Eye observation wheel in 2006. Despite its struggles at the Towers, it still made a large profit when it sold Tussauds to the Merlin Entertainments Group for £1 billion in March 2007. The deal created the second biggest operator of visitor attractions in the world, behind only the mighty Disney.

Merlin was headed by a familiar face. Nick Varney, who had been marketing director at Alton Towers during the creation of Nemesis, was the firm's chief executive. Varney had moved from Tussauds to Vardon Attractions, a division of health and fitness operator Vardon PLC, in 1995. The division had been formed in March 1992, when Vardon acquired the London Dungeon and the York Dungeon. Later that year, it also bought up nine Sea Life centres. After Varney joined as managing director, an aggressive expansion plan saw the number of Sea Life centres grow to twenty-three, across continental Europe and the UK. In early 1999, he headed a management buyout of the firm (backed by private equity investment group Apax Partners), breaking away from Vardon PLC and renaming the firm as Merlin Entertainments.[341]

In February 2004, UK-based Hermes Private Equity bought Merlin for £72.5 million. It didn't hang on to it for long, selling it on to another private equity firm, the Blackstone Group, for £102.5 million in May 2005.[342] Blackstone, which already owned a 50 percent stake in the Universal Orlando Resort, had grand plans for Merlin. In July 2005, it acquired the four Legoland theme parks in England, Germany, California and Denmark for 375 million euros, and merged them with Merlin's existing line-up. The Lego company and its founding family retained a 30 percent stake in the combined group.[343]

In 2006, the rapidly-expanding Merlin generated profits of £56.8 million, compared to just £7 million in 1997 when it was still part of Vardon.[344] Tussauds, meanwhile, was by now generating £100 million in annual profits. Following the merger in 2007, Blackstone took a 50 percent stake, DIC kept 20 percent, Lego also held 20 percent and management owned the remaining 10 percent. Varney held on to the chief executive role, and now presided over four of the top five theme parks in the UK (Alton Towers, Thorpe Park, Chessington World of Adventures and Legoland Windsor), as well as the popular Dungeons and Sea Life chains.[345] "It [the deal] allows us to become a major European force and compete on the world stage with the big American operators such as Disney and Universal", he said at the time.[346]

Alton Towers would now form the model for the other three parks, which Merlin planned to turn into "resort theme parks". Indeed, by 2013 all of Merlin's UK theme parks would boast on-site accommodation, and all are now promoted as short break destinations. The company operates three divisions – Resort Theme Parks, Legoland Parks and Midway Attractions (which includes the Dungeons and Sea Life centres).

Just four months after acquiring Alton Towers, Merlin sold the property to entrepreneur Nick Laslau's investment vehicle

Prestbury as part of a £622 million deal that also included Thorpe Park, Madame Tussauds London and Warwick Castle. Merlin, though, would continue to operate all of the attractions under a 35-year lease deal. Blackstone used the proceeds to fund investment and pay off debt.[347]

When Merlin acquired Alton Towers, 35 percent of the park's visitors were families, with a majority being young adults and thrill seekers, according to the Merlin-appointed marketing director Morwenna Angove.[348] Just as Tussauds had done in the early 1990s, the company planned to reposition the park so that it would attract more families. A range of family-friendly updates were made to the resort, including the addition of new baby changing facilities (complete with music and lights), a blanket smoking ban except in designated areas and more hotel rooms themed to appeal to young children. The monorail trains that delivered guests to the park's gates were updated in 2008 to feature brightly-coloured designs based on characters and areas in the park. All employees, meanwhile, were sent on a course to learn the "appropriate manner" to interact with families.

The operator's first major addition to the theme park, which opened in time for the 2008 season, reflected the new focus. "Kids love getting soaked on a water ride," said Angove, and they could do just that on Battle Galleons, a pirate-themed Mack Splash Battle ride located in the Ingestre Lake. Riders float around a fixed circuit in miniature ships, equipped with water cannons to blast other guests. Landlubbers can join in, with further cannons located around the water's edge. The "shabby" Merrie England area was updated to become Mutiny Bay, with the former Tea Cup Ride becoming Marauder's Mayhem (with barrels replacing the tea cups) and child-friendly flat ride Heave Ho! joining the line-up.[349] Merlin spent a total of £6 million on the new land.

The company also stepped up marketing efforts for the park. Its television advertising campaign emphasised the resort's credentials as a short-break destination, and targeted family shows on Saturday evenings. A new-look logo was introduced, along with the strapline "stay for days when you escape to the Alton Towers Resort".[350] The goal, said general manager Russell Barnes, was to convince the public that the combination of a major theme park, two hotels, a water park, miniature golf and a spa was "simply not available at any other location within the UK". The ads' soundtracks would feature *In the Hall of the Mountain King*, a tune long associated with the Towers but dropped from many of its ads during the DIC era.

The results were immediate, with attendance recovering to an estimated 2.6 million in 2008.[351] More importantly, the visitor mix changed dramatically, and by 2010 half of all visitors to the resort were families. The average length of stay at the hotels grew from 1.3 nights in 2007 to 1.7 three years later, while sales of two and three-day tickets grew six-fold during the same period.[352]

Merlin has a policy of incorporating its "midway attractions" into its resort theme parks. It relocated a small Sea Life Centre to Chessington World of Adventures in 2008, and was happy with the results. In 2009, it repeated the trick at Alton Towers, spending £4 million on the conversion of a previously mobile Sea Life Centre into the permanent Sharkbait Reef attraction on the site of the former 3D Cinema in Mutiny Bay.[353] Visitor numbers rose again to 2.65 million.[354]

Since taking them over, Merlin has been careful to target its UK theme parks at specific markets. Legoland Windsor caters for families with children aged 2-12, while Chessington World of Adventures features attractions appropriate for families with slightly older kids. Nearby Thorpe Park is focused purely on teenagers and young adults. Alton Towers, being the largest and most popular resort theme park, can afford to market itself to both families and thrill-seekers.

While the parks target different audiences, Merlin has homogenised some key elements since its takeover. This can be seen most clearly in the catering area, with near-identical restaurants such as Burger Kitchen and the Fried Chicken Company operating at Alton Towers, Chessington and Legoland Windsor. Theme park fans are now able to buy Merlin Annual Passes, which allow entry to all four parks plus all of Merlin's midway attractions and the London Eye.

The use of *In the Hall of the Mountain King* wasn't the only tradition brought back under Merlin. The Secret Weapons were also back, with the "SW6" moniker being applied to the Corkscrew's eventual replacement after its removal in 2008. John Wardley also returned, being brought out of retirement by Varney to work as a consultant on the new ride.

Just as Tussauds had required that the original Secret Weapons offer something unique, so would Alton Towers' new operator. "Merlin like to ensure that there is some sort of compelling proposition to every ride," says Wardley.[355] He was clearly pleased to be working with Varney once again: "Nick Varney understands his rides. He understands that quality and finish are important. Merlin have always devoted sensible budgets to rides so that things can be done properly using the best quality ride hardware, by putting the best creative talent onto a ride to be able to conceive and execute the theme, right down to composing special theme music. That's why I am so pleased to still be involved with Merlin after my retirement."

Morwenna Angove explained the marketing concept behind the revived Secret Weapons in a 2010 interview: "Our strategy with the new big rides begins with the idea that it should be a world first, both technologically and in terms of the ride concept, which is becoming ever more challenging nowadays. It has to be 'Alton-esque', with the fantastical escapism sparkle to it." [356]

Secret Weapon 6, the first major roller coaster to be added to Alton Towers under the Merlin regime, would come with a hefty price tag – some £15 million, the most the park had ever spent on a coaster. John Wardley designed the basic footprint and layout, but credits Merlin Studios' Candy Holland as its true designer. "I have been given a lot of credit for this ride that I don't really deserve," he said, "It's very embarrassing". Wardley, though, would be the public face of the design team, with Merlin taking advantage of his vast experience of dealing with the media.

He explains where the initial concept for SW6 came from: "We looked around and it was obvious that we needed a ride that would appeal primarily to the teenage market but that would also work for the families that visit Alton Towers. As the years go by, we find that the younger family market is more robust, and will ride attractions that a few years ago they would have found intimidating. We wanted to create a ride with a relatively low height limit, so that young people, if they felt they wanted to ride it, were able to." [357] This immediately ruled out several types of coaster.

There was a need to replace the Corkscrew, and the planning authorities dictated that the former site of the coaster was the only place in the Ug Land area of the park where a major ride could be built. To enable the coaster's circuit to be longer than that of the Corkscrew, Alton Towers proposed that it be allowed to run the track into the adjacent woodlands as well. The planners agreed to this, as long as the woodlands weren't disturbed.

Merlin was determined that the ride would be unique, but this was a problem for Holland, Wardley and the design team: "We had already done nearly everything," says Wardley.

"One of the criteria that Merlin applies to any project when it comes to capital investment is that there needs to be a fundamental, compelling proposition to that attraction, which has to be more than just the mechanics of the ride." [358]

Several years earlier, Wardley had designed a spinning roller coaster for the park, which was to feature a trick track section in it – one that would tip unexpectedly just before riders went up the lift hill. The idea was dropped, primarily for budgetary reasons. However, it would be revisited for SW6.

Intamin was consulted about the new ride. As part of a brainstorm, a recent project at Merlin-owned Heide Park was discussed, during which an Intamin-built panoramic tower had been converted into a freefall drop ride by adding a new gondola and magnetic brakes. It was suggested that the same concept could be applied to a roller coaster – taking a piece of track and allowing it to freefall. "Provided we could hide it from guests and do it in a very dramatic way, preferably in the dark, it would come as a complete surprise to riders," said Wardley.[359]

Achieving this would be complicated, but Intamin already had most of the required technology. "It's one thing to take a six or eight-person carriage and take it high up on a tower and drop it down. But a full size roller coaster train and its track would have a tremendous amount of mass," says Wardley. A balance needed to be struck between the height of the drop and its speed – higher velocities would require too much braking. In the end, the example of the small freefall drop tower, Extremis, at the London Dungeon was examined. The attraction, manufactured by ABC Rides, only dropped riders around 6 metres, to simulate being hung from the gallows. In the dark, though, says Wardley, it was a "very satisfactory effect".

Following testing, it was decided that a 5 metre drop was enough for the roller coaster. "You achieve weightlessness after a freefall of just a few metres," Wardley explains, "therefore it doesn't matter whether it's 5 metres, 10 metres or 20 metres, in the dark the effect is more or less the same." To add to the drama, a "false drop" of half a metre would precede the main drop.

As with Oblivion and Air, maintaining capacity would be a major issue. SW6 was designed to have a realistic throughput of 1,100 riders per hour, in order to keep queues to a minimum. There would need to be no delay in the coaster entering and exiting the drop sequence. Intamin's design allowed for the weight of the track and train to locate the track securely in its lower position, meaning that there was no need for any locking mechanism. Instead, sensors would immediately disable the hydraulic drop system, and riders would be launched backwards through a tunnel section. At the end of this, another launch section would fire the train back into the station. To enable the trains to be accelerated quickly, they could not be too heavy. Intamin therefore employed its Mine Train Coaster model, which boasts relatively lightweight trains and track.

The woodland setting would lend the ride its theme: "There was absolutely no question of us felling any trees and we had to take the ride through the woods," explains Wardley. "The theme is quite dark, but basically it's that the woodland has taken over the Towers." [360] The drop sequence would be housed inside a mock crypt, which would provide a dark setting as well as hiding it from the view of waiting riders. After the train entered the building and the door closed behind it, riders would see mysterious shrouded figures on either side. Sound effects and air cannons would accompany the false drop and the main freefall.

The new ride was named Thirteen, suggesting that guests would suffer from bad luck if they dared to ride it. The surrounding Ug Land area was rethemed as the Dark Forest (a name that is strikingly similar to the existing Gloomy Wood), with nearby Rita receiving a new theme based around escaping from the danger within. Ug Swingers was moved to Cloud Cuckoo Land, an updated version of Cred Street (the former Talbot Street area) that had opened in 2009.

Whereas Nemesis had featured an elaborate backstory, Thirteen would feature only the basic concept that the woodland had "taken over" the Ug Land area, with Merlin Studios aiming for an "edgy" theme. The ride buildings, notably the crypt, would be designed to resemble the Towers themselves, given their close proximity to the old mansion. "The mythology was very loose. We didn't go into great depth as we did with Hex," says Wardley.[361] "It's a back story; a story that you don't actually need to understand. If you try to do be too clever, invariably your guests do not take it on board and you fail dismally." [362]

Wardley felt that the vast majority of Alton Towers visitors would not take any notice of the ride's storyline: "It's a case of building up atmosphere rather than telling a story. The story would be wasted on the riders in any case. They get so hyped up in the moment that they are not really receptive to the subtleties of a storyline." [363]

That didn't stop roller coaster enthusiasts and Alton Towers fans from speculating about the theme on Internet forums. "There was great fun and games on the internet though with people reading far more into the story than we ever meant," recalls Wardley.[364] In particular, television advertisements featuring a mysterious girl and the slogan "if you go down to the woods today" sparked questions about the nature of the girl and her role in the ride. However, there was actually no direct link – it simply made for an appealing advert. "There is a lot more depth and meaning put into things than is actually the case [by Internet forums]," believes Wardley. Similarly, mystery surrounded the hooded wraiths that featured in the adverts and the ride itself, but "they are there – that's it! If you try to be too clever, the media will start to ridicule it. The basic idea of some strange power in the woods with a ghostly crypt containing spirits was about as far as it went." [365]

As with Oblivion, Alton Towers was determined to maintain secrecy around the nature of Thirteen's "world first" element. This was partly for publicity reasons, but the park also wanted guests to be surprised when they first experienced the coaster: "It's rather like revealing the outcome of a whodunit before an audience has even watched the play," says Wardley.[366] Once they had ridden, however, there was a danger that they would reveal the secret to other guests. The park even considered adding a sign at the end of the ride asking riders to keep quiet, but opted against it as it was feared that some guests would deliberately rebel against it. However, most prefer not to tell others about the drop, according to Wardley: "The average rider gets some sort of sadistic delight out of ensuring that the next rider gets the same element of surprise." The policy of secrecy worked: "On opening day, I think it was true to say that 99.9% of people who went on the ride got a complete shock." [367]

Thirteen debuted, as planned, on the opening day of the 2010 season. Despite the pouring rain and the inexperienced ride operators, it exceeded the capacity challenge laid down by Wardley. During the first hour of operation, 1,260 people passed through the ride – higher even than the theoretical capacity of 1,200 that it had been designed for. "The queue was moving at a constant walking pace. I never dreamed that they [Intamin] would be able to move the trains as quickly and slickly as they have," recalls the designer.[368] Inevitably, there was some downtime, but the coaster was "gobbling up guests almost as fast as they can get to it."

Some roller coaster enthusiasts expressed disappointment with the new ride, and particularly with the Dark Forest theme. Early concept art had shown much heavier theming, with "near-misses" in the woodland section and a queue line surrounded by foliage. In reality, Alton Towers had simply applied some creeping vines to the existing Ug Land buildings, and the saplings alongside the queue line had not yet had time to reach maturity. Unlike Nemesis, Oblivion and Air, for much of the queue Thirteen itself was barely visible to those waiting to ride it – and, of course, the crypt hid the freefall drop.

The marketing of the ride was also called into question. The park had described Thirteen as "the world's first psychoaster", billing it as "the scariest ride in the UK". However, the actual ride had been designed to appeal to a family audience as well as teenagers. Although they could meet the height limit, some children were put off by the Dark Forest theming. "A little boy in front of us was in tears," recalls Natalie Sim, who attended the opening day. "His dad was only able to persuade him to go on the ride after we reassured him that there was nothing to worry about. At the end of the ride, he begged his dad to take him round again!"

Despite criticism on the Internet, Wardley was happy: "I personally think that they [Merlin] have done a good job of promoting the ride." Guest satisfaction scores from visitors to the park also met expectations: "The ride is delivering to the general public. There is no doubt about it." [369]

Thirteen had a big impact on Alton Towers' attendance figures, with numbers exceeding 3 million for the first time in more than a decade. 2011, though was the first year in the park's history that no new attractions were added, and the Themed Entertainment Assocation estimated that visitors numbers dropped to 2.6 million. In 2012, despite the £6 million dual additions of the Nemesis Sub-Terra drop tower (a virtual clone of Extremis at the London Dungeon) and the licensed *Ice Age Dawn of the Dinosaurs – The 4-D Experience* movie, the estimated attendance fell further to 2.4

million. Undoubtedly, poor weather and the London Olympics had taken their toll.

Something major was required, and indeed had been in the planning stages for several years. In late 2012, the park began the removal of the long-empty Black Hole tent, and revealed that it would be replaced by another roller coaster – Secret Weapon 7. This time, the budget had been set at a huge £18 million. As with Thirteen, Candy Holland would lead the design team, with John Wardley acting as a consultant and producing the basic ride layout.

Once again, Alton Towers claimed that its new coaster would be "the only one of its kind in the world." Coaster fans pored over plans submitted to the local authorities, which showed the ride's layout, with speculation focusing on the vertical section in the middle of the ride. Given its location close to Oblivion, could the new coaster boast a vertical launch section? Some wily enthusiasts, though, pointed out that the curves prior to the vertical section were simply too tight to support a vertical launch.

It was clear from the plans that the ride would be a Gerstlauer Euro-Fighter model, a type of coaster that had already been employed at fellow Merlin park Thorpe Park in the form of Saw – The Ride. Alton Towers, though, wasn't about to retread old ground. Instead, it had chosen the ride system due to its ability to execute inversions in very tight spaces. SW7 would boast a record-breaking fourteen inversions, packed into a relatively small 1.5 acre site.

The suggestion to go for the inversion record was made by Merlin's Chief Development Officer Mark Fisher. John Wardley recalls: "Mark said 'shall we build an 11 inverter?' I replied 'you can bet your boots someone around the world is trying to beat Colossus [at Thorpe Park, which previously held the record with 10 inversions] and is doing 11 or 12. We don't want to build 13 for bad luck, and you have got a ride called that in any case. Let's go for 14."

Even for Euro-Fighter, the compact site was a problem. "It was necessary to have a two-lift ride [in order to generate the required speed], and we would pack in as many inversions as possible. This was a huge, huge problem - if you didn't get the exit from any given inversion absolutely perfect there was no room whatsoever to correct it before you entered the next inversion. Normally, after you've gone through one inverted configuration, you allow yourself a few metres of track to correct yourself before you enter the next. Here there was going to be no space for that." Somehow, the track layout – originally designed by Wardley, and tweaked by Werner Stengel – managed to achieve its aims.[370]

Unlike Thirteen, The Smiler's debut did not go smoothly. Alton Towers was forced to delay its opening date by two months due to construction delays, and last-minute glitches led to a high-profile breakdown on the media day in May 2013. After finally announcing May 23 as the ride's opening date, the park was again embarrassed when technical problems forced it to miss that date, too.

Wardley says of the delays: "The Smiler was incredibly behind schedule - the technical problems that they faced with that ride were enormous. There were geological problems with the site, there were floods, there was snow. It was a very complicated project indeed."

"From the moment you get on the ride you will never know where you are and it has some great surprises for riders," said Wardley prior to the ride's debut. "It has more track per square metre than any other roller coaster ever designed." [371]

The theme for the new addition would be based around the mysterious Ministry of Joy, a mock-Orwellian organisation that wanted to turn the population into "smiling advocates". This led to the ride's name – The Smiler. Sitting at the heart of the coaster would be an enormous robotic spider, known as "The Marmaliser". Each of its five legs would contain a "mind-manipulating" special effect, such as bright lights to confuse and disorientate riders and enormous rotating discs that would "hypnotise" them. "Whereas other roller coasters play with your body, this will play with your mind. It's more than just a physical roller coaster," promised Wardley.[372]

"We know people get a thrill when they ride roller coasters, but in order to heighten that feeling of excitement we needed to design a roller coaster that also incorporates a variety of mental cues," said the consultant. "The Smiler will be different from other traditional coasters in that it will combine intense physical effects to put the body through its paces, along with the unique mental elements to mess with the mind. After riding the coaster they will have experienced full mind and body 'marmalisation.'"

The delayed schedule meant some close calls during The Smiler's launch period. "The marketing people agreed that the ITV News people could have their weather forecast people do the first run live on television," says Wardley. "Whenever we've done first runs in the past, it's all been a bit of a cheat. There were multiple 'first runs' for Nemesis. On this particular occasion it was really quite bizarre, because we'd promised them that they could have the first run and we assumed that we'd have run the ride and we'd have been riding it for several days if not weeks beforehand."

However, come 2am on the day of the broadcast, no human being had ridden The Smiler. It would be 5.15am before the commissioning engineer from Gerstlauer and Alton Towers' inspection engineer got on board. ITV's Laura Tobin was only the third person to ride the coaster, live on *Daybreak*.

When The Smiler did finally open to visitors, on May 31, 2013, it was met with almost universal acclaim from roller coaster enthusiasts and the general public alike. "The Smiler is not only one of the most influential roller coasters ever built in Britain, it stands up to anything on the world stage, too," said coaster fan Adam Bysouth.

For Wardley, though, it would be his last involvement in a major ride at Alton Towers. Having already "retired" once, he planned to finally do so again – for real, this time. "I am very proud of what I have achieved at Alton Towers and memories of creating Nemesis and riding it for the first time will live with me until the day I die," he said. "It is time for me to hand over to someone else, nobody wants an old fart getting in the way. It is time to bow out gracefully." He will now spend his time traveling the world with his wife Jenny, and is confident that the park's future coasters will live up to expectations: "The roller coaster design team is brilliant, it is in safe hands. It's up to the next generation to decide where roller coasters go next and I will be watching and riding with interest!" [373] He admits, though, that he could still be tempted back: "I love rollercoasters and they have been my life, now my contractual agreements are all finished. But if the phone ever rings and somebody wants my help designing a ride, who knows?"

Some coaster fans have suggested that The Smiler outdoes Wardley's own Nemesis. The designer disagrees: "The Smiler is a good ride, if your idea of a good ride is just being turned upside down as many times as possible in as short a space of track as possible. For my money, at least, Nemesis takes you on an adventure - you go somewhere, you feel as though you are achieving something. Whereas The Smiler is basically just a very intense experience." [374]

Since taking over Alton Towers, Merlin has continued its impressive growth spurt. The opening of new Legoland theme parks in Florida and Malaysia helped it deliver a 16.5 percent increase in profits in 2012, with the company making

£258 million on a turnover of some £1.07 billion. More than 54 million people visited its various attractions, which now number over 100, over the course of the year. The group – which now owns 94 attractions in 21 countries - is rumoured to be planning a stock market float in London or New York in late 2013 or early 2014, which could see more than 2,000 employees enjoy a financial windfall.[375]

Not everybody is happy with Merlin's dominance of the UK theme park market. In particular, the firm has been dubbed "M£rlin" by some theme park fans, who feel that it is trying to squeeze every last penny out of them through schemes such as the Fastrack queue-jumping system and exorbitant car parking fees.

John Wardley, though, believes that the sheer size of the company bodes well for the future: "Merlin are the only people with the budget to enable big coasters to be built, and also they're the only people that have the imagination to put aside ride manufacturers brochures and start thinking outside the box and creating something different and something special. I would say that Merlin are uniquely placed to be able to take roller coasters forward in Britain, and if it were left just to the competition I don't think that would happen." [376]

Spinball Whizzer twirls its way around a winding circuit.
Image: Natalie Sim

Rita overtook much of Ug Land when it opened in 2005.
Image: Natalie Sim

Battle Galleons was Merlin's first addition to the park.
Image: Natalie Sim

Thirteen emerges from its "crypt".
Image: Natalie Sim

For more images, visit
http://www.themeparktourist.com/tales-from-the-towers/

7. Waking up the neighbours

Alton Towers has been an important part of the local economy for hundreds of years, with the estate having provided a livelihood for many locals during its time under the ownership of the Earls of Shrewsbury. Residents of the surrounding villages have been able to visit the gardens since the mid-nineteenth century, and the establishment of a tourist attraction on the struggling site in the 1920s provided an economic boost to nearby businesses. In 2010, Staffordshire County Council estimated that Alton Towers brought in almost £43 million of income in the local economy, and over £87 million in the regional economy.[377]

In more recent years, though, the relationship between the owners of the Towers and some residents has soured. Two major factors have led to the animosity – the visual impact and noise generated by theme park rides and attractions, and the growth of motor car ownership. Raging battles over planning permission for new attractions are now commonplace, while the park has also faced legal action aimed at forcing it to curtail noise and even remove or relocate some of its most popular rides.

While John Wardley has cited the innovation forced by planning restrictions as a key reason behind the success of rides such as Nemesis, he has also seen his designs for some attractions adjusted or thrown out altogether as a result of disputes with residents. Roller coaster enthusiasts and fans of the park have been up-in-arms as a result – but do the local residents actually have a valid point about the impact of the park on the area?

The roller coaster that kickstarted Alton Towers' growth into the sprawling theme park it is today, the Corkscrew, was opened by John Broome without first gaining planning consent. The ride did receive retrospective planning approval in 1981 – a year after it opened – by which stage Broome could argue that it had helped to create a vast number of jobs.

This was typical of Broome's cavalier approach to the planning system. Perhaps the best example is the installation of the Alton Beast and the Alton Mouse in the "Coaster Corner" area close to the Flag Tower. Both rides debuted in 1988, with *Neighbours* star Kylie Minogue on hand to open the Beast and Winter Olympics star Eddie "The Eagle" Edwards leading the celebrations when the Alton Mouse opened. While the Alton Beast was granted retrospective planning consent for a temporary period until March 31, 1989, the application for the Alton Mouse was declined.[378] However, the Staffordshire Moorlands District Council decided not to take enforcement action against the park pending discussions with its management.

Local resident C.T. Thorley wrote to the planning authorities to complain about the Alton Beast, saying: "As heard from the Red Road, Alton, the noise from this equipment is unbelievable. Every minute or so a noise similar to a lorry shedding its load of steel plates is heard. In the first instance, it was ludicrous to allow a fairground in the middle of a conservation area and this latest development proves the point. The noise from this fairground has been steadily rising over the years. I have lived in the valley for 25 years and now shrieks and yells with incessant drum beats and public address systems are clearly audible. The council seems oblivious to the additional noise that is steadily rising and casting a blight over the entire valley."

"The concrete footings for a second ride are already in place. I ask the question: Why can Alton Towers Ltd prejudge the issue on their own favour to the extent that they spend a considerable amount of money on the footings if their planning application is not a foregone conclusion?"

Andrew Hollingsworth, the park's managing director, responded by writing: "There has been a complaint from a resident in the Red Road area concerning the noise from the Beast, so we are modifying the wheel assembly on this ride to alleviate any problems there may have been."

The park's solicitors, meanwhile, were adamant that the Alton Mouse was needed to provide additional capacity on busy days: "The capacity of the existing ride has proven to be such that it only partially solves the problem at Alton Towers on peak days, and therefore, our clients wish to install a further small ride in the same area." The "small ride" would stand at 17 metres tall, a similar height to the Alton Beast.

The solicitors had also advised Broome that no planning consent was required *at all* to keep the rides in Coaster Corner. Hollingsworth wrote: "You are aware that we have received consistent advice from our solicitors that this application did not need planning consent because it was covered under class XXIX of the General Development Order 1977 as amended [essentially, that it fell within the agreed bounds of the existing amusement park and did not require separate planning consent]. David Cooper on the company's behalf made a statement to the effect that it would go through the planning process as if Class XXIX did not exist but should your authority refuse the application then they reserve the right to invoke Class XXIX and carry out the development regardless. That undertaking was given in the spirit of the undoubted cooperation which has existed between this company and your authority over many years and indeed it came from John Broome himself that that relationship should be maintained at all cost and that your authority regardless of Class XXIX should be continuously involved in the future expansion of Alton Towers."

The council disagreed, and in March 1989 it ordered the removal of both rides by December that year.[379] Broome responded by submitting a planning application for a permanent "gravity ride" in the same area, promising to remove the Alton Beast and Alton Mouse in 1992 *if* permission was granted. Local resident Sheila Parrington was furious, writing: "We are not all teenagers wanting the plastic thrills of the rides at Alton Towers." The Lower Churnet Valley Conservation Group also chimed in on The Beast, saying: "The quiet of the Churnet Valley which attracts so many walkers has been literally shattered by this ride. The visual beauty of the Farley and Ramshorn areas has already been ruined by the Alton Towers complex and this noise can be heard a mile away in that direction."

The Coaster Corner application marked one of the first disputes between Alton Towers and the Roper family, who own nearby Farley House. Stephen Roper said to the Uttoxeter Advertiser of the plans: "The company seems to be at liberty to ride roughshod over residents' views and environment issues and indeed the wishes of the planning authority. What so angers me is the sheer arrogance of John Broome that he can come up time and time again with retrospective planning and that includes this new attraction of his, the Britannia Building Society Farm [opened in 1989], sited at the park. It appears that anything goes up there. I hope that this planning refusal will be the start of a new wave of thinking about Alton Towers and the disastrous effect it has on the visual and noise disturbance of the surrounding area."[380]

In the end, both rides were ultimately removed from the park, although not until long after the original December 1989 deadline after Broome won his desired extension. The Alton Mouse was removed in 1991, while the Beast was moved to Thunder Valley where it remained until the end of the 1997 season.

Broome's next big plan for Alton Towers was the installation of a Center Parcs-style holiday village, complete with an enormous leisure centre and 107 chalets. The park's outline planning application was, surprisingly, submitted *before* construction work began, and was approved after being referred to the Secretary of State. A subsequent, more detailed application, however, featured several significant alternations.

Local residents Mr and Mrs Green picked up on one of the biggest changes: "Permission for the chalet units was granted following a public enquiry. But this has now been converted into *double* units [with two storeys], catering for around 1,700 people [the actual capacity was 1,200], creating a village almost as large as Alton itself."

"Despite stating in its application that the development will have 'minimum visual impact on areas outside the estate', there is to be a restaurant with 'magnificent views over the Staffordshire Countryside'. The two comments are hardly compatible. The highest building [the leisure centre] is to be built on the highest part of the site, with an unsympathetic glass roof. It will be easily visible from outside the estate, especially when lit up."

The Greens weren't entirely opposed to development at Alton Towers: "Please consider our views to be realistic; we do not wish to prevent Alton Towers from operating, merely to try to restore to the valley the natural quiet that it had only a few years ago. With a little more thought and planning of location and screening, we feel that Alton Towers could go ahead with many of its plans without affecting the valley and surrounding villages. It is disgraceful that the individual has to comply [with planning regulations], while the large, profit-making company is allowed to flout the planning laws repeatedly, without either enforcement or penalty."

Sheila Parrington, who had opposed Coaster Corner, questioned Broome's trustworthiness: "Alton Towers has also been granted permission for a hotel in the valley on the site of Alton Mill (1000 years old) with 56 bedrooms [this was a separate application to the chalet complex]. Subsequent plans have a sitting room added to many of these bedrooms; these will no doubt become bedrooms in due course."

It wasn't just at Alton Towers that Broome demonstrated his "build first, ask later" style. During the period when he planned to develop Trentham Gardens into a sister park for the Towers, similar issues arose. In 1983, Broome submitted an application to install a giant concrete slab, which would accommodate large temporary tents and allow Trentham to host events such as The Bike Show, the Holiday and Home Show and the Sports and Leisure Exhibition.

A letter from John Shyrane, County Planning and Development Officer for Staffordshire County Council, to the local planning authorities relating to the concrete slab application stated: "I would like to draw your attention to the premature execution of these proposals which were seen to have been completed at the time of Mr Preston's site visit on 18th November, 1983. A number of instances have occurred in recent years at Trentham and in Staffordshire Moorlands District in which the applicant and the applicants' related company Alton Towers Ltd have undertaken major development without planning permission. This casual attitude is particularly disturbing in view of the magnitude of their proposals for Trentham Gardens and the potential impact on the historic interest of the estate. You may, therefore, wish to draw to their attention the importance of complying with the requirements of planning law and to the penalties which may be incurred if such requirements are ignored." A handwritten note scrawled by Borough Planning Officer Keith Platt on the letter states: "They know this already".

The addition of the 4 Man Bob, Spider and Ferris Wheel to Trentham's fairground following Broome's takeover did not go down well with the planning authorities. In a report, they noted that: "During recent summer months several rides have been installed which do not appear to accord with the form or high standard of the illustrated layout. However, the applicant indicates that these unauthorised developments have been carried out as a temporary expedient to bolster summer attendances." Of course, Broome was happy enough with the appearance of the rides to move them to Alton Towers when he sold Trentham to the NCB.

At the Battersea Power Station, too, Broome was accused of ignoring planning laws. The Battersea Power Station Community Group claimed that the entrepreneur knocked down parts of the listed building without planning permission, leaving it without a roof for years.[381]

It is arguable that without Broome's approach to the planning process, Alton Towers might never have evolved into a theme park at all. Certainly, Tussauds' later experience with Woburn Abbey would suggest that gaining planning consent to install rides on a historically-significant site has become much more difficult since the early 1980s.

When Tussauds took over Alton Towers' in 1990, it took a more constructive approach to working with the planning authorities than Broome. The chalet complex application was quietly withdrawn, along with that for the "gravity ride" next to the Corkscrew. The company's first application to install new rides – the Runaway Mine Train and Haunted House – was far more detailed than Broome's previous submissions. For example, it contained a thorough assessment of the noise that the coaster would generate, based on the similar ride at Chessington World of Adventures. The ride itself was designed to minimise noise, with polyurethane wheels on a metal track and a quiet electric motor for the train. Screaming would be minimal, as the coaster was not a white-knuckle attraction.

Tussauds agreed to remove the Alton Mouse and re-site The Alton Beast, and appealed to the planning authorities to allow it to maintain capacity by adding the two new rides. It did not expect a huge attendance boost from the new additions (though it got one), but did plan to add a major ride two years later (this ultimately developed into Nemesis). Unlike Broome, who acted quickly, Tussauds was happy to take its time over the Nemesis project, ensuring that it took environmental concerns into account in its planning application. The resulting coaster, buried in an underground pit to minimise its visual impact and noise generation, stood in stark contrast to Broome-era creations.

Nemesis would feature a lift hill that was "suitably coloured" to blend in with the landscape, despite not being visible through the treeline. The second planning application for the ride reduced the complexity of the circuit, featuring two high points instead of three, and fewer inversions, to help reduce the noise impact. The loops in the original design were "tighter", which would have increased wheel noise as well as – the authorities felt – generating louder screams. The second application also included provision for a large mound to shield the coaster from views across the valley towards Alton and Denstone.

Responding to one resident who complained about the plans, the council's Assistant Chief Planning Officer, D.A. Jager, wrote: "My experience has been that on the whole the new management at Alton Towers do take their responsibilities seriously and in my view the planning applications that have been submitted recently have been thoroughly researched and well presented on all the relevant planning issues. I do not know whether you have had the opportunity of viewing the latest developments which have taken place in the area of the water rides and in particular the Runaway Train and Haunted House but I am sure you would agree that the quality of the work that has taken place and in particular the new landscaping has done much to improve the appearance of that part of the estate. I feel confident that the same high standards will be achieved in respect of this latest development."

Tussauds could not avoid controversy indefinitely, however. Its first big clash with local residents came over the retention of the Thunder Looper, which it had agreed to remove by the end of 1995 as a condition of the approval of the Nemesis application. Temporary planning permission had been given to retain the ride until then, with the warning that the authorities "do not regard this development as being appropriate for this particular site." The height of the coaster's tower and its noise levels were cited as the reasons for this viewpoint.

By 1995, however, it had become clear to Tussauds that the Thunder Looper was still a hit with visitors – indeed, it was still the second most popular ride at the park behind Nemesis. It applied to the council to keep the coaster in place for a further two years, giving it time to build a suitable replacement elsewhere (Oblivion would not open until 1998).

Once again, members of the Lower Churnet Valley Conservation Group were not happy, writing: "Permission was only granted for the Thunder Looper on a temporary basis and has already been extended beyond its original timescale. No doubt Alton Towers will always find a reason for requesting renewal and have no intention of removing it in the foreseeable future. As the ride extends above the treeline it is also an eyesore and completely out of character with the valley."

Resident Gillian Smallwood was also unhappy: "I do not think that Alton Towers should be allowed to renege on this agreement. The Thunder Looper lives up to its name by being the most noisy of all the rides and it is also visually intrusive." Mrs J Penrose agreed: "I am rather worried that if they can manipulate the authorities to allow them to do as they like, and bend the rules as they like, it is going to be a pretty poor outlook for the people of Alton in the future."

1995 had seen weak attendance at Alton Towers, and Tussauds therefore claimed that it was "anxious to make use of current investment" by retaining the Thunder Looper. It accepted, though, that due to the size of the coaster and its age (which made it costlier to maintain), that it would have to be removed eventually. It appealed to the council to give it time to replace it with a ride that created a similar experience.

The plea was only partly successful. At its meeting on September 21, 1995, the planning committee agreed to permit the retention of the Thunder Looper for a further 12 months, and not the two years that the park had asked for. The committee made clear that the extension would not be repeated. With Oblivion not due to open until 1998, Alton Towers compromised by adding the Ripsaw flat ride to Forbidden Valley in 1997. The Thunder Looper's position was occupied by The Blade, a rethemed version of the Pirate Ship that had been moved from Fantasy World to make way for the new coaster.

Tussauds' biggest fight was yet to come. On March 3, 2003, it submitted an application to the Staffordshire Moorlands District Council to build a "wooden roller coaster with ancillary station, maintenance and retail buildings and landscaping". This was to lead to a pitched battle between outraged local residents and environmental groups on one side, and roller coaster enthusiasts and Alton Towers fans all over the globe on the other.

John Wardley had designed the roller coaster, which would feature a station located close to the Corkscrew. From there, it would plunge down a valley through Grade I-listed woodland, turning around close to Air before completing a return trip through the valley. Intamin had been engaged to produce the ride, which would have opened in 2005.

The local press immediately seized upon the controversy, with a Staffordshire Sentinel headline screaming "Roller coaster sparks conservation anger". The newspaper quoted council officer Steve Massey as saying: "It is considered that the proposed development would have significant adverse impact on the ancient woodland, wildlife species and habitat on the character of the conversation area and the visual amenity of the wider landscape and countryside. It is totally inappropriate to allow the introduction of a major development on this site." Another officer agreed: "It will cut an open swathe right through the landscape. I would be very concerned that if this was granted a precedent would be established making it difficult to resist further development."[382]

Whereas opposition to many previous plans had been ad-hoc, this time local residents and environmental groups were highly organised. A meeting in the village of Alton attracted 120 people, and more than a thousand letters of objection were sent to the council. The majority of these were based on a standard template, which read:

I write to object to the above planning application on the following grounds:

1. *Visual and aural intrusion into the Churnet Valley and village.*
2. *Its planned location in a Grade 1 Historical Landscape of high quality, ancient woodland and Grade 1 County site of Biological importance.*
3. *The precedent on future development of the woodland.*

4. *The impact of increased visitor numbers on an already congested and unsuitable road network.*

Whilst being appreciative of the benefits that the theme park brings to the area I feel that this is a step too far and sincerely trust that you will recommend the planning permission be refused.

J.S. Bennett, along with several others, pointed out that "the ride would appear to be in direct contravention of the Alton Towers Supplementary Planning Guidance published by your authority in September 1987. The publication states that the southern wooded slopes of Alton Towers should not be developed. The destruction of almost 20 acres of ancient woodland…will no doubt lead to the start of even more erosion of the woodland."

Several letters drew attention to the potential impact on Alton Towers' landscaped gardens, with Lesley Thompson pondering: "How many people would visit these gardens with a roller coaster roaring over their heads – not very romantic? [In reality, the coaster would have passed through woodland alongside the gardens, but not through the gardens themselves]. As a final thought what are your children and grandchildren going to say when they inherit an enormous noisy monster called a roller coaster that is responsible for the destruction of our countryside and for which the countryside has had nothing in return. I believe they will wonder where our brains were!" Annette Bastock agreed, saying: "I trust this ludicrous scheme will not go ahead."

One resident, a Dr D Eardley, went as far as photographing balloons that were floated above the site of the coaster's second lift hill, close to Air. He claimed that "the leaves are on the trees and the roller coaster ride will be clearly visible from the village of Alton." Several residents contacted the office of HRH The Prince of Wales, although Prince Charles wisely responded that his position "naturally precludes him from intervening personally in such issues as these are a matter for the local authority".

Alton Towers conceded in its planning application that the proposed ride was located within a Grade 1 site on the register of historic parks and gardens. However, it pointed out that the coaster's circuit would be located 100 metres to the east of the formal gardens, within existing dense woodland. The ride structure would be located 180 metres from the nearest garden structure, the Pagoda Fountain. The station, meanwhile, would be on the site of a former quarry, while the second lift hill would climb no higher than Air's existing lift hill.

The park also admitted that the erection of the coaster would require the removal of 146 trees, which either lay directly in its path or could not be reshaped. The majority of these, it claimed, were of "lower grades" and would need to be removed anyway. The park's noise assessment claimed that noise levels were unlikely to represent even a marginal complaint at the nearest properties. The Campaign for the Protection of Rural England dismissed the noise report, claiming that "local residents may be more annoyed by noise from this activity than noise from an activity which is considered essential or socially beneficial. This factor may warrant a lower annoyance threshold than normal being considered."

In response to the complaints from local residents, Alton Towers fans determined to see the wooden coaster plans become a reality roused support on the Internet. Some also wrote letters to the council, with James Hume's submission stating: "I am writing to convey my dismay at the ability of some narrow-minded villagers being able to stop the progress of the new wooden roller coaster at Alton Towers theme park. I have a number of years of experience of this type of coaster, which Alton Towers are proposing to construct. My experience tells me that this coaster will be quiet and discrete, hidden behind the tree line. You will not be able to hear it from the park entrance let alone the village. I hope you will consider the happiness of the whole of the UK when you make this decision."

Mr T Jones pointed out the improvements that have been made in wooden coaster technology in recent years: "The park have contacted the ride manufacturer Intamin who have already built a wooden coaster in Germany which has a new track system which reduces the noise from the running rails. It is made from wood and would blend into the surroundings much better than a brightly painted steel coaster (which the park would turn to if the wooden coaster does not get the go-ahead)."

Messages of support were gathered via two online petitions. One attracted 963 responses, with examples including "A new ride will attract more people to the area and provide more income for local business," and "The ride would be a refreshing and quieter change to the influx of steel coasters in recent years." [383]

One respondent challenged the residents' comments, saying: "From the complaints that I have seen I don't think there is much room for the Alton residents to complain. The objections they have raised so far have already been addressed by the plans submitted. The noise pollution is not an issue due to the type of wood being used. The track will be kept below tree level and the wooden structure will blend into the surroundings anyway. Churnet Valley's natural heritage will not be lost as the vast majority of the trees being taken down would have been removed regardless due to the park's preservation scheme. There is no cause for concern." Another went a step further: "As for the trees, I'm wondering if the locals can even see the trees that are being cut down? Do they know how many are cut down to make their stupid letters to the planners?"

The Alton Environment Group took note of the petition, writing to the council: "We have recently become aware of an Internet petition supporting planning permission for a new wooden roller coaster at Alton Towers. Whilst we endorse the right of anyone to support or object to consent for planning permission, we would like to point out that this petition is from fans of roller coasters anywhere and everywhere. By the organiser's own admission, many of the signatures were registered from as far afield as the United States, Canada, Australia and Russia. We therefore suspect that many of these people have little idea of the beauty of the Churnet Valley, nor even where it is. Local residents are not objecting to the roller coaster per se but on planning grounds such as conservation and noise pollution are objecting to its proposed location." The group organised its own petition to "demonstrate the strength of opposition to this proposed roller coaster in Abbey Woods".

For the most part, the arguments put forward by both sides were constructive. There were exceptions, though. One rogue signature on the coaster fans' petition screamed: "Shut the park down for good! [The coaster] will be an eyesore and bring drugs and vandals to the town." One American respondent to the online survey offered: "For those who don't like it, move and let me buy your house."

Faced with intense opposition, Alton Towers withdrew the plans for the wooden roller coaster. At the time, it said that it would prepare a revised scheme for submission later that year. An updated plan never emerged, however, and Rita opened in 2005 instead.

If the wooden coaster plans were controversial, the Charterhouse-owned Tussauds' next planning application for a new ride at Alton Towers seemed to have been positively designed to arouse anger from residents' groups. In November 2003, Alton Towers proposed installing a tethered hot air balloon, which would float as high as 400 feet above the park. Clearly, given the well-known restriction on rides rising above the tree line, the application had no chance of success. Nevertheless, it attracted dozens more objection letters, with one stating that it was "frankly insulting to a local resident and visitors to the area." On February 27, 2004, the application was dropped.

While Alton Towers' battles with residents over new rides have been fierce at times, they pale in comparison to the long-running war over the construction of a "relief road" to divert traffic that currently passes through the villages of Alton and Farley on its way to the park.

While Alton Towers attracted more than 30,000 visitors in a single day as far back as the Grand Fetes of the 1890s, the majority of these arrived via the Churnet Valley Railway. With the line's closure, and the growth of private car ownership, the balance has now changed dramatically. The park's own surveys have found that 85 to 90 percent of visitors now arrive by car, passing through the narrow streets of the two neighbouring villages.[384]

Back in 1995, Alton resident P A Barnes complained to the planning authorities that: "The exhaust fumes from the trail of coaches and cars leaving the Towers and slowly grinding up the hill out of the village towards Uttoxeter and the motorways is poisonous and the noise is unending." Fellow resident Gillian Smallwood complained: "It is very difficult to cross the high street especially with two young children in a double buggy – I'm hardly able to make a quick dash as the traffic is continuous. The road is narrow and bendy with in places no pavement at all or a very narrow pavement. Any developments that will potentially increase the number of visitors and hence traffic through the village should be discouraged until a proper access road to the park is provided...Once such a road is provided I would very much support the development of further environmentally sound rides as the park and its visitors provide an important source of income to the local economy."

Ironically, it was Alton Towers (under John Broome) which initially identified the need for a relief road and proposed a route. Indeed, much of the correspondence about the chalet complex that was proposed in 1989 actually relates to the relief road, rather than the holiday village itself. Broome had grand plans for the resort, and expected it to attract more than 4 million visitors per year by the 1990s. This would lead to attendances of 40,000-plus on peak days.

Broome proposed a new access road to the east of the park, and promoted the use of the route of the disused Churnet Valley Railway. Staffordshire County Council, though, preferred an alternative route between Alton and Denstone, with a major highway linking the park to the B5030. However, construction machinery manufacturer JCB had its world headquarters close to Alton Towers, and owned some of the land through which the relief road would pass. It objected to the proposal, and would not agree to sell its land to allow its construction.

Further investigations were carried out throughout the 1990s and 2000s, looking at various different potential routes that would have a lower environmental impact than the council's initial plan. Alton Towers would be required to fund the vast majority of the cost of the new road, which has variously been estimated as between £10 million and £30 million.

Following its takeover by Merlin in 2007, Alton Towers began the preparation of a long-term development plan, which would enable the Staffordshire Moorlands District

Council to prepare a new Supplementary Planning Document against which future planning applications would be considered. The plan included a detailed transport study, and emphatically ruled out the construction of a relief road.

The park cited several reasons for its decision, including complications due to land ownership, engineering difficulties (the options considered included crossing the River Churnet and passing through woodland), the huge cost and the environmental impact of the construction work itself. It pointed to the apparent success of alternative traffic management measures and encouragement of overnight stays at its hotels, and claimed that local roads could accommodate existing and future traffic levels. It drew special attention to the fact that the park had attracted an average of 2.4 million visitors over the previous 10 years – nowhere near the 4 million figure predicted by Broome when the relief road was first proposed.

Alton Towers' head of development Mark Kerrigan said of the decision: "No business would be expected to invest such a substantial sum of money for something that may only make a difference for a month or six weeks of the year."

Some local figures welcomed the long-term plan, which would see millions of pounds invested in new rides, hotels and heritage projects. Councillor John Wakefield said: "The 10 -year plan is good news, with a strong commitment to deliver extra investment which will have significant benefits to the local and regional economy and jobs." Others, though, expressed disappointment at the dropping of the relief road plans. Tony Moult, the chairman of Alton Parish Council, admitted that: "£15 million is a lot to have spent on a road. They could probably build another ride with that amount to replace The Corkscrew. People do come into Alton and visit pubs. Alton Towers does help trade in the village." [385]

Waking up the neighbours

Other residents reacted with outright disgust. One wrote to the Staffordshire Sentinel to say: "Their heart has never been in it – there is no question about that. The final blow to the hopes of many Alton residents was totally expected. Alton Towers have never had any intention of providing a relief road to avoid the horrendous congestion Alton and surrounding villages endure throughout the summer months – not a month or six weeks, as stated by a spokesperson for Alton Towers. Seeing the damage to the wall on the White House corner [in the village], after it had been totally demolished and rebuilt, is sufficient reason to know there has to be an answer. There are long scratches of red and blue paint on the new, costly stone already and the wall opposite has now also been reduced to rubble. The so-called feasibility schemes over the past 20-odd years have just been a smoke-screen and we have all been taken for fools – again."

Not all villagers are in favour of the relief road, as Moult explains: "There are some elements in the village who want it and some who do not. I do not think the decision came as a surprise to many people, who did not expect Alton Towers to spend all that money. It will be interesting to see now what the district and county councils do. I have said many times that Alton Towers has been allowed to develop by the district and county councils. They are the ones who have granted planning permission and allowed the theme park to develop in a conservation area between two small villages. I think they have got a lot to answer for. They have got to look closely at this new long-term plan and make sure some infrastructure is put in." [386]

Indeed, the council did demand that Alton Towers stump up £100,000 for road improvements before agreeing to the construction of The Smiler in 2013. The money was used to fund measures designed to alleviate traffic congestion caused by an increase in visitor numbers that the ride was expected to generate.

241

The furore over the relief road erupted again in 2012, when a revised version of the long-term development plan was released. Figures revealed that roads in Alton and Farley attract more than three times the level of traffic during the main summer season, compared to the November-March off-season. Once again, calls for a relief road were made, and once again they were declined by Merlin. Moult responded: "They charge about £6 to park at the resort at the moment and that must bring them millions in revenue. That money could have been used to fund the relief road, which we have been asking for, for a long time." [387]

The battle over the relief road looks unlikely to end, with villagers having blockaded country lanes in the past to make their point. For now, though, it is not on Merlin's agenda. Its own projections suggest that the resort's focus on attracting guests for longer hotel stays and off-peak visits will ensure that even if it is successful in meeting its goal to attract 3.3 million visitors in 2019, the increase in car journeys will be marginal.

Moult sighed in 2008: "We live in a conservation area but there's not a lot we can do about it as a parish council, when you have the country's largest theme park on your doorstep and the district council and the county council gave their permission for it to expand over the years. It is just very disappointing."

For its part, Alton Towers has tried several schemes to improve its relationship with local residents. The park's medical and security teams are First Responders trained by the West Midlands Ambulance Service, and are available to attend local emergencies at any time of day, 365 days a year. The resort donates £50,000 worth of theme park tickets every year to local communities and charities, sponsors local sports teams and donates prizes to charity events. It also provides litter pickers to help maintain the appearance of local villages.[388]

In 1999, a £120,000 closed circuit television security system was installed in nearby Cheadle town centre. Designed to deter crime, it was monitored 24 hours a day by staff at Alton Towers' main security control room. Bob Curry, Engineering Manager for Staffordshire Moorlands District Council, said: "Without Alton Towers offering to monitor the system the project would not have gone ahead. They have recognised their commitment to the local community and I believe everyone in Cheadle will benefit." [389]

In the same year, the park sold off property lost by visitors to the resort to its staff to raise money for local charities. In addition, it handed over cash from staff donations and on-site wishing wells, helping to fund a new helipad at North Staffordshire Hospital.[390]

Some residents, though, are not placated by such "corporate social responsibility" exercises. Stephen and Suzanne Roper are the most prominent example, having engaged in an ongoing battle with Alton Towers' various owners over the past three decades.

The wealthy Ropers bought Farley House, a large house in the village of Farley, in 1968 – 12 years before the park developed into a theme park, although at the time it already attracted significant numbers of visitors. In addition to vocally opposing the addition of the Alton Mouse, the couple objected to many other attraction developments during John Broome's reign.

The final straw appears to have come in 1998, with the opening of Oblivion. The Ropers, unhappy with the noise levels generated by the ride, began to look at legal options. Some six years later, in 2004, they won a civil claim against the park. Giving evidence, Stephen Roper said: "Outstanding would be Oblivion. I find it hard to believe that Alton Towers went beyond the feasibility study for that machine. The noise levels have been absolutely disgraceful. Metal clanging and clattering like living next door to a breaker's yard at times. The level of screaming seems to have grown out of all proportion in the last six to seven years; continuous screaming from 9am until sometimes 7pm."

Some neighbours gave supporting evidence, with Beverley Ryan, a resident of Farley since 1986, complaining about the annual fireworks events: "The sound levels have increased, the commentary is louder, there is music before and after and special sound effects during the displays. From my property, as the evening wears on, you can hear the increase in volume and there's a definite increase 30 minutes before the show. It is louder than any thunderstorm. It makes it sound like a war zone. It is horrendous. I have to take special precautions because of my horses which are frightened by the noises. Last year I moved the horses out of the village and found alternative stabling. It means moving them out one week before the fireworks and moving them back one week after."

Not all local residents were on the Ropers' side, however. Graham Blackburn, who lives nearby, said: "Of course you hear noise from the park. Screaming and the noise of people who are in there. General everyday noise. We know there's a theme park there. Noise is there all the time. I don't notice the noise now. It doesn't affect my life. You can hear people enjoying themselves." He said that the firework displays were excellent and that he watched them from home.[391]

Judge Timothy Gascoigne visited the Roper's home, and said: "I could clearly hear the screams from the riders on Oblivion. The fundamental problem with Oblivion seems to me is its design. The ride stops just over the edge of the drop.

Obviously the 'Don't look down' message played as the car hangs over the edge is designed to heighten the white knuckle effect. This includes screaming. I find that the screams and mechanical noise is intrusive and constitutes a nuisance." He also criticised the park's fireworks events, saying: "Alton Towers, in a conservation area, aims to set off the loudest fireworks in Britain." He slapped the park with a £5,000 fine and imposed noise restrictions.[392] Tussauds' appeal against the verdict was dismissed in 2005, although the company was successful in getting the fine reduced to £3,500 and the maximum noise level increased to 40 decibels from 30 decibels.

In anticipation of the noise abatement order, Alton Towers had instigated "Operation Hush" in 2005. A resort-wide survey was carried out to identify the impact of amplified music and commentary systems. Recommendations included the replacement of live announcements with pre-recorded messages, with audio limiters in place to control their volume. Loudspeakers were removed from the upper queue line from Nemesis, as well as from Oblivion's drop section. Guests would no longer hear the "Don't look down!" message. The park also reduced and eventually cancelled its fireworks after the 2006 event (they would later return in 2010).[393]

The Ropers were successful in pursuing an updated noise abatement order in May 2007. This was followed up by a criminal action against Tussauds. The couple claimed that the firm had failed to comply with the order, and that noise levels were still too high. Local businesspeople raised concerns about the court battle, with the owner of Bulls Head Inn in Alton, Janet Gibson, quoted as saying: "I thought it was all sorted. Every case the Ropers win does have an effect on trade. It was a shame to see the fireworks stop. I haven't noticed any increase in noise." [394]

The couple were forced to drop the criminal action after Merlin took over the park in 2007, and once again pursued civil action. In January 2011, a claim for a further noise injunction and damages dating back to 1998 was thrown out of court, with the judge citing delays in the Ropers pursuing the case. However, this verdict was overturned on appeal and the couple are now planning to take on Alton Towers in the High Court. If successful, they could force any rides that breach planning consent to be closed or even removed. Mr Justice Hickinbottom, delivering his verdict, said that he had upheld the appeal "with a heavy heart" and warned the Ropers that the costs to them would be substantial if they were to lose the case.[395] At the time of writing, it is yet to come to court.

Ironically, the Ropers themselves are no strangers to noise complaints. Stephen Roper is a former CEO and Chairman of Churchill China, which is based in Stoke-on-Trent.[396] At one stage, in 1999, he owned 22.3 percent of the company.[397] Before his retirement in May 2007, the firm was frequently accused by residents close to its Tunstall High Street factory of allowing noise levels to increase.[398]

Roper remained a shareholder in Churchill China after retiring, and the company's second warehouse in Sandyford caused another dispute, with resident William Bourne complaining in 2009: "I have been campaigning against the expansion of the Churchill factory since the officials first set foot in the field behind my house in 1989. They wanted all their operations on one site instead of spread across the city. But now we are stuck in the middle. We have noise all the time and once the factory starts full production there will be traffic 24 hours a day, pollution, vibrations from the machinery and constant noise. It's like being stuck in the middle of the industrial revolution. The field used to be full of cattle and horses – now it has a 25-metre high warehouse…Churchill has taken away all the pleasure of living in this house." [399]

Fellow residents Terry Cope and Craig Pond wrote in 2008: "Why is it that the stench of hypocrisy hangs over the Churchill China factory in Sandyford? Mr Roper – he who complains of the noise coming from Alton Towers…builds a giant warehouse surrounding the residents of Birchall Avenue, not more than 100 yards away from the rear of their houses. Add to this the future constant comings and goings of 40-ton heavy goods vehicles, the noise of forklifts loading and unloading, an internal tannoy system and radios, and you start to get the picture of what the residents of Birchall Avenue will have to put up with, not to mention the health and safety risks of carcinogenic diesel fumes wafting their way into the homes of residents, and their children's lungs…One other local resident, also known to me, has been fighting this case for thirty years but is constantly blocked by the City Council and Churchill China's insistence on getting their way come hell or high water." [400]

The Staffordshire Moorlands District Council has faced a tough job over the last few decades, balancing the concerns of residents with the economic benefits of the Alton Towers Resort. While it has thrown out or forced the withdrawal of several planning applications, it has in most cases been able to come to a compromise with the park's owners that enabled new developments to go ahead. With a new hotel on the drawing board, and several major new rides planned over the next decade, expect the objection letters to keep on coming.

Parts of the Thunder Looper ready to be installed, 1989.
Image: Glen Fairweather

John Wardley's overhaul of Katanga Canyon went down well
with the planning authorities. Image: Natalie Sim

For more images, visit
http://www.themeparktourist.com/tales-from-the-towers/

8. The business of theme parks

Since John Broome introduced a "pay one price" policy in 1980, revenue from ticket sales has been Alton Towers' primary source of income. However, there are now many other aspects to the resort's business model. In addition to revenue from hotel stays, this includes sales of merchandise and food, special events and promotions to draw in visitors during off-peak periods, private parties and concerts, and "upsell" opportunities such as queue-jumping passes. Marketing and public relations are also key to the resort's success, with regular coverage in the press, online and on the television being vital in raising awareness of its latest offerings.

It's something of a theme park cliché. Still high on adrenaline, riders spill out of an attraction…and directly into a shop. If the ride has delivered on its promise, the park hopes, the hapless guests will be powerless to resist the merchandise on offer. T-shirts, fridge magnets, on-ride photos – anything even vaguely related to the ride experience – are available at pumped-up prices. All in the name of increasing the average spending per guest.

Alton Towers, of course, has experimented with all kinds of ways of encouraging visitors to open their wallets. Over the years, the park has offered everything from high-class arts and crafts through to branded contraception aids in its stores. As technology has progressed, the merchandise has become increasingly personalised – but not always with successful results.

As a region, Staffordshire has been associated with the art of pottery since the seventeenth century. Even now, the nearby

Stoke City football team are known by their nickname of "the Potters". Inevitably, then, one of Alton Towers' earliest merchandising efforts revolved around its own on-site pottery, which operated from the 1950s until its closure in 1994.

Rather than being simply a shop, the pottery was a mini-attraction in itself. Guests could see potter Steve Parry-Thomas in action producing ceramic crafts on his wheel, which can now fetch hefty prices on auction websites such as Ebay.

The pottery was moved to the Farm area in the 1990s, and closed in 1994 as Tussauds took the park in a new direction. Indeed, some of the merchandise produced by the park's new owners was of a radically different nature, and more in-keeping with the park's new focus on thrills than its history as a stately home.

By 1981, under John Broome's tenure, the park was advertising "quality, themed shops" in its brochure. A wide range of hand-crafted basketware and expensive clothes were available from Shopping World in Aqualand, while Toyland offered "Toys of Character".

In 1990, just ahead of the Tussauds' takeover that saw many of Broome's high-end shops stripped out of the park, there was an eclectic mix of merchandise on offer from more than 50 outlets. The majority of the retail stores were clustered in Talbot Street and Towers Street.

On Talbot Street, guests could grab Henry Hound toys, mementos and souvenirs from Maison Talbot, browse a variety of cuddly creatures in the Raven's Den or dress up in period costumes for a sepia photo in the Photo Studio. On Towers Street, meanwhile, they could peruse the "crème de la crème of exclusive international leather goods", along with watches, perfumes, clocks and jewellery from firms such as Yves St Laurent, Gucci and Cartier in the elaborate Bond

Street Boutique. Further down the street, they could watch skilful glass blowers demonstrating their art in the Glass and Ceramics Shop, where they could buy chinaware from the likes of Coalport, Aynsley and Wedgwood. Toyfair offered an "Aladdin's Cave" of toys and games, while World Bazaar sold such exotic items as Polynesian lampshades, Russian dolls and Chinese lacquered boxes. The Athena Shop offered postcards, birthday cards and framed pictures, while guests could hire a camera for free from the Film Shop.[401]

Elsewhere in the park, the farm hosted the Windmill Souvenir Shop, housed in a faithful recreation of an agricultural landmark. The park even sold its own range of leisureware – dubbed "The Alton Collection" - which was "specially commissioned from one of the country's top fashion design studios to ensure quality and durability". Each unisex design – available via mail order as well as in-park – carried a unique Alton Towers designer label, and was available in a "series of fashionable colourways".

For many theme park visitors, it's a point of pride to be able to prove to their friends that they have braved a towering roller coaster or survived a soaking on a log flume. Alton Towers was quick to pick up on this trend, and during the 1980s guests were awarded "ride certificates" as lasting evidence of their bravery.

What was really needed, though, was photographic proof. These days, all of the most popular rides at Alton Towers offer guests the chance to purchase an on-ride photo, at extremely lucrative prices (a fridge magnet from The Smiler, for example, costs some £10). Striking a pose for the camera has become an essential part of the ride for groups of teenagers, anxious to demonstrate that they are capable of looking good even as they race through a vertical loop or plummet towards a watery pool below. They can often be seen gathered around the screens at the ride's exit, pointing out the expressions on their friends' faces.

It wasn't always quite so straightforward, though. In the park's early years, guests would be handed a small slip on which was printed a reference number. After providing their name and address, they would wait for days for their (as yet unseen) photo to arrive in the post. It was not uncommon for them to subsequently discover that the image was actually that of another group of guests entirely.

With technology moving on, it was only a matter of time before a video version of the on-ride photo was introduced. The first hint of this came in 2006, when the Sunday Express reported that Alton Towers was planning to tag and track its guests using a network of "Big Brother cameras". The ominous report claimed that visitors would be "watched" as they navigated the park, with goals including cutting crime and tracking lost children.[402]

Even if the original aims of provider Venue Solutions were somewhat ambitious, the reality was more commercial and slightly less invasive of guests' privacy. YourDay eventually launched in 2007, capturing footage of guests as they rode on Air, the Corkscrew, Congo River Rapids, The Flume, Nemesis, Oblivion, Rita and Spinball Whizzer. Wristbands equipped with Radio Frequency Identification (RFID) tags were used to pinpoint guests as they whizzed past the cameras. At the end of the day, guests could pick up a personalised DVD for £19.99 from the YourDay store on Towers Street.

Alton Towers had high hopes for the YourDay system, and by 2008 Venue Solutions shares had soared from 0.35p to 0.88p.[403] The system was set to be expanded into other parks in continental Europe and Australia, and the future looked bright.

Unfortunately for the park and its technology partner, YourDay didn't quite capture the public's imagination as they had wished. This wasn't helped by a delayed launch, with the full line-up of attractions not being fully supported until 2008. Some guests also complained about the amount of "stock" footage that was mixed in with the actual video of them enjoying the rides. By March 2009, the supplier had gone bust and YourDay was no more.

Alton Towers hasn't yet given up on video souvenirs altogether, though. By 2011, it was again selling footage of riders on the Air roller coaster, although inflation had seen prices rise to £12 for just this single attraction.

Soft toys are a staple part of any theme park's merchandise line-up. These days, guests who experience *Ice Age: Dawn of the Dinosaurs 4-D* and Sonic Spinball (both of which feature recognisable, licensed characters) can expect to pick up a cuddly friend designed to look like Scrat, Sid or Sonic himself. In years gone by, though, Alton Towers had its own characters to promote.

Henry Hound (more on his in-park incarnation later) and his loving wife Henrietta Hound were based on the iconic Talbot hounds, heraldry of which can still be found around the Towers themselves. Until finally being dropped in 2007, the loveable hounds appeared on a wide variety of items, and stuffed Henrys are likely to be found tucked away in attics across the UK. As well as his duties on-site, Henry also acted as the figurehead for the Alton Towers Fun Club in the 1990s. He was the proud star of the *Wonderful Times* magazine, even receiving his own comic strip.

While he is now enjoying his retirement, evidence of Henry's days at the park can still be found tucked away in the Towers' gardens. In the area surrounding the former Swiss Cottage restaurant, non-biodegradable cups emblazoned with Henry's image continue to defy the forces of nature.[404]

The installation of Nemesis in 1994 saw then-owner Tussauds branching out into new fields with merchandise relating to the ride. In many cases, the aim was not simply to raise cash to claw back the enormous cost of installing the coaster, but to promote the Nemesis brand both in and out of the park.

The elaborate backstory to the ride, long since forgotten by most riders, is based around an alien that was discovered when the site was excavated, and subsequently pinned in place by the masses of steel that make up the coaster. It was available in comic book form from the Nemesis store, and has since become a collectors' item.

Not content with riding the coaster and taking in its plotline, though, guests were also able to literally "taste" the Nemesis experience. Evidently, the taste of Nemesis was blackcurrant and liquorice, for this was one of the flavours of "Nemesis Cola" that were on offer as part of a partnership with Coca-Cola. Sold both inside and outside of the park, the fizzy beverage was available until 1996.

The marketing campaign for Oblivion in 1998 was just as extensive as that for Nemesis four years earlier. Tussauds had lost none of its flare for unusual and quirky ride-related merchandise during the intervening period, and Oblivion launched with an even more bizarre array of branded products that its predecessor.

While it did not revive its partnership with Coca Cola, Alton Towers instead enlisted Lynx, the popular brand of deodorant. Naturally, guests waiting to plummet over the edge of Oblivion's vertical drop would be perspiring heavily. Luckily, the ride's shop, X-Sell, was on hand to sell them various different varieties of antiperspirant, including "Rush" and "Zero-G". Again, the promotion extended well beyond the park, and major chemists such as Boots offered the product. There was no escape from Oblivion in the summer of 1998.

Tucked away elsewhere in X-Sell, randy Alton Towers fans could find an even greater treat – and one that brand-conscious rivals such as Disney would surely never contemplate. Designed for a different type of "ride" altogether, the Durex-manufactured Oblivion condoms were available for just £1 per pack. Evidently, the feeling of soaring through the air is just as likely as dropping into Oblivion to arouse theme park-loving couples, as Air also featured its own range of condoms when it debuted in 2002. Who knows how many discarded wrappers from these limited-edition family-planning aids can be found strewn around the park's gardens.

The standard cost of visiting Alton Towers has risen substantially over the past few years. Research by the charity 4Children found that the cost of entry to the park for a family of five has risen by a huge 57 percent from £126.50 in 2009, to £198 in 2013.[405]

In its defence, Merlin pointed out that "virtually no-one" would pay the prices quoted, with most taking advantage of discounts for pre-booking tickets online or "2-for-1" deals offered by newspapers and voucher websites (author's note: our Theme Park Tourist website receives millions of visitors every year looking for such offers). They can also buy tickets using vouchers from the Tesco Clubcard loyalty scheme.

In the past, Alton Towers has worked with brands including Kelloggs, The Sun, the Daily Mail, McDonalds, Kleenex Tissues, KFC, Pizza Hut, moneysupermarket.com, Cadbury, Walkers, Tesco and WH Smith to offer such deals. In most cases, they are based on a "tit-for-tat" exchange of benefits – for example, newspapers agree to provide a certain amount of coverage of the park over the course of a year in exchange for being able to offer 2-for-1 vouchers. If you've ever wondered why some of the resort's more outlandish PR stunts are reported as fact by major newspapers, this may be the explanation.

In general, the resort runs such promotions at the start and middle of the theme park season, partnering with major brands that complement it in terms of target market and size. It has gone as far as offering completely free tickets (for a specific date) via The Sun, a promotion which first ran in the 1990s and was resurrected in 2008. Merlin credits the offer with bringing new visitors to the park, who will return as paying guests in later years.[406]

The popularity of voucher deals has led to the regular appearance of "voucher touts" in the Alton Towers car park. After purchasing a vast number of copies of The Sun or grabbing a handful of vouchers from a shop, these touts offer to sell them to guests who have failed to plan in advance. The resort has taken steps to protect the integrity of its deals with partners, and in June 2012 it successfully prosecuted a man who broke an injunction against the activity. The Manchester resident was sentenced to four months in prison by a judge at Stoke-on-Trent County Court. Commenting on the ruling, Ian Crabbe, Divisional Director at the Alton Towers Resort said: "It sends out a very strong message to anybody else involved in this type of activity that we will not stand still and allow touts to 'hijack' our business. The judge was very clear that a court injunction is not something that can be ignored and we will continue to pursue these individuals to the full extent of the law to ensure that they are suitably punished."

It may not extract the full gate price from every guest, then, but Alton Towers has found other ways to push up the cost of a visit. One of the most controversial measures was the introduction of a £2 parking fee in 2002, which had risen to £6 by 2012. Initially, holders of all Merlin Annual Passes received free parking, but since 2011 this has been restricted to Premium Pass holders. The resort itself estimates that around 400,000 cars park at the theme park every year (excluding guests parking for free at the hotels and water park).[407] Even accounting for annual passholders, this is likely to equate to more than £2 million pounds of additional income each year.

The resort has also looked to save on costs by reducing the operational hours of its rides. The most recent attempt came in 2012, when the park revealed that it would shut as early as 4pm during quieter months early in the season. Rides including Air, Thirteen, The Flume, Battle Galleons, Congo River Rapids, Charlie and the Chocolate Factory and Driving School would all open an hour after the rest of the park. The inclusion of Thirteen – which had only opened in 2010 – in the late-opening line-up was a particular cause of concern for fans, who complained vociferously. After just five days, the cutbacks were reversed.

In the early 2000s, Alton Towers followed a trend set by Universal in the US and introduced a ride reservation system known as "Virtual Q". Guests could head to a popular attraction such as Nemesis, Air or Oblivion and grab a time-stamped ticket. When their time window came up, they could return to the ride and bypass the regular queue. By restricting the number of passes given out for a particular time slot, the system ensured that guests using it could have a short wait for even the most popular attractions.

Whereas Disney currently still offers its similar Fastpass system for free to all guests (though it will soon move to an alternative version that enables advance booking of ride slots), it did not take Alton Towers long to begin monetising Virtual Q. From 2002, "Virtual Q Mobile" was offered alongside it, as part of a deal with London-based Mobile Maximiser.[408] For £5 per person, guests could receive SMS messages on their mobile phone informing them of when they could skip the queue for major attractions. Frequently, when the free Virtual Q tickets ran out for the day, a van would appear at an attraction's entrance to sell Virtual Q Mobile subscriptions instead.

The park had experimented with paid-for queue-jumping options before, selling "Accelerator Passes" in 2000 at a cost of £65. These allowed guests to enter via the exit to any attraction, avoiding queues altogether, and just 30 were sold per day. Dominik Diamond, writing in the Daily Star, said of the system: "It's a surefire way of illustrating the class divide - separate queues for rich and poor. Imagine the poor parents standing there with four bored kids who don't understand why they can't jump to the front." [409]

By 2005, the free Virtual Q system had been scrapped altogether, in favour of a premium "Shortcut" pass. For £5, guests could buy queue-jumping privileges for Air, Nemesis, Oblivion and The Flume. Almost immediately, the park was accused of over-selling the tickets, resulting in long waits for Shortcut pass buyers and even longer standard queues.

The Shortcut system has evolved into today's Fastrack, which is also offered by Merlin at Thorpe Park and Chessington World of Adventures. Prices are higher, with a "Fastrack Scream" pass for Air, Nemesis and Nemesis Sub-Terra costing £12. A "Fastrack Silver" pass for Air, Nemesis, Oblivion, Rita and Thirteen costs £21, while for a huge £50 the "Fastrack Gold" pass includes virtually all of the park's most popular rides, including the newly-opened The Smiler.

Fastrack continues to be an emotional subject that angers many Alton Towers' visitors, as they watch those who have purchased the passes race past them as they wait in the standard line. This was accentuated by a 2011 decision to begin selling the passes at the entrances to attractions, and to advertise them on queue time boards. Naturally, this has led to accusations that the park is exploiting the limited capacity of its own rides for profit. Nevertheless, premium queue-jumping options are unlikely to be phased out any time soon.

Feeding the millions of guests that visit Alton Towers every year is a major undertaking. The park estimates that 260 tonnes of chips are consumed in a season – an amount that would comfortably outweigh the Statue of Liberty. To quench the thirst caused by all that salt consumption, it is claimed that the amount of fizzy drinks sold each season could fill around 1,500 bathtubs.[410]

As with the retail outlets at the park, the restaurants have evolved significantly since the days of John Broome's ownership. During the 1980s, guests could head to the Swiss Cottage, sitting indoors or on an outdoor patio overlooking the landscaped gardens. There, they could enjoy a "superb silver service restaurant", which remained one of the only locations to serve alcohol after Broome's drinking purge. The restaurant closed after the Tussauds takeover, and the building now sits largely empty. Adventurous visitors can find an abandoned toilet block up a steep slope not far from it.

Elsewhere, the 1980s offerings included "traditional-style food" at the Ingestre Restaurant, gourmet pizza from the Pizza Express restaurant in Talbot Street, steaks from the Railcar Brunch Bar in Festival Park and burgers from the "largest fast food restaurant in Europe", the Talbot Restaurant.

Tussauds overhauled the park's catering infrastructure after its takeover. First, it introduced the "Alton Eats" brand across virtually all of the park's food outlets, which were operated by in-house teams. In 1998, though, the firm abruptly reversed direction and began to outsource the operation of eateries in prime spots throughout the park. Deals were struck with McDonalds, Kentucky Fried Chicken and Pizza Hut, which took up residence in locations in Forbidden Valley, X-Sector, Merrie England and Katanga Canyon. The overhaul of the former Talbot Restaurant into the Cred Street McDonalds was particularly popular, with heavy theming applied both inside and out. A 2002 deal saw Costa Coffee arrive at the park, with Costa's managing director Mike Tye explaining the rationale: "The Tussauds Group entertains more than 10 million visitors a year. Our aim is to introduce as many as possible to the Costa experience." [411]

By 2006, the outsourcing approach appeared to have backfired badly. In October of that year, food hygiene investigators from the district council visited the park, inspecting 19 restaurants. Only 15 of these met the required standards, with levels of cleaning in kitchens being labelled as below par. The KFC outlet in Katanga Canyon and the McDonald's in Merrie England were both highlighted as having "poor" cleaning standards, with the KFC restaurant falling below legal requirements and the McDonald's requiring "a thorough deep clean and disinfection". [412] KFC staff were accused of having a poor level of food hygiene awareness, with a spokesman for the firm saying: "The recommendations of the council have been taken on board and we are confident that the store will meet our strict company hygiene standard when it re-opens in the spring."

Across the park, the inspectors found dirty sweet scoops, damaged work surfaces, ceilings, carpets and skirting boards and a lack of hot water. Problems were even found with the theme park's own staff restaurant. A council spokesman said: "Officers will be monitoring the situation closely in the coming months and have the power to take enforcement action if necessary."

Alton Towers' in-house restaurants faired relatively well, with a spokesman saying: "Alton Towers takes the health, safety and welfare of its visitors and staff very seriously and we do not compromise on anything that could affect this. With respect to the food units on site which are operated directly by Alton Towers, while there is nothing in the most recent report to cause any concern, there are a few very minor areas in which we can improve, and action has already been taken to ensure that we do so before we re-open next March."[413]

The park hinted at a future with fewer outsourced restaurants, with the spokesman continuing: "We are of course disappointed that one of the independently operated franchise units [the KFC] has had issues highlighted, and we will be discussing these with the appropriate senior management to ensure that they comply with the requirements outlined."

McDonald's also defended itself, with a statement reading: "Hygiene and food safety is an utmost priority at McDonald's and we have stringent and established hygiene and food safety procedures in place in every restaurant. Naturally then we are disappointed on the rare occasion when a restaurant does not meet the high standards we set ourselves and take immediate action to investigate and resolve potential issues. With regards to the Alton Towers restaurant specifically, all recommendations identified by the environmental health officer have been implemented and we will continue to take on board recommendations put forward from the environmental health department of the council with whom we have a good working relationship."

Nonetheless, McDonalds was unceremoniously booted out in 2008, being replaced by rival Burger King. Guests now faced higher prices, with Burger King charging service station rates rather than high street rates for its meals. The theming of the Cred Street McDonalds was also torn out, replaced by a blander interior and exterior.

The food hygiene scandal wasn't the only bad press for Alton Towers' food operations in 2006. The Soil Association conducted a survey which saw a "secret mum" head to 14 different tourist attractions across the UK, scoring them on criteria such as "availability of healthy drinks in vending machines" and "how long it took to find fruit". Alton Towers fared badly, scoring 0 points out of 5 in the "healthy food promotion" category and just 5 points out of 25 overall. The park responded with a statement, saying: "Given the irregular nature of most people's visits to a theme park, and the fact that it is regarded as a one or two day 'treat', Alton Towers does not feel that we can take serious nutritional responsibility for our visitors while they are with us. That said, we work hard to ensure we offer an extensive choice of food for our guests to enjoy at a range of high street prices. Our own restaurants and kiosks offer everything from sandwiches to full meals; as well as a wide range of snacks including fresh fruit - with menus based on visitor research and actual sales."

A year before the outsourcing deal, in 1997, Alton Towers itself had faced criticism from *Which* magazine, which found traces of the E.coli and Staphylococcus aureus bacteria in an egg sandwich bought from the Bagshaw's Family Restaurant, as well as traces of Staphylococcus aureus in a ham baguette from the Corner Coffee Shop.[414]

Following its takeover of Tussauds, though, Merlin showed confidence that it could operate its own restaurants effectively. Pizza Hut was replaced by the in-house Explorer's Pizza and Pasta Buffet in 2010, while KFC was ejected in favour of Merlin's Fried Chicken Company in 2012. Burger King was the last franchise out of the door, being replaced by the cheaper Burger Kitchen in 2013.

Alton Towers has long used special events as a way of bolstering attendance, particularly during off-peak periods. These range from one-off concerts and performances, to annual events that have become a fixture on the resort's calendar.

Christmas events have been a source of out-of-season visits from Alton Towers' earliest days as a theme park. Back in 1990, the park was transformed into a "Winter Wonderland", with Dickensian characters meeting guests on Towers Street, Santa waiting in his grotto and the Spectacular on Ice show featuring live music, top skating professionals and – of course – Henry and Henrietta Hound.[415] Modern day events are focussed around "Santa's Sleepover" short breaks at the resort's two hotels, with guests receiving a Christmas dinner, meeting Santa and his reindeer, watching Christmas films in a small cinema and enjoying a handful of children's rides in the theme park itself.

At the other end of the season, Alton Towers has experimented since 2008 with pulling in guests early by opening a limited selection of rides during the February half-term. Cheap entry prices and the promise of shorter queues are designed to entice visitors, although the curtailed opening hours and absence of some major attractions put off some. Prior to this, the park had offered "Adrenaline Weeks" at either end of the season, focusing on thrill rides.

By far the biggest success stories have been Alton Towers' Halloween and fireworks events, which have resulted in the October half-term week becoming the busiest in the park's calendar. Eyeing the popularity of Halloween "haunt" events at US theme parks such as Knott's Berry Farm and Universal Studios Hollywood, the park expanded its Halloween offerings from a basic outdoor show to a full range of attractions for the "Halloween Spooktacular" in 2000 and 2001. A Halloween-themed ice show was held in Storybook Land's big top, while many rides stayed open until 7pm, allowing guests to enjoy them for the first time in the dark.

2002 saw the introduction of the Terror of the Towers horror maze in the Towers themselves, which was clearly aimed at drawing more teenagers and adults to the Halloween events.

After a brief hiatus from 2004 to 2006, Alton Towers relaunched its Halloween events in 2007, with the introduction of "Scarefest". Terror of the Towers returned, while the new Haunted Hollow attraction was populated with live actors. Kids could meet-and-greet a line-up of spooky-but-friendly characters, including Skelvin the skeleton, Phil the mummy, pumpkin-headed Patch and Franklin the monster. Outside the park's gates, guests could pay extra to experience the expansive Field of 1000 Screams maze or to stay in one of the Alton Towers Hotel's "Scare Rooms". They could also brave the Room 13 maze in the hotel's conference suite, which had debuted in lieu of the main Halloween event in 2006.

Scarefest proved to be an immediate hit, and over the following years new mazes such as The Boiler Room (in which guests were pursued by murderous twins) and the Carnival of Screams (a distinctly unpleasant circus) were introduced. From 2011, the mazes were moved from the grounds of the hotel into the park itself, making use of the vacant Black Hole tent and the Towers building.

Not everybody was happy with the introduction of the Carnival of Screams maze in 2010. Groups of clowns – likely encouraged by Alton Towers' marketing department – chained themselves to the park's gates, protesting that the attraction "demonised" their profession.[416] One participant, Fips the Clown, said: "We feel it is an unfair depiction of clowns. It only serves to reinforce stereotypes of clowns as evil. This will do for clowns what *Jaws* did for sharks. I can't believe this - it has taken us years to get over Stephen King's *It*." [417]

One-off music concerts have been held at the park since its opening, with artists such as Chris de Burgh and Bryan Adams appearing on a stage in front of the main lake during the 1990s. In 1999, the BBC's Live and Kicking Roadshow came to Alton Towers, bringing with it such luminaries as S Club 7 and former *Coronation Street* star Adam Rickitt.[418] In more recent years, the summer Alton Towers Live events have caused gridlock on local roads, as fans pour into the area to see the likes of Olly Murs and Little Mix.

In summer 1999 and 2000, the park's lake hosted a live action spectacular – just as it had done during the Grand Fetes a hundred years earlier. Special effects firm Artem was brought in to bring the story of a post-apocalyptic world to life. The plot revolved around a colony of rebel survivors who had built a giant water purification plant on the lake, which was by now one of the last remaining sources of uncontaminated water left on earth. They fought off an attack from the "Oblivion Master" and his stormtroopers, who were seeking to seize the planet and "hold mankind to ransom".[419]

Other one-time-only events have included 2005's Playstation Weekender, which saw guests doing battle in inflatable sumo suits in the gardens, sliding down a zip wire from the top of the Towers and duelling with laser guns inside the mansion.

The following year, the park hosted an evening "ghost hunt", with 870 volunteers walking through the mansion in darkness, keeping watch for any strange sounds, sights or sensations. Ghost hunter Martin Jeffrey, who organised the event, explained that a ghostly woman in a black wedding dress was the most likely spirit to be encountered: "She was first seen in the 1950s by a man who walked into the library with his dog and the dog suddenly started barking. He looked up and saw this woman with a thin black lace veil covering her face staring down at him. These stories have continued year in and year out - from the staff and members of the public, who sometimes think she's a guide! More recently, a female worker saw a tall dark gentleman wearing Victorian clothes pass her then disappear through the chapel roof. Poltergeists have also been reported. Visitors and staff have had small stones and objects thrown near them from a horizontal position." No new spirits were turned up by the hunt.[420]

Not all special events are open to the public, with the park occasionally being hired out in its entirety by private groups. In June 2003, telecommunications firm BT spent an estimated £1 million on a celebratory bash for employees who had worked for the company for 30 years or more and their families. Live bands were laid on, while the general public were told to stay away. The park was later admonished by the Advertising Standards Agency for claiming that "Alton Towers is open every day from 5th April to 2nd November", when it was actually closed for two days to accommodate the BT event. The park had advertised the closure and allowed people who did turn up to enter, but the ASA still found in favour of the complainant. That didn't stop management from renting the park out to BT again the following year.[421]

In July 2006, The Independent reported that Alton Towers was among the latest venues chasing the so-called "pink pound". It was claimed that the park, along with Thorpe Park, would close its doors to the general public for a day in September to welcome exclusively gay men and women over 18. Tussauds was working with the dating and lifestyle website Gaydar to promote the event.[422] In the end, guests of any age or sexuality were allowed in, and no major problems were reported between the estimated 8,000 gay and lesbian visitors and the other guests at the park. A spokesperson for Tussauds said: "Both the gay and straight communities enjoyed the fact that the event was non-exclusive and that the mix of both communities created a 'party' atmosphere just as we had promised." [423] In the following years, unofficial "gay days" have been advertised, with guests asked to attend wearing specific items of clothing, such as red t-shirts.

Another private event planned for 2006 proved to be more controversial. The Sun newspaper reported that:

Britain's biggest fun park has sparked a race row – with a MUSLIMS-ONLY day.

Up to 28,000 are expected at Alton Towers on September 17 when there will be no music, booze or gambling.

*Instead there will be prayer areas, Muslim stalls and all food served will be **HALAL**.*

Non-Muslims phoning the Staffordshire park have been refused tickets. One, George Hughes, 19, who rang up for 15 tickets for a pal's birthday, said: "I couldn't believe it. It's the only day we can go, yet I can't because I'm not Muslim. Can you imagine all the fuss if there was a Christians-only day?"

George, of Crayford, Kent, added: "My Muslim friends think it's outrageous. What's the world coming to when people are being banned from flying the St George's flag yet this sort of day is allowed? If it must be held, then why not on a weekday rather than a busy weekend?" - The Sun, June 30, 2006

Fellow tabloid the Daily Star was also up in arms, reporting that a couple marrying at the Alton Towers Hotel would not be able to go on rides together at the park due to a clash with the Muslim day. Amanda Morris and fiance Scott Lee had reportedly been told that they and their 60 guests would have to obey all Muslim rules, including segregation between men and women on major rides. Alton Towers had written to the couple to warn of the clash, saying: "While the park will remain accessible to you on this day, due to the numbers expected you may wish to change your booking." The resort later said: "We sincerely apologise for the way in which the wedding party were informed. We are currently discussing all options available with the party and are confident we will ensure their wedding weekend is everything they dreamed." [424]

In response, one open-minded reader wrote to the paper to say: "I agree with all those passengers from Malaga, if they can hav [sic] Muslim only days at Alton Towers lets hav muslim only flights then maybe we'll feel safer." [425]

There were major inaccuracies in the reporting of the Muslim Day, most notably in The Sun's story. Despite being located under a banner headline that read "Muslim-Only Alton Towers", the story conceded that a spokesman for Islamic Leisure, the company organising the event, had insisted that the day was open to guests of all faiths. Abid Hussan said: "We're trying to get Muslims to go to this day because they wouldn't normally go somewhere like Alton Towers. We're trying to integrate Muslims into the wider community. People can come down and see the way we live. It will be a peaceful family environment." For its part, Alton Towers confirmed that any organisation could hire the park for a day. Tickets could not be purchased directly from the park – by Muslims or non-Muslims alike. Instead, they would have to purchase them through Islamic Leisure – standard practice for a private event.

Ultimately, the Muslim fun day was cancelled, with Islamic Leisure citing poor ticket sales.[426] This has not stopped the myth of Muslim-only days at the park being perpetuated by false reports on the Internet over the last few years. Alton Towers had hosted a Christian music festival, the Ultimate Event, for over 15 years until 2010, seemingly without attracting similar coverage.

In addition to spending millions of pounds on advertising every year, Alton Towers also seeks to gain coverage in national newspapers and on television by investing in public relations activities. The opening of a new ride is sure to grab some column inches, but the park also engages in a wide variety of publicity stunts to keep itself in the public eye.

Often, the aim is to attract guests to the park while at the same time grabbing attention from reporters. In 2004, the resort launched the ihatework.co.uk website, urging browsers to "escape the workplace rat-race". Non-weekends, it said, were the perfect time to visit the park, "with the kids out of the way and back at school and the ride queues at an all-time low."

The website caught the attention of the Federation of Small Businesses, which accused Alton Towers of encouraging absenteeism. Spokesman Stephen Alambritis said: "We do not take issue with their right to market an offer, but enticing people to leave work is not the way forward. It is irresponsible. They are getting people to toy with the idea of taking a sickie. It is also demoralising for other workers who are likely to find out that a colleague has bunked off work to go to somewhere like Alton Towers."

The park's own research revealed that up to one third of its midweek adult visitors were on "unofficial" leave, although it did say that it did not condone people lying to have time off work. It did, however, suggest that midweek guests were "doing other visitors a favour" by spreading trips to the park more evenly across the week and reducing queues at busy weekends.[427]

A year later, the park offered free entry to up to 1,000 visitors who brought a garden gnome to the park throughout the month of May. The move was made in response to the publication of *Bollocks to Alton Towers*, a book which encouraged alternative days out to attractions such as Gnome Magic and the British Lawnmower Museum.

The BBC was among the outlets to report that this promotion "unwittingly created a gnome mountain", with forgetful guests leaving their porcelain friends behind. The park claimed that it was seeking to find homes for more than 200 abandoned gnomes, and that it had set up a "gnome crèche" to take care of them in the meantime.[428]

Later in 2005, Alton Towers was accused of "rewarding failure" after offering free entry to any A-Level students who failed all of their exams. To take advantage of the offer, young guests would have to prove that they had racked up at least three unclassified grades. Marketing manager Mike Lorimer claimed that the scheme was a "celebration of the underdog, underachievers and all those A-Level students staring at the U."

Predictably, education organisations couldn't resist responding. Nick Seaton, chairman of the Campaign for Real Education said: "Obviously youngsters who do not pass their exams will feel they need consoling but I think that most people will think it is ridiculous to reward failure in this way, instead of encouraging success. It sounds like a very trendy idea, but I would have thought that it was giving completely the wrong message to young people." [429]

In 2009, the park again offered a consolation prize, this time to gamblers who had backed a losing horse in the Grand National. The first 100 guests to produce a losing betting slip were allowed in for free, with the park saying that it was "confident a fantastic day out with all the family will ease their disappointment." [430]

Major sporting events such as football's World Cup and the Olympics can have a seriously adverse effect on attendance at Alton Towers. During Euro 2004, the park redecorated one of Oblivion's trains with the St George's Cross, numbering its seats and labelling them with the name of the England player due to wear that number. The ruse was designed to remind guests that the park would be showing the tournament's matches on big screens, so there was no need to stay away.

For the Royal Wedding of Prince William and Catherine Middleton in April 2011, Alton Towers laid on a "British street party", as well as showing the ceremony on a giant screen and serving Pimms and lemonade on the lawn in front of the mansion. Four years earlier, when William's father Prince Charles married Camilla Parker-Bowles, the park had renamed Rita – Queen of Speed as Camilla – Queen of Speed for one day only.

Just as a clash with a major event can cause poor attendance at the park, so can a prolonged period of rain. In August 2007, Alton Towers claimed that it planned to "beat washout summers" by controlling the weather, employing "cloud seeding" technology to freeze clouds as they approached the park. Organisers of the Beijing Olympics in 2008 planned to use the technique - which involves releasing chemicals into the clouds to encourage precipitation - to prevent rain during the opening and closing ceremonies.

Russell Barnes, the park's general manager at the time, said that the aim was to prevent a rerun of the wet summer of 2006: "After we read about Beijing, we thought we'd investigate. The wet weather definitely puts off families and our aim is not to be held hostage to the increasingly extreme weather conditions." [431]

Alton Towers' use of cloud seeding, it was reported, would cause rain to fall on nearby towns such as Stoke-on-Trent instead. Locals were said to be furious, with student Matthew Williams, 22, saying: "What gives Alton Towers the right to play God with our weather? It sounds like something Dr Evil [of *Austin Powers* fame] would do. Anyway, what's the sense in stopping it raining when people head straight for the log flume?"

Another attempt to overcome poor weather, this time in 2012, was less complex. The park simply promised that it would give £1,000 each to eight randomly-selected guests who braved the rainy conditions.

Attitudes to beauty contests have changed significantly since Alton Towers hosted The Mirror's pageants in the 1970s. The resort was accused of sexism, though, when it hosted the Miss Alton Towers contest in 2006, with winner Alana Cunningham claiming a place in the Miss England finals. The park was again accused of demeaning women in 2011, when it launched a search for thirteen "Coaster Cuties" to star in a new calendar.

Other firms haven't been shy about using exposed female flesh to promote their wares at Alton Towers. After the park's marketing team claimed in June 2009 that women were suffering from "wardrobe malfunctions" on its roller coasters, Ultimo sent a "bevy of babes" to brave the rides. The underwear firm claimed that its bras "could take the pressure".[432] Unsurprisingly, tabloids were happy to publish photographs of scantily-clad models racing around on Rita and other attractions.

The models needn't have bothered wearing anything at all. In 2004, the world record for "the most nude people on a roller coaster" had been set on Nemesis, with 32 naked riders racing around its circuit.[433] The record was lost, though, when 102 thrill-seekers bared everything on the Green Scream roller coaster at Adventure Island in Southend in 2010.[434]

Merlin's attempt to refocus Alton Towers on families led to a flurry of PR activity designed to play up the resort's family-friendly credentials. First up was a "ban" on smartphones during the 2008 May half-term week, with the aim of helping parents to disconnect from the office and reconnect with their loved ones.[435] The ban was not enforced, of course, but attracted comments from psychologists such as Dr Pat Spungin, who said: "We all need to use weekend breaks to reconnect and invest in our most important relationships in order to restore our work/life balance and put the fun back into going away."

Next up was a ban on men wearing figure-hugging, Speedo-style swimwear at the Alton Towers Water Park in August 2009. Customers were ordered to switch to shorts, with marketing director Morwenna Angove saying: "Our water park team observed an increase in the number of men wearing tighter trunk-style swimwear. We feel this small brief style is not appropriate for a family venue so we are advising male bathers to wear more protective swimwear such as shorts. We are also looking into offering complimentary male waxing, which will ensure we preserve the dignity of all our guests."[436]

The following year, the park went a step further by banning sex in rooms in some sections of its on-site hotels. One visitor was quoted by the Daily Express as saying that the noises coming from the room next door were "louder than the screams from the Nemesis ride" and had ruined their trip. The paper pointed out that the new policy meant that there were now "no rides for adults" at the resort.[437]

Many PR stunts are designed to build anticipation for the launch of new attractions. Rita's debut in 2005, for example, was greeted with the sight of 20 transvestites riding the coaster on the pages of national newspapers. The Daily Star reported that "The glam daredevils clung on to their wigs yesterday as the ride rocketed from 0 to 60 miles per hour in just 2.5 seconds." Many were wearing full make-up and high heels. Spokeswoman Liz Greenwood said that the group were the perfect choice to prove that it takes "real balls" to take a ride on Rita.[438]

When Spinball Whizzer was renamed as Sonic Spinball as part of a licensing deal with Sega in 2010, Morwenna Angove's team were on hand with a story that a rogue squirrel had been conducting a month-long "reign of terror" during the testing process. The squirrel, fittingly nicknamed Sonic, was said to have ridden the coaster during unmanned testing, and then snatched food belonging to riders and staff during manned tests. A high-pitched alarm – conveniently inaudible to humans – was claimed to have been installed to keep the creature away.[439]

The debut of Thirteen in 2010 was accompanied by an unprecedented number of PR schemes, again fronted by Angove. First, the park announced that it had asked Google Earth not to photograph the site, in order to keep its "world's first" element a secret. Then, it hired pop mogul Simon Cowell's former bodyguard to stand guard over the under-construction ride.[440] "I wanted to keep secret the "magic" element – the freefall drop – in order to increase anticipation and speculation," says Angove. "People said I would never be able to manage it."

Not all of the publicity was deliberate. "We put up posters around the site before we'd decided on the ride's name with cryptic words like 'Surrender' and 'Demon of the Dark Forest' in order to advertise it without giving too much away. Online forums went crazy musing on the possibility that it was connected with dogs in some way, because of a small silhouette of what looked like a dog on one of the posters. In reality that was just an ink drop mistake from the printers," Angove claims.

Thirteen was billed as "every roller coaster you've ever dreamed of rolled into one", despite featuring a low height restriction of just 1.2 metres. "In theory, an eight year old could go on Thirteen," says Angove. That didn't stop the park from claiming that the ride would be so terrifying that only those aged 16-55 would be allowed to ride, with healthy young guests being limited to one ride per day, such was the horror they would have to endure. Visitors would be offered hypnotherapy to overcome their worries about riding it, after a builder was said to have been "paralysed by fear" while working on its construction.[441]

Despite accepting that riders over 55 would be able to handle Thirteen, Alton Towers still wouldn't let the "horror" of the new coaster go un-hyped. Ahead of the ride's debut on March 20, the park introduced a special new ticket option. For an extra £1, guests could add "health insurance" to their ticket, covering them for "physical and psychological trauma". The price even included access to a medical expert stationed close to the ride - though as with most of Merlin's unusual promotions, the option seems to have been quietly dropped. Staff did, though, hand out "protective" rubber pants to visitors before they boarded the coaster, to prevent any unfortunate accidents.

Thirty people were invited to a pre-launch "boot camp" at the park hosted by cage fighter Alex Reid, undergoing endurance exercises and psychometric tests. The winners' inaugural ride was broadcast to millions of viewers on ITV's GMTV. The opening day saw celebrities such as Jennifer Ellison, Gail Porter and Sarah Harding wheeled out, although one of the biggest names – Jonathan Ross – missed the event after the doors on his train jammed and he reportedly ended up in Stockport 40 miles away.[442]

Alton Towers, and Angove in particular, came in for heavy criticism from some fans for billing Thirteen as "the scariest roller coaster in the world" when it was, in reality, a family ride. Angove defended the approach, saying: "The bulk of our marketing campaign has been aimed at teenagers to make it aspirational as they represent the largest number of people riding Thirteen. It is important to note that the ride scores well among both families and young adults. In terms of the marketing leading up to the ride launch, we need to ensure maximum exposure before the ride opens. This means we need to have a range of PR stories that are of interest to the media and our target audience." [443] Given the huge boost in attendance at the park for 2010, Angove could justifiably claim success.

The promotional campaign for Nemesis Sub-Terra, the park's next new ride, took a similar slant. This time, the park called in the British Board of Film Classification, which provided its first certification ever applied to a theme park ride. The attraction received a rating of "12A", meaning that it was recommended that children under 12 should only ride if accompanied by an adult. The organisation said: "The BBFC's Guidelines at '12A'/'12' allow moderate physical and psychological threat, provided that the disturbing sequences are not frequent or sustained. Nemesis Sub-Terra contains some intense moments, in some respects comparable with scary scenes which may be experienced in horror or science fiction films at 12A/12. But while some people will no doubt find this a frightening experience, the personnel monitoring the site are soon on hand to guide the public to safety."

In reality, the language used by the BBFC was quite subtle. It advised Alton Towers based on how it would classify a movie were the impact to be the same, however there is no mandatory classification for theme park rides whatsoever. The press lapped up the story regardless.

The stunts were back for the launch of The Smiler in 2013, with the ride's "smiley face" logo being emblazoned on flocks of sheep across the country.[444] Technology now plays a bigger role, though, with Alton Towers releasing *The Smiler: The Game* for iPhone, iPad and Android devices, allowing guests to take control of the coaster's trains. Unfortunately, some factors are outside of marketing teams' control. The game's release coincided with a two-month delay to The Smiler's opening date.

Alton Towers has featured on television extensively over the years, with images of Anneka Rice braving the rapids in an episode of *Treasure Hunt* and Yvette Fielding searching the mansion for spirits in *Most Haunted* having been broadcast across the UK. The park was even chosen as the venue for the first ever televised version of the *UK's Strongest Man* contest in 1999, which saw twenty-four heavyweight competitors lifting Ford Focus cars and doing push-ups with a giant log.[445]

One of the first shows to be hosted at the theme park was *Hold Tight*, an ITV production that ran from 1982 to 1987. It saw two teams of schoolchildren competing to answer questions to which the answers were letters and numbers. Getting the right answers meant advancing up a four-storey Snakes and Ladders board that was installed in Talbot Street, while getting them wrong meant sliding down a snake. Schools would bus in large numbers of supporters for their teams, and one round involved riders attempting to spot letters from a word while racing around on the Corkscrew. Pop bands also performed live at the park, with the final series – dubbed *Hold Tight: The Altons* - featuring no game show element at all.[446]

Hold Tight was presented by Pauline Black, formerly of the pop group Selecter, and physical education lecturer (and TV newcomer) Colin Cripsen. A much higher-profile cast took part in the next game show to be hosted at Alton Towers, although many of the stars involved probably wish that they hadn't agreed to appear on the infamous *It's a Royal Knockout* (also known as *The Grand Knockout Tournament*).

Hosted by Stuart Hall (since convicted of indecently assaulting thirteen women), the charity show was based on the format of the BBC's *It's a Knockout*. It was the brainchild of Prince Edward, then 23, who promised: "The games will be slightly different from the old *It's a Knockout*. We've deliberately kept a sense of decorum." Some viewers may have questioned this statement as they watched the royals don outfits including Elizabethan tights and codpieces.[447]

The line-up of royal contestants included Prince Edward himself, Prince Andrew, Princess Anne and Sarah Ferguson, although the Queen, Prince Philip, Prince Charles and Princess Diana declined to take part. Celebrities including

John Travolta, John Cleese, Cliff Richard, Gary Lineker, Jane Seymour, Christopher Reeve and George Lazenby joined the royals. They were challenged to complete bizarre tasks by comedian Rowan Atkinson, playing the role of "Lord Knock of Alton". In one round, the teams dressed up as giant vegetables and threw fake hams at one another. Another saw them chasing each other through giant tanks of water.

Immediately after the event, Prince Edward – who had organised the programme through his production company Ardent – asked assembled journalists: "Well, what did you think?" The response was nervous laughter, which led to Edward storming out and yelling: "Oh, what's the bloody point?" The show was panned by critics, with some commentators going as far as describing it as the beginning of the decline of the Royal Family's popularity.[448] On the plus side, the event did succeed in raising more than £1 million for charity.

The plan to show the human side of the royal family had backfired badly. A courtier told royal biographer Ben Pimlott afterwards: "It was a terrible mistake. The Queen was against it but one of her faults is she can't say no."

In May 2010, Alton Towers was reported to be in talks with production company Endemol to recreate the show to celebrate the park's 30th anniversary. A spokesman said: "We are planning a variety of Eighties-themed activities, and the chance to revive *It's a Knockout* could be the jewel in the crown. We are in talks with several broadcasters to see if this would be of interest." The idea came to nothing.[449]

Unlike rivals Disney and Universal, Alton Towers and its owner Merlin do not have access to their own back-catalogue of intellectual property upon which to base new rides. Instead, the park has entered into a number of licensing agreements with third-parties over the years, enabling it to bring in characters such as *Barney the Dinosaur*, *The Tweenies* and *Sonic the Hedgehog*.

Not all of these deals have paid off. In 1997, the park launched Nickelodeon: Outta Control, a new attraction in Cred Street that featured characters from shows on the children's TV channel. It saw groups of kids and their parents being guided around a building, with each room featuring different attractions. One challenged guests to make as much noise as possible, while another allowed them to throw balls into a toilet. All the while, guests were being recorded, and the resulting footage was played back in a small theatre at the end of the ride. Despite being the headline attraction of the newly-rethemed Cred Street, the attraction featured disastrously low throughput and shut after just two years at the end of the 1998 season. Rather than replace it, Alton Towers left most of the interior intact and simply placed the Frog Hopper ride in front of the building.

Talbot Street, seen here in 1986, was home to a range of retail outlets. Image: Glen Fairweather

Oblivion condoms, still on sale in 2013.
Image: Nick Sim

A friendly welcome to Duel: Live at Scarefest 2009.
Image: Natalie Sim

The not-so-funny clowns of Carnival of Screams.
Image: Natalie Sim

For more images, visit
http://www.themeparktourist.com/tales-from-the-towers/

9. When things go wrong

Alton Towers receives millions of visitors every year. Its rides, many of which rocket around their circuits at high speed, are designed to cope with being used almost non-stop throughout the summer season. Dedicated maintenance staff in its Technical Services division are employed to deal with any issues that cause breakdowns, as well as inspecting the rides for faults each morning. Major maintenance work takes place during the winter off-season, and can be very involved. Rita's trains, for instance, are dismantled and put back together again, right down to the last bolt.

Inevitably, though, things will go wrong occasionally. Even relatively minor incidents, such as power outages and roller coasters' safety mechanisms bringing them to a halt, are often reported in the press in sensational terms. In April 2010, for example, the Daily Star melodramatically proclaimed that "terrified families were left stranded in mid-air on white knuckle rides" when a power cut hit the park.[450] "Everyone was screaming to get off," said one visitor. "It was really upsetting as people panicked." In reality, the park stuck to its standard emergency procedures and evacuated riders safely. The outage lasted for just forty minutes.

The park is powerless to prevent "urban legends" developing around some of its more famous attractions. The Black Hole, for example, was said to have decapitated test dummies during early testing. People are claimed to have fallen into Oblivion for real, rather than in the safety of the coaster's trains.

The reality, though, is that Alton Towers' attractions have a very good safety record, with no deaths having been attributed to the rides themselves (deaths from natural causes do occur at the resort, of course, just as they do anywhere else). In a park with so much high-tech machinery, however, things do occasionally go wrong. During the park's decades of operations there have been some high-profile incidents, which have at best caused embarrassment in the media, and at worst caused physical injuries to those involved.

Given its billing as the UK's answer to Disney's Space Mountain, the Black Hole was always going to attract a lot of publicity when it opened in 1984. Not all of it was welcome, or positive, however. On April 24, 1984 – just weeks after its debut – the ride hit the headlines for all the wrong reasons.

As it traversed the indoor circuit, one of the coaster's original single-car trains shuddered to a halt and partly came off the track.[451] Five children were injured in the incident, with one being kept in hospital for two nights for treatment for head injuries. The Black Hole was immediately closed to guests, with inspectors from the Health and Safety Executive (HSE) being called in to look it over. Representatives from the ride's German manufacturer were also summoned to help identify the fault.

Newspapers immediately labeled the Black Hole as "controversial", with much of the attention being focused on the fact that it was bought "second-hand" by Alton Towers, having previously operated in Germany.[452] The insinuation was that an "old" ride was somehow less safe, despite the fact that Schwarzkopf Jetstar II roller coasters (of which the Black Hole was an example) were common and frequently moved between different locations. A spokesperson for the park emphasised that "the German authorities have regulations which are even tougher than ours. There is no suggestion that it was ever involved in an accident of any kind and it has a completely clean log book."

With its £2 million new attraction out-of-action, Alton Towers was keen for the investigation to be wrapped up quickly. It was also hopeful that the negative publicity surrounding it wouldn't put visitors off riding it. The spokesperson said: "I don't think what happened will deter people from using the Black Hole when it opens. When it was installed, we took safety measures which were far above those recommended by the manufacturers. Of the 140 rides of this type, we are the only ones that have fitted seat belts."

In the end, the Black Hole reopened just four days after the accident, having been granted a new safety certificate.[453] There was no sign that the press coverage had caused any significant damage to its reputation, with riders once again queuing up to whizz through outer space. "We did not notice any greater or less demand for the ride yesterday and we think people have accepted that it was something that was investigated thoroughly" was the park's defiant statement.

The results of the HSE report were not publicised, although an official stated before its completion that the accident was likely to be connected with the failure of a restraining device designed to keep the car on the track. There was further controversy, though, when Peter Morrison, Minister of State for the Department of Employment (of which the HSE was a part) visited the park on a carefully-orchestrated tour less than a month after the accident – and before reading the report.

The minister was happy to be pictured on the Black Hole itself, riding with owner John Broome. "I have not seen the HSE report yet," he said, "but obviously the department and Alton Towers are equally concerned that everything is as safe as possible. This is a family place and families want to come and enjoy themselves. I am here today to enjoy myself and I am looking forward to going on the Black Hole." [454] Broome had made use of his political connections to help salvage the reputation of his new coaster. The same connections would later secure Margaret Thatcher's backing for his doomed Battersea Power Station project.

Some changes were made to the Black Hole at the end of its debut season, although it is not clear that any of them were related to the accident. The ride's first drop was modified, while lights were added to the lift hill so that riders would not be too surprised by the sudden drop. The coaster would later be completely rebuilt in 1988, adding dual-car trains.

The partial derailment on the Black Hole wasn't the only well-publicised accident at Alton Towers in 1984. A month later, 14 people were injured when a road sweeping truck careered out of control on a hill and ran into a group of visitors.[455] Then, during the summer season, a 12-year-old boy suffered head, pelvis, arm and leg injuries when he fell from another new ride, the Magic Carpet. Darren Fewing was taken to North Staffordshire Royal Infirmary to undergo treatment, but the injuries were not life-threatening.

The HSE were again called in to inspect the ride, and were seemingly satisfied that the boy fell because he was attempting to do something that he shouldn't have. Alton Towers reopened the Magic Carpet again the very next day, with a spokesman saying: "There is absolutely nothing wrong with the ride. We have checked it and double checked it and there is no reason why it should not open today. We are certain that this accident was not due to an equipment failure - with that in mind the ride will be operating today. It is to be inspected by the HSE Officers today and we expect them to give it a clean bill of health."

Another Broome-era addition, the Alton Mouse, suffered a problem during its final season at the park in 1991. A car stalled at the bottom of the coaster's second drop, causing it to shut down. However, a ride operator restarted it, with the car still trapped at the bottom of the drop. As a result, a second car crashed into the back of it, causing injuries to several riders. The HSE fined Alton Towers, citing inadequate training for the ride operator.

A seemingly much tamer ride, the Miniature Railway, suffered an accident during its penultimate year of operations in 1995. The train skidded into a safety buffer as it approached the Merrie England station, causing minor cuts and scrapes to 11 riders. It reopened two days later.[456]

Alton Towers' first major roller coaster, the Corkscrew, was at the heart of several incidents that caught the attention of the media during its lifetime. In 1997, four members of staff were trapped on the ride as they carried out a routine test ride, and had to disembark using a ladder. Four years later, a technical fault led to the train stopping between the two corkscrew elements – mercifully, it was not upside-down. 28 riders were trapped onboard for 90 minutes, although all were evacuated safely without injury.[457] The Corkscrew reopened two days later.

Introduced alongside the Corkscrew in Ug Land in 2005, Rita – Queen of Speed hit the headlines almost immediately. The mother of Amelia Seiga, 12, claimed that the 62 miles per hour coaster had caused "appalling injuries" to both of her daughter's wrists as it rounded a bend. Jane Seiga said that her daughter was treated by a nurse at the park, who "dismissed" her injuries as "badly sprained wrists." The next day, she was seen by doctors at a hospital in North Wales, who again sent her home. Finally, a week later, her parents again took her to hospital, where an X-ray found that both wrists were broken.

Mrs Seiga demanded that the park impose a new height restriction on Rita, preventing those as young as her daughter from riding it. She said: "There is no way I would have let my daughter on the ride if I knew she was going to be injured. She passed all the checks and restrictions, so how can this happen? The health and safety people have suggested Amelia may have weak wrists - but she didn't break her wrists, the ride broke them. Because of her age, her bones are not hard so they didn't snap, they buckled. It was horrendous. She will never go on one of those rides again. There's a TV advert for Alton Towers and she feels sick every time it's on."

Mrs Seiga's claims were widely reported by national newspapers, who speculated that the g-forces that riders are subjected to on Rita were to blame. The HSE inspected the coaster, however, and found no evidence to suggest that this was the case. A spokesperson said: "No fault was found with the ride and there did not appear to be the mechanism in place to cause such an injury in the normal cause of operations of the device. As it is a new ride, Alton Towers will continue to monitor it closely and report any further incidents. In such circumstances, we would of course reopen our investigation."

A spokesperson for Alton Towers added: "The investigation concluded the ride is safe and no changes to the ride, height restrictions or operating procedures are deemed to be necessary." [458] No other riders have since reported breaking their wrists on Rita.

On July 24, 2012, the cable used to launch Rita's train snapped during normal operations. Nobody was injured as a result. A number of previous cable-snapping incidents have been reported on Intamin accelerator coasters, with the most serious having occurred on the Xcelerator coaster at Knott's Berry Farm in 2009. On that occasion, the snapped cable created a cloud of debris and caused a laceration to a 12-year-old boy's leg. The incident on Xcelerator was investigated by the California Division of Occupational Safety and Health, which found that it could have been avoided if Knott's Berry Farm had been up-to-date on its maintenance schedule at the time. Manufacturer Intamin also received criticism for "shortcomings" in its instructions for inspecting and maintaining the cable, which failed to specify whether it should be inspected every month, or every six months.

Following the 2012 incident, Rita received a new catch-tray from Intamin. This was designed to prevent a recurrence of the aftermath of the cable-snap incident, which saw the cable dangling onto the pathway below.

John Wardley's Secret Weapons have remained remarkably accident-free, despite carrying tens of millions of riders over the past two decades. The only incident of note involving Nemesis came in 2002, when a young boy was struck on the head by one of the ride's trains. He was taken to North Staffordshire Hospital by air ambulance with laceration injuries, but these were not life-threatening and he remained conscious throughout. The boy had entered a restricted area close to the station, and while operators shouted warnings to him and activated the ride's emergency stop system, they could not prevent the collision. The HSE allowed Alton Towers to continue operating the ride, while Alton Towers said in a statement: "The immediate reaction of the staff resulted in less serious injuries than might otherwise have been sustained." [459] Aside from this incident, the main hazard for riders on Nemesis continues to be losing their property – the park has previously claimed that such diverse items as prosthetic legs and arms and artificial eyeballs have been found in ponds underneath the coaster.[460]

Oblivion has a similarly unblemished safety record. The coaster did hit the headlines in May 2012, though, when a 20-year old man climbed over safety fences and found his way onto a ledge close to its vertical drop. He was rescued by three fire crews and subsequently arrested for a public order offence, with Oblivion returning to action soon after. Alton Towers said: "As with all our rides the area surrounding the Oblivion track is securely fenced off and ride operators reacted immediately in line with our well-rehearsed safety procedures."

Arguably the most serious accident ever to occur at Alton Towers took place on the Runaway Mine Train on July 20, 2006. As the train entered the tunnel section of the ride, two of its carriages became separated. After losing power, the front section of the train rolled back and collided with the back section. Witness Matthew Toast said: "It was all very dramatic. The ride was packed full and you could hear the excited screams from people. Then suddenly there was a big bang and you could hear a lot of groans instead... People were pretty frightened up there, and you could hear some shouting to get down." [461] Debris could be seen on the ground on the path near Katanga Canyon's Pizza Hut.

The coaster was immediately shut down, and the 38 passengers were evacuated by staff over a period of 40 minutes. Six were taken to hospital, including two women with whiplash injuries who were transported by air ambulance. 25 others were treated on-site for cuts and bruises caused by the impact.

Jenny Crisp was in the park's first aid centre fetching a bandage for a friend when the injured began to arrive. She said: "There were six girls practically in tears, and two guys. One of the guys was wearing an eye patch and the other had a bloody scratch running down the side of his face. His eyes were really bloodshot. The girls were shaking like leaves. One of them was then sick and they were led by first-aid staff off the site. It was terrible."

Newspapers seized upon the incident, with the Daily Express' story labeled with the headline "Roller coaster of terror".[462] Some of the reporting was wide of the mark, with the Daily Star claiming that the collision happened at 80 miles per hour (the top speed of the Runaway Mine Train is actually just 22 miles per hour and it was travelling much slower than this when the two train sections struck each other).[463]

In response, Alton Towers released a statement in which it said: "The train has a complicated structure and we are still investigating exactly how the accident managed to happen. The ride has been closed and will remain so while a thorough investigation is carried out by the park's management team together with the HSE."

The HSE's investigation found that a previously unidentified step in a track joint had triggered the accident, causing one of the three bolts retaining the coupling bar bracket between the two cars to fail. The remaining two bolts then also failed, causing the bracket and coupling bar to fall onto the track. An operator, hearing a bang, activated the ride's emergency stop system, shutting down power to the train and carriages (each of which features an individual motor). This did not bring the ride to an immediate stop (which would be dangerous in itself), but progressively slowed it as it rounded a 360-degree helix and a further turn before the back section came to a stop in the tunnel. The front six cars carried on up a slight incline, and then rolled backwards until cars 6 and 7 collided. As would be expected, the most serious injuries were to the occupants of car 7, which took the brunt of the impact. The train was in bad shape, with several other coupling bars failing, and the track was also damaged.

The coupling bar bracket was redesigned to feature four bolts, as well as tie wires to supplement it in case of a failure. The HSE confirmed that the coaster had been up to date with maintenance, had undergone the required daily checks and had the necessary safety certificate. Inspectors described the crash as an "isolated incident" and said: "This is an established ride with a good safety history. This failure can be quickly remedied and simple measures can be put in place to prevent a recurrence of such an incident."

Despite being cleared of blame for the crash, Alton Towers erred on the side of caution and kept the Runaway Mine Train closed for the remainder of the 2006 season. Head of

Technical Services Terry Dunn said: "Obviously, health and safety is our most important consideration. There is still a lot of work to be done to the track following the unfortunate incident earlier this year. In addition, we have sent the carriages back to the manufacturer in Germany for a complete refurbishment, which is a time-consuming process. We don't want to rush anything, so we have decided to delay the re-opening until next season." While the park did consider retheming or even replacing the coaster, it returned to action in 2007.[464]

Alton Towers' two major transportation systems, the Skyride and the Monorail, have not caused any major injuries since opening in 1987. Those who suffer from vertigo, though, may not want to think about the methods used to evacuate riders from the Skyride on the rare occasions when it does break down. The well-rehearsed procedures were put into practice in 2004, when 69 people were trapped on the attraction after a gondola's guide wheel failed to slot into the correct place as it approached the Forbidden Valley station, causing it to grind to a halt. The fire brigade was called, but its services were not required as park staff helped nine guests *abseil* down to the ground below. The ride was then restarted (running backwards), with the remainder of the riders – who had been stranded for around three hours – able to exit normally. They were greeted with offers of a refund or tickets to return to the park.[465] In the event of a complete breakdown, the abseiling technique would be used to evacuate all riders who are not within range of a fire brigade's ladder.

The Skyride helps guests at the park save on shoe leather by providing a shortcut across the landscaped gardens. However, visitors have been left facing energy-sapping walks for extended periods twice in recent years by fires in the ride's stations. The first, which occurred during the Scarefest Halloween events in 2007, left the Forbidden Valley station without a roof and damaged the workings of the attraction. Fortunately, the incident occurred while the ride was shut and came close to the end of the season. The Skyride was back up-and-running again by mid-2008.

Just months after it received all-new gondolas, the Skyride was hit by another blaze in July 2009. This time, the fire – caused by an electrical fault - completely destroyed the Cloud Cuckoo Land station. Again, no-one was hurt, but the ride was closed for the rest of the season.

While the monorail system at Walt Disney World has seen several accidents and one fatality, the shorter line at Alton Towers has not been the scene of any serious injuries. At least two incidents have occurred, though, with one in 2003 seeing a train crash into the back of another while travelling at a slow speed.[466] Both trains were empty of passengers, and the drivers were unhurt, though the nose cone of one train was badly damaged. The Monorail reopened later the same day.

A second accident, in August 2012, occurred when staff were in the process of adding two trains (Trains 1 and 2) to the monorail's running line. One train (Train 6) had just passed the Duel attraction and was approaching the access track switch that was being used to add the additional trains. The System Controller failed to ensure that this train had passed the access track switch before giving permission for Train 1 to access the system. The driver of Train 1 started to rotate the access track switch from the running line direction to the access track direction, which could potentially have caused a derailment of Train 6. Fortunately, the driver of Train 6 noticed the track starting to rotate and hit the emergency stop button. The train was unable to completely slow down and stop before it hit the part-turned track switch, causing it to come to an abrupt stop. 27 of the 74 passengers on-board complained of minor injuries, with 12 being treated by Alton Towers' on-site medical team. Additional controls have been put in place to prevent a repeat of the incident.

Not all safety incidents involve rides. In 2005, during the park's end-of-season fireworks extravaganza, a rocket misfired, causing another one to fire at an incorrect angle. It flew into the crowd, and eight people required eye wash treatment as a result. At least two were sent to hospital, receiving further anti-biotic eye baths.

The incident occurred near the end of the display, run by specialist company Millennium. Its staff shut off the section of the fireworks which had malfunctioned immediately. Alton Towers laid the blame on the rocket's manufacturer, which it said had been improperly packed. A spokesperson said: "We have been having these shows for about 15 years now and we have set off hundreds of thousands of fireworks and this is the first time something has gone wrong...The fireworks are very carefully monitored, it is very unfortunate that this has happened but there was very little we could have done about it." [467]

Earlier in 2005, the Daily Star featured the banner headline "Gang raped at fun park".[468] The accompanying story told of a 15-year-old on a school trip, who claimed to have been repeatedly raped by a group of boys from another school. The girl said that the six boys had approached her as she walked around the park by herself after a disagreement with friends, leading her away from a main pathway and then assaulting her. She said that she eventually managed to escape, before being treated by park medical staff.

A spokesman for Staffordshire Police said: "The park staff managed to contact staff from her school and she returned home with the rest of her party. The boys weren't thought to be armed but the girl said she was scared because there were so many of them."

Meanwhile, the park itself said in a statement: "There was no report made on the day to either Alton Towers' security department or our fully trained medical team. A girl was treated for the after effects of drinking alcohol on that day. But no other injury was reported by her or observed by our medical staff."

More than a year later, in October 2006, police announced that no further action was to be taken following the completion of an inquiry.

Humans have escaped without serious injury from most incidents at Alton Towers. Animals, however, aren't always quite so lucky. In 2001, an outbreak of foot-and-mouth disease spread across the United Kingdom. More than 2,000 cases of the disease were reported, with over 10 million sheep and cattle being culled before it was brought under control. Among the unfortunate victims were a cow, six sheep, three pigs and eight goats that lived in Old MacDonald's Farmyard, which were slaughtered as a precaution.[469] It was six years before animals began to be reintroduced to the agriculturally-themed area.

Spare a thought as well for the staff of Alton Towers in the days before it became a theme park, when health and safety laws were not so strict. In 1884, 19-year-old under-gardener Robert Nash ventured upon the ice-covered lake near the house's farm. When he reached a point twenty yards from land, the ice gave way, leaving him immersed in the freezing cold water. Before assistance could be rendered him, he drowned.[470]

10. Creating the magic

On busy days, Alton Towers can attract upwards of 20,000 guests. Beavering away to keep them happy and safe are around 2,000 employees, with roles as diverse as ride operators, marketing managers and costumed characters. Working at a theme park can be tough, involving long hours in hot or freezing weather, wearing uncomfortable uniforms and dealing with angry, frustrated customers. It can, however, also be rewarding, with staff often having the chance to meet a celebrity, make someone's day or even – in extreme circumstances – save a visitor's life.

Staff are split across a number of departments. The theme park and hotels share Finance, Sales and Marketing, Entertainments, Corporate Events, Retail, Security, Medical, Uniform, Human Resources, Health and Safety, Retail and Food and Beverage teams. The Technical Services and Experience teams maintain and improve the rides and attractions in the park, Housekeeping ensures that the hotels are kept clean and Leisure Operations runs the water park and spa. An IT department oversees more than 500 computers, 700 internal and external telephones and an array of smartphones.[471] The rides themselves are designed by Merlin's "Magic Making" teams, of which there are 13 around the globe – including one at the Towers.

Every summer, Alton Towers advertises around 1,000 seasonal jobs. Despite the perceived downsides, competition is fierce. In 2010, for example, there were 17,822 enquiries for the 1,200 roles on offer.[472]

In order to secure one of the available posts, hopeful applicants must pass through an interview process that can vary from lightweight to grueling. "My initial interview was kind of rushed with no assessment centre," says one long-time Alton Towers Water Park employee. "My most recent interview was very formal, with a full assessment centre and structured team-building activities."

The assessment centres consist of group activities, such as making a short presentation as a team. These are designed to weed out those who don't work well with others. A more standard interview with management focuses on dealing with the public and any relevant past experience. "The interview process was quite good," says a ride operator, "just normal interview stuff and team building exercises".

Once they've signed up, employees can look forward to being indoctrinated by the two-day "Welcome to the Beating Heart of Fun!" induction course. Before starting work, they'll then receive anything from a few days to several weeks of further, role-specific training. Ride hosts must study and memorise large sections of a manual for the attraction, including evacuation procedures, typical queue times and what to do in a variety of situations. Lifeguards at the water park, meanwhile, must attain the National Pool Lifeguard Qualification, and then take a further 3-day course specific to Alton Towers.

Pay levels are not exactly sky-high. Staff, though, can look forward to receiving a number of perks, including discounts at Merlin-operated hotels, money off at some high street retailers and childcare vouchers. They also receive a free pass to all Merlin attractions, which the company promises will ensure that they "have never been so popular".[473]

Many of Alton Towers' employees are local (living within 20 miles of the resort), and have the option of using company-provided transport to get to work. Those from further afield can take advantage of accommodation in two converted mills in nearby Leek. The Well Street Mill hosts 39 bedrooms with en-suite facilities, while nearby Alexandra Mill hosts a further 26 rooms. One employee describes the atmosphere in the buildings as being "like a student hall", with plenty of alcohol-fuelled hijinks and teenage romance.

The permanent roles at the resort can be very different to the seasonal ones, with management ranks often made up of those with qualifications in Business Studies or Marketing.[474] Managers can expect to get their hands dirty, though, according to former Marketing Director Morwenna Angove: "There's no hierarchy between office based and customer facing staff here. The marketing department brings in the visitors so, when things get really busy, we'll lend a helping hand to the operational team. If you had airs and graces you probably wouldn't last very long here. This is not a nine-to-five or a Monday-to-Friday workplace – we all work very hard." [475]

Angove, who oversaw a team of 80, insists that management are on the same side as rank-and-file employees: "We'll stand at the entrance in costumes handing out bacon butties or small gifts to employees as they arrive on a day that we know is going to be really busy," she said in 2010. "In July, when schools tend to have their summer jolly, the whole of the marketing team will be out litter picking or helping on admissions. For the launch of Thirteen I planted trees and I've even been known to clean toilets. This certainly isn't an ivory tower role, nor would I want it to be. You have to be ready to pick up anything." [476]

Working as a ride operator is often perceived as one of the more glamorous and exciting roles at Alton Towers. In reality, it takes some time for an employee to work their way up to the actual job title of "Ride Operator". They'll begin as a lowly Trainee Ride Host, being kept under close observation until they have completed a required number of hours and passed any relevant tests. Once they've qualified as a Ride Host, their responsibilities will range from everything including managing queues, ensuring guests board the ride safely and even emptying bins.

Ride Operators themselves outrank Ride Hosts, and are essentially team leaders. They control the operation of an attraction from a cabin and are responsible for filling in paperwork, starting with "smaller" rides such as Blade before graduating to larger, more popular attractions such as Air and Nemesis. Once they have gained significant experience, they can become a Ride Assessor, helping to train other operators. Rides are grouped into different areas, with an Area Coach overseeing the various Ride Operators. The highlight of working as a Ride Operator was clear to one former staff member: "Pressing the magic 'go' button!"

The month prior to the park's opening day – when the park is devoid of guests - is actually one of the busiest of the year for those working on Alton Towers' rides. In addition to training and studying ride manuals – which can be hefty for larger rides such as roller coasters – they will also learn emergency procedures and learn how to perform basic tasks such as measuring the height of children. Ride hosts and operators also help out with other tasks such as cleaning and ensuring signage is in place.

Health and safety is a priority for the resort, as is reflected by its impressive record of zero fatalities caused by its rides. Rules have been tightened up since the park's early days, though. One Astroglide operator from the late 1980s recalls smearing silicon polish onto one of the ride's mats for an early-morning test run, resulting in an explosively fast journey down the slide and the loss of skin from both arms.[477]

Other roles can be less entertaining. In particular, on busy days, working in one of the park's restaurants or dining outlets is described by one former worker as "mind-numbing". When it's hot outside and guests are in a hurry, it can be "hellish, when you get people complaining." [478]

Following its takeover of the park in 1990, Tussauds began to adopt a Disney-style approach to operating the park. Terms such as "On Stage" (meaning "in view of guests") began to be used by management, and the overall aim was to "create the magic for everyone". Staff were based in "Magic HQ" and were told to behave as ambassadors for Alton Towers. The company even had a definition of what "the magic" was: it was the same feeling that children experience on the night before Christmas.[479]

Menial roles such as emptying bins were given grand job titles such as "Cleansing Assistant". Staff were told to smile at all times, although Cleansing Assistant Frank was less than enthusiastic: "For £3.40 an hour you don't have a lot to smile about." [480]

Employees were dressed in formal uniforms, projecting a consistent image to guests. The uniforms were, though, extremely hot and staff campaigned to have them changed. A more lightweight design was finally introduced in 1998, by which time Tussauds was now under Charterhouse's ownership and the emphasis on "the magic" had begun to wane.

Special events bring with them a host of part-time jobs. During Scarefest, for example, the park employs a number of "Scare Actors", whose job it is to terrify guests in the various horror mazes and scare zones. Alton Towers promises that successful applicants will "get the chance to make people's nightmares come true".[481] It won't always be comfortable, though – as well as wearing masks, prosthetics and make-up, the Scare Actors will also spend much of their time working in smoky, dark, strobe-lit environments. There's also the ever-present risk of terrified guests overreacting to a jump-out scare.

The Christmas period, too, can offer up some unusual job opportunities. After winning a landmark discriminations case against Kwik Save in 2005, 4 foot 4 inch tall Scott English landed a position as one of Santa's Little Helpers at the Alton Towers Hotel. "After years of hell at Kwik Save, I'm thrilled with my new life," he said. "Finally, I'm appreciated somewhere because of my size." His duties included providing "professional elf service" and "madcap greetings" to hotel guests, as well as reciting specially-written poems and reading bedtime stories. Guests could also look forward to his "rapid elf unpack" service, in which he slung visitors' clothes into wardrobes in a manic fashion.[482]

Not all workers at the park are employed directly by Merlin. The operators of the various games stalls around the park, for example, have been provided by external supplier HB Leisure since the 2007 season. The lucrative games can bring in thousands of pounds per day, so Merlin could have done without the dreadful publicity focused upon them by the BBC's *Your Money, Their Tricks* programme in July 2013.[483]

The broadcaster sent undercover reporters into Alton Towers' sister park Thorpe Park to work for HB Leisure, and highlighted a number of questionable practices. As an example, the programme showed how the odds on the "Mad Milk" game could be manipulated. The goal of the game is to knock down some bottles with a single throw of a ball. The manager explained that the number of bottles could be increased to make the game harder: "You are not actually cheating anyone."

Later on, things became much more sinister. On "Rebound", guests were shown how a ball could be bounced off a board and into a box, claiming a prize. However, the ball that was used for the demonstration was weighed down by a coin - making it easier to use than the actual balls given to the customer. This was blatant false advertising - and HB Leisure was forced to admit that it didn't "sanction, condone or encourage this practice." Similarly, it was unhappy with hosts on another game shouting loudly to distract customers, labeling it "inexcusable".

"People used to get into trouble for giving out too many prizes and not making enough money," said former HB Leisure employee Charlene. "Games hosts would do certain things to make the games harder for people. I was really shocked."

An HB Leisure manager said: "All the games have to be made in such a way that they are possible to win. But you can increase the difficulty level of the game. You can shout in such a high voice that you just distract the person."

For its part, Merlin sought to manage the response to the allegations via its social media accounts, bringing in marketing agency We Are Social to handle the response. It addressed concerns on Twitter with posts such as: "We're investigating and will take action if we find any evidence of malpractice," and "we absolutely do not condone this and we are investigating thoroughly".[484]

HB Leisure, meanwhile, promised measures to enforce fair operation of its games, which operate at Chessington World of Adventures, Legoland Windsor, Drayton Manor and Paultons Park in addition to Thorpe Park and Alton Towers. The firm recently expanded into the United States, winning the contract to run the games stalls at Merlin-operated Legoland Florida.

Costumed characters play a smaller role at Alton Towers at present than at Disneyland and other family-oriented theme parks. Rather than operating park-wide, they generally stick to specific areas, such as the *Ice Age* characters that meet guests in Cloud Cuckoo Land or the Pirates of Mutiny Bay. In the past, though, they were a major feature of the park's offerings, meeting-and-greeting guests throughout the day and starring in the daily parade.

Merlin now works with an outside company, Rainbow Productions, to develop the costumes for its characters (the company's other credits include creating the costumes for the mascots of the London Olympics and Paralympics in 2012, Wenlock and Mandeville). The process starts with Merlin providing artwork to Rainbow, before deciding on the height of the costume in relation to the performer. Material swatches are sent to Merlin for approval, before costume makers start work on sculpting the head and body at Rainbow's studio in southwest London. When these are completed, Rainbow can provide training including health and safety advice and guidance on how to care for the costume. The entire process takes around 6 to 8 weeks.

At Alton Towers, Rainbow has helped to bring to life characters including Rastamouse, Scratchy and Zoomer (a trio of crime fighting rodents who appear at the Caribbean Beach Party weekend events), Fin the Shark (who can be found in Mutiny Bay) and – of course – Henry Hound in his most recent incarnation in 2005.

In his prime during the late 1980s and early 1990s, Henry was featured prominently in the park's marketing, starred in several shows and was the headline performer in the parade. His partner Henrietta joined him for many of these tasks, often flouncing around in a colourful dress. Both characters, along with Henry's son Junior, were based on the Talbot Hounds, which are found on the Talbot family's coat of arms. Talbots were large hounds with long hanging ears and a heavy jaw, making for an appealingly dopey-looking mascot.

Though Henry was the lead act, many other characters joined him in the park. The Cuddly Bears actually pre-dated him, and were present for longer than him, too, leaving the park in 1997. Oversized frogs represented the gardens in the parade, while Jack the Scarecrow looked after the farm. Friendly vampire The Count appeared in Henry's cartoon adventures in the Fun Club magazine, and helped to launch the Haunted House in 1992.

Henry was dropped in 1993 ahead of the major marketing campaign around Nemesis and Toyland Tours the following year, and was absent for more than a decade before a brief return between 2005 and 2007.[485]

Inside the wide array of characters that entertained guests at the park during Henry's golden years were a group of around 20 to 30 young staff. Among them was Alistair Farrant, who landed a summer job at the park in the early 1990s through a friend. He recalls: "You just turned up each day and didn't know what you were going to be doing. One day you might be Henry Hound, the next day you'd be a bear and the next day you'd be a pirate or something."

What were the costumes like to wear? "Not that pleasant," recalls Farrant. "They were quite claustrophobic. You could only really see out of the little holes for the eyes, nose or mouth. They were hot and sweaty, and they weren't cleaned that often. If you went out on a blazing hot summer's day, you got pretty sweaty and horrible. You changed around a bit, so someone else might have been wearing the costume in the morning and you had to get into it in the afternoon."

"Within reason, you could wander wherever you wanted. We used to go out in pairs, because you were only able to see so much and there were kids that would try and do things to you. I had people kicking me up the backside, they'd pull my tail, they'd try to pull my head off or smack me round the head. I once had a lit cigarette shoved into my costume's nose. I was dressed as a bear and it ended up dangling only an inch or so away from my actual nose, which was a bit scary."

Performers wouldn't always take such abuse lying down. "You couldn't do much - the minders would try and put them right. We used to find certain kids were worse than others. During the parade, they would come and try to kick and punch us. There were 20 or 30 of us and we knew certain parts of the route where nobody was really watching you, so we might retaliate slightly. There were some little shits and it was hard to resist."

Not all of the park's furry residents are humans in costume. Feral cats can be found in several locations, with at least eight of the felines having been spotted on the roof of the Mexican Cantina. As at many other theme parks, they are neither encouraged nor discouraged to stay by staff, and can play an important role in killing the vermin that are attracted to litter around the estate.

Celebrities frequently make visits to Alton Towers, from Kylie Minogue and Eddie "the Eagle" Edwards in the 1980s to the likes of Katie Price and Jonathan Ross in the 2000s. For staff, this offers them the chance to meet famous people up-close, whether serving them in a restaurant or helping them to board a ride.

One of the most infamous visits made by a "VIP" to the park was by Margaret Thatcher – a long-time supporter of John Broome – during her election campaign in 1987. Thatcher declined Broome's offer of a ride on the Grand Canyon Rapids, but did board the newly-opened Skyride. The Labour MP for nearby Stoke-on-Trent, Mark Fisher, expressed the hope that the "Iron Lady" would fall into the Black Hole and stay there.[486]

Security arrangements were tight for the Prime Minister's visit, which came exactly a week before her third General Election victory and was the first ever trip by a serving Prime Minister to Alton Towers. Members of the SAS and sniffer dogs were present to keep Thatcher safe, while snipers sat on the roof of the Towers and other buildings.[487]

Nevertheless, Thatcher could hardly escape attention – some wanted, and some less so. More than 100 journalists tailed her and her husband Denis around the park, and at one point she was encircled by a crowd of openly hostile guests. Denis was unfazed, saying: "It's all part of the campaign, old boy." [488]

Thatcher's tour was followed just 10 days later by the *It's a Royal Knockout contest*, bringing with it a huge line-up of royals and other famous figures. The show's host, Stuart Hall, actually met Thatcher during her trip. He was dressed in a doublet, rehearsing his role.

Princess Diana was frequently pictured in newspapers on visits to the park with her sons Prince William and Prince Harry. Former archivist Les Davies accompanied the trio on several occasions, and remembers: "When Princess Diana came with her two boys, their first visit was official and again security was tight. But on later occasions Diana and the princes mingled with the crowds and were hardly recognised." He has fond memories of Diana and the boys: "We took the three of them for a meal at the kids' restaurant. We talked to her about children and things like the history of the Towers. She was a fan of the water rides and compared them with skiing. The young princes had no airs and graces and both of them gave me a kiss when they left." [489]

Not all "celebrities" seen at Alton Towers are genuine. In 2011, the park offered guests a special "Reality of Alton" package, which enabled them to experience fame for a day. Packs of paparazzi would follow them around the park, while a film crew would make an hour-long "reality" show about their visit.[490]

Most of Alton Towers' predominantly young seasonal staff enjoy their time at the park, with Alistair Farrant recalling: "All my friends worked there, so it was just like hanging out with your mates." Sometimes, though, things can turn serious.

A water park lifeguard recalls: "The most memorable incident I remember and dealt with was around 3 years ago. A guest began to have a seizure in the water park. After around 5 minutes of fitting, the guest stopped breathing and we had to begin CPR. After a further 10 minutes we got the guest breathing again and kept him safe until the ambulance arrived. At the time our training kicked in and we dealt with the situation as we were trained to do so. Only afterwards did the realisation of the severity hit us. Essentially we brought a man back to life. If he had been in any other situation he might not have been as lucky. The man went on to make a full recovery in hospital."

Henry Hound prior to his retirement.
Image: Dave Smith

The parade route could be hazardous for Henry and his friends. Image: Dave Smith

For more images, visit
http://www.themeparktourist.com/tales-from-the-towers/

11. What might have been

Over the past three decades, Alton Towers has conceived dozens of different concepts for new rides and attractions. While many of these have eventually been fully developed and installed at the park, a large number of them ultimately never saw the light of day. Some may be revived in the future, but most will only ever exist as drawings and concept artwork. The theme park and resort could be a very different place today if some of these abandoned projects had gone ahead.

Towards the end of his reign as owner of Alton Towers, John Broome was facing a pitched battle with local residents and planning authorities to keep The Alton Beast and the Alton Mouse, both of which were located in Coaster Corner. The prospect of losing the coasters was not an attractive one, as it would leave the park woefully short of ride capacity to absorb the crowds on peak days. Even moving the rides would not provide much of a solution to the capacity problem – the Alton Mouse was capable of handling fewer than 500 riders per hour, and was only ever intended to be a temporary addition. The Beast could handle much greater numbers, but there was still a need to expand the park's line-up to avoid queue times becoming out of control.

Broome had been ordered by the district council to remove the Alton Beast and the Alton Mouse by the end of December 1989. In May of that year, Alton Towers submitted an application for a new "gravity ride", to be located on the Abbey Woods site next to the Corkscrew. Typically of Broome, he offered to remove the existing two coasters from the Coaster Corner site *if* – and only if – the application was approved. Even then, the two rides would be kept in place until the end of the 1991 season to allow construction of the permanent replacement to be completed.

The council acquiesced, and approved Broome's application for the gravity ride. Predictably, the park's neighbours were furious. Cyril Thorley, a resident of an eighteenth century sandstone cottage nearby, described the council's actions as a "betrayal". Councillor Sheila Parrington echoed this sentiment, saying that the decision was "appalling". Planning Officer Michael Sutcliffe disagreed, saying: "The council has a responsibility to the economy of the area as well as its conservation. Alton Towers says the new ride is essential if they are to keep ahead of their rivals, and we accept that." [491]

"Too much queuing does not encourage tourists to make a return visit," said Broome. The coaster, then, would be designed to have a staggering capacity of 2,500 riders per hour – much higher than the modern coasters at the park today. To achieve this, seven trains would be employed, with several in motion while others were loaded. In a sop to the complaining residents, the rails would be synthetically lined to reduce wheel noise.

Broome promised that there was nothing else comparable at the time anywhere else in the world, and the plans for the coaster suggest that he was not exaggerating. Unlike the Corkscrew, the Black Hole and the Alton Beast, the gravity ride would not be an off-the-shelf model. Instead, it would feature a completely custom design and a number of innovative features.

Legendary German ride designer Anton Schwarzkopf, who was behind the Jetstar models that were used by the Black Hole and the Alton Beast, had been called upon to design the new addition. It was to be similar in style to the Lisebergbanan at Liseberg in Sweden, which had opened in 1987 and is often cited as Schwarzkopf's favourite roller coaster, but on a larger scale. Like the Lisebergbanan, it would make use of the contours of the ground and natural vegetation surrounding it to generate thrills. It would boast no fewer than three lift hills, with two of them running parallel to each other. Synchronising the dispatch of trains would enable them to "race" or "duel" around sections of the circuit, including climbing the parallel lift hills together. There would be no inversions, but several tight helices and turns would take riders close to the trees.

The gravity ride would have been one of the largest steel roller coasters in the world at the time. Schwarzkopf's own company had gone bankrupt by this stage, so it would have been built in conjunction with Zierer as had several previous Schwarzkopf-designed creations.

When Tussauds took over Alton Towers in 1990, it stuck to its agreement to remove or relocate the Coaster Corner rides by the end of 1991. However, despite the Schwarzkopf coaster having received planning approval, it opted to scrap the project. John Wardley was involved in the decision, and claimed that the projected capacity of the ride was unrealistic. He did not believe it would be possible to dispatch every train without delay, warning that this would have led to an "operational disaster".

Following the progress of Alton Towers' latest "Secret Weapon" project has become a regular pastime for roller coaster enthusiasts. The park has used the label as the codename for most of its major coaster projects over the past two decades, from Nemesis ("SW3") through to The Smiler ("SW7"). But where did the "Secret Weapon" moniker come from? And whatever happened to SW1 and SW2? The answer lies in the plans formulated by Tussauds following its acquisition of the park.

While it had dumped Broome's plans for the Schwarzkopf coaster, Tussauds knew that it needed to introduce a major new roller coaster to Alton Towers. To really grab the public's imagination, the park would need to install a coaster that was unique and ground-breaking. At other theme parks, this was relatively easily achieved by pushing the envelope on the ride's size and speed, enabling marketing teams to promote it as the "world's tallest" or "Europe's fastest". This was simply not an option at Alton Towers, with strict planning regulations ruling out any record-breaking additions.

Rather than looking to go taller or faster than its rivals, then, Alton Towers would have to differentiate its new roller coaster in other ways. To help achieve this, Tussauds turned to a long-time partner, one with a track-record of industry-changing innovations: Arrow Dynamics.

Originally known as Arrow Development, the manufacturer had a formidable reputation. As long ago as 1959, it had worked with Walt Disney himself to produce the world's first tubular steel track roller coaster, the Matterhorn Bobsleds at Disneyland. The ride is still a favourite with guests at the park today. It followed this by installing the world's first log flume, El Aserradero at Six Flags Over Texas in 1963, a ride which has subsequently been copied by theme parks all over the globe. The world's first mine train coaster (complete with an underwater tunnel), the Runaway Mine Train, followed at the same park three years later.

Another of Arrow's major achievements had directly contributed to the success of Alton Towers itself. The Corkscrew, which debuted at Knott's Berry Farm in 1975, was the world's first modern inverting roller coaster and the first to take riders upside down twice. While Alton Towers' own, identically-named Corkscrew was manufactured by Dutch firm Vekoma, it was closely based on the template developed by Arrow.

Fresh from the successful project to add the heavily-themed suspended coaster Vampire to the Tussauds-owned

Chessington World of Adventures, Arrow was keen to engage with Alton Towers' owner once again. This time, it had a new trick up its sleeve: the pipeline coaster.

The chief innovation of the pipeline coaster (and the one from which it derived its name) was the positioning of the ride's trains. Rather than sitting on top of the track (as with a traditional coaster) or beneath it (as with a suspended or inverted coaster), the vehicles would instead sit *in-between* the rails. The u-shaped track, with the trains running down the middle of it, had the appearance of a pipeline.

Strictly speaking, Arrow's in-development new product wasn't an entirely novel type of coaster. Japanese firm TOGO had developed a pipeline coaster known as the "Ultra Twister" in the early 1980s, with the first example opening at Nagashima Spa Land in 1984. There was one key difference, though: the TOGO coasters were unable to make turns, and thus were all "shuttle" coasters, with the trains racing around the track in one direction, and then traversing it again backwards (TOGO did eventually promote a full-circuit version during the mid-1990s, but it was never built[492]). The Arrow version would not suffer from this limitation.

Because of its position embedded within the track, the coaster's train would have the ability to roll around its longitudinal axis. This would place its centre of rotation close to the riders' mid-sections, and, Arrow believed, allow the creation of a "totally new experience". The pipeline coaster would be capable of manoeuvres similar to those performed by stunt aeroplanes, such as snap rolls and steep dives.

Arrow had high hopes for the pipeline coaster concept. It proudly proclaimed that having introduced the log flume in the 1960s, the Corkscrew in the 1970s and the suspended coaster in the 1980s, the pipeline would be its major contribution to the world of theme parks for the 1990s. The company began to display the ride's train at the International

Association of Amusement Parks and Attractions (IAAPA) annual convention, and to actively seek engagement with theme park operators – including Tussauds.

In 1989, Arrow started construction of a prototype of the pipeline coaster concept at its headquarters in Utah. By June 1990, it was ready for its first test run, which the company boasted it had passed "with flying colours". Shortly thereafter, Arrow employees Dal Freeman, Larry Miller and Mike Smith were joined by Randy Geisler from the American Coaster Enthusiasts group for the first manned trip around the circuit. Bizarrely, the prototype had no lift hill, so the group were seated in a train on a section of track and lifted 120 feet into the air by a crane. From there, they passed through several "rollover" inversions and a steep drop towards the ground.

According to Arrow, the early test runs were a huge success. "Awesome", "smooth" and "totally different" were among the superlatives apparently thrown at the new creation by those lucky enough to try it out. Coaster enthusiasts eagerly awaited the first installations at theme parks – and Alton Towers was first in line.

Tussauds management were, it seems, suitably impressed by Arrow's marketing claims. They set John Wardley to work on a design for a pipeline coaster, which would occupy a site close to the Thunder Looper in Thunder Valley. Wardley, inspired by the ride's bullet-shaped trains, developed a theme based around a secret military research establishment, surrounded by a barbed wire fence.[493] The ride itself would represent a "Secret Weapon" – and thus the naming convention for Alton Towers' roller coaster projects was born. The initial design for the pipeline coaster was dubbed "SW1".

Problems, though, began to emerge when Wardley was invited to Utah to ride the prototype. He found it to be a huge disappointment, later describing it as "very slow and rather boring".[494] The primary issue was the level of friction generated by the ride's trains as they traversed the track, which made it very energy inefficient. Compared to other types of coaster, the pipeline coaster simply didn't go very far or very fast. Not only that, but its visual appearance – something that Wardley has always placed heavy emphasis on – was "rather cumbersome".

For Alton Towers, which couldn't afford to build a towering lift hill to compensate for the ride's limitations, this was a major problem. Wardley calculated that if the coaster's lift hill topped out at tree level (and it would have to, since this was one of the key planning restrictions placed on the park), its circuit could only run for a mere 300 metres. Naturally, this was unacceptable.

Ever creative, though, Wardley's team suggested a solution. What if the park simply built *downwards*, into the ground? He proposed a new design, "SW2", which sprawled across a wide area that includes parts of the sites that currently house Air and Nemesis Sub-Terra. Most significantly, it would involve the excavation of an enormous pit to house much of the ride's circuit.

Despite Wardley's complaints about the pipeline coaster ride experience, Tussauds pushed ahead with the concept. Outline planning permission for a tree-height coaster and the creation of the pit was secured, and Thunder Valley would never look the same. It seemed that Arrow's pipeline coaster dreams were still alive.

Wardley, though, was never happy with the SW2 plan, owing largely to his experience riding the Utah prototype. When he was able to persuade Bolliger & Mabillard to divulge their plans for an inverted coaster at Six Flags Great America, the concept that eventually became Nemesis was born – and SW2 was dead in the water. Fortunately, the planning work that had already been carried out around the pit was not wasted, and Nemesis' unique location became a significant contributor to its success.

While Secret Weapons 1 and 2 were ultimately never built, Arrow's pipeline design did still exert an influence on Alton Towers' future plans. A similar theme was applied to Oblivion in 1998, and the Secret Weapon codename lives on.

Unfortunately for Arrow, it was never able to iron out the flaws with its pipeline coaster concept. The combination of high friction and uncomfortable over-the-shoulder restraints meant that no actual rides based on the model were ever built. It wasn't the only manufacturer to experiment with the pipeline design and fail – Swiss rival Intamin also invested significant effort in developing its own version, which was a total commercial failure. The firm sold just one, to a theme park in South Korea, and it was later moved to Kuwait before being closed for good.

While it never managed to sell a full-circuit version, TOGO did succeed in selling seven of its Ultra Twister models before going bust in the early 2000s. Five of these are still in operation today – four in the company's native Japan, and one in Kuwait.

The wasted investment on the pipeline coaster helped push Arrow Dynamics towards the brink of bankruptcy in the 1990s. It was the company's next big development, though, that tipped it over the edge. It produced a "fourth dimension" coaster, which boasted trains with seats that were able to rotate 360 degrees during the ride. Unfortunately, the first installation – X at Six Flags Magic Mountain – was a disaster. It suffered from serious problems even before its opening day, eventually opening half a year late. The delays to the debut of the prototype coaster, combined with subsequent modifications that were required to its trains, eventually forced Arrow out of business in 2001. The rump of the firm was snapped up by ride manufacturer S&S Power, and it carried out a successful modification of the ride (now known as X2) in 2008.

Before his "retirement" (and subsequent re-hiring by Merlin), John Wardley's last design for Tussauds was for the infamous cross-valley wooden roller coaster that generated so much ire among local residents and environmental groups. Setting aside the issues over whether or not the ride should have received planning approval after the application in March 2003, there is no doubt that it would have been an extraordinary creation and different from any other wooden coaster in the world.

The ride experience largely consisted of two enormous drops – each over 200 feet – down into the wooded valley between the then-Ug Land area (now the Dark Forest) and Forbidden Valley. The station was to be located on the site of a former quarry close to the Corkscrew. Riders would sit in trains consisting of five cars, each capable of holding up to six people.

After exiting the station, the trains would climb a 22-metre (72 feet) lift hill up to the top of the tree line, before plunging down into the valley below, racing past trees on either side of the track and likely hitting speeds of well in excess of 70 miles per hour. After rising up the other side and emerging close to Air, the train would perform several turns, climb another lift hill and plummet down a second drop parallel to the first. After turning a final time, it would return to the station.

The train would have run on steel tracks, but these would be mounted on a timber deck approximately three metres wide and supported by a timber structure. Alton Towers promised that the wooden structure would "fit particularly well in visual terms" with the surrounding woodland, and would make for a "stimulating and unique ride experience".

After the plans were withdrawn in the face of fierce opposition, Wardley was left disappointed. However, all hope may not be lost. In a 2010 interview, former marketing director Morwenna Angove said that a cross-valley coaster was "something that we are [still] interested in exploring".[495] Merlin's long-term development plan for Alton Towers, last updated in 2012, earmarks two major new rides for 2016 and 2019. Intriguingly, one of these is a "Cross Valley Ride", described as a roller coaster that would link the Forbidden Valley and Dark Forest areas.

Wardley does not feel that concept was dropped due to opposition from residents. Instead, he points the finger at Merlin CEO Nick Varney. "Nick said to me: 'What is the unique selling point?' I said that it was going to be a fabulous ride, but that wasn't good enough. I don't think the cross-valley coaster is dead in the water at all. The planners were coming round to our way of thinking." [496]

Tussauds' next planning application for a new attraction at Alton Towers came in November 2003, when it proposed the installation of a tethered hot air balloon. Similar to attractions at Disney's resorts in Florida and Paris, the balloon would have floated some 400 feet (120 metres) above the park below, providing stunning views across the surrounding countryside.

It is very likely that Alton Towers would have charged extra for rides on the balloon, given its limited capacity. The manufacturer, Lindstrand, suggested that a typical ride would last 15 minutes, enabling around 1,000 people per day to ride on peak days. It also proposed a £10 per passenger fee, so the park could have raked in an extra £10,000 per day if the plan had gone ahead.

The balloon was proposed as a replacement for the Dynamo flat ride, which was removed from Forbidden Valley at the end of the 2003 season. However, the plans also refer to a site in the Cred Street area (now Cloud Cuckoo Land).

Alton Towers planned to use a Lindstrand HiFlyer balloon, a model which was first introduced in 2006 and has since been installed at more than 50 locations worldwide.[497] Filled with helium, the balloon would feature a diameter of 75 feet (23 metres), although this would expand to 79 feet (24 metres) when on the ground. It would stand at some 118 feet (36 metres) tall. A high-tensile wire cable would enable the 30 passengers to be raised into the air, with a sophisticated electric winch returning them back to earth.

Lindstrand boasts that "featuring a sponsor's logo/ branding on this highly visible aerial advertising platform provides an excellent opportunity to seek advertising revenue. The envelope can be used as a backdrop for video projection and laser advertising." Alton Towers' plans, however, show the balloon decorated with a simple Alton Towers Resort logo and mock trees. The balloon could also be illuminated at night, via a system suspended internally from the top of the envelope.

The application was never likely to be successful, given that the balloon would have emerged above the treeline even when at ground level. It was quietly withdrawn, and Spinball Whizzer was the only major addition to the park in 2004.

In 2005, Alton Towers installed a zip wire from the roof of the Towers mansion to the lawn below for the Playstation Weekender event. In April the following year, it applied for permission to place a launch platform and gantry on the roof of the building for a further two-and-a-half years. Riders would start on the flat, modern roof, before sliding down to a landing platform on the opposite side of the main lake.

Dubbed "Vertigo", the zip wire attraction appeared on the park's official map for the 2006 season. However, it never actually operated, and the park withdrew its planning application.

Alton Towers struggled during the period that Tussauds was owned by Dubai International Capital, with falling attendance figures and staff lay-offs. Excluding Rita, which was well into construction before DIC took over, the firm only added the Peugeot 207 Driving School, the rethemed Charlie and the Chocolate Factory, and the minor There's Something in the Dung Heap and Haunted Hollow attractions to the park during its tenure.

Things looked much more positive during the early days of DIC's ownership, though, with rumours about the mysterious "Project Dolphin" circulating online. This was said to be a 10 year development plan for the resort, which would see major investment in the theme park, the hotels and other attractions. The goal was to create "once in a lifetime experiences" to keep the resort ahead of its rivals.

The codename "Dolphin" was said to be derived from swimming with dolphins, an experience that many would consider to be once in a lifetime. The concept appears to have been inspired by Discovery Cove, the exclusive SeaWorld-owned park in Florida that limits attendance to 1,000 guests per day and offers dolphin swim experiences as well as other interactions with marine life.

Alton Towers' ambitions didn't extend quite as far as replicating the dolphin swim experience, but swimming with tropical fish *was* put forward as one of the Project Dolphin concepts. The attraction would have taken the form of a combined aquarium / swimming pool, with areas including the Lost Lagoon, Shimmering Shoals and Quay Tropicalia. A "child-friendly" rock pool and play areas would have been included, with concept artwork appearing to show the entire attraction being housed inside a giant Eden Project-style bubble. Guests, it was promised, would be "brought face-to-face with tropical fish wherever possible".

Another potential addition under Project Dolphin was the Lost Temple, which would have occupied the Ice Arena in Storybook Land after its closure at the end of the 2005 season. Artwork for the attraction shows a heavily-themed interior that resembles the set of an *Indiana Jones* movie, with kids enjoying a number of interactive activities including puzzles and touchscreen displays embedded into the scenery.

Many different concepts were put forward as part of Project Dolphin, with Alton Towers promising that they were being "developed with customer feedback". Ultimately, though, few would see the light of day. While it has been claimed that Sharkbait Reef was inspired by the tropical fish plans, in reality Merlin was always likely to seek to add one of its Sea Life Centres to the resort following its takeover.

Concepts put forward for the 2007 season include Alton Woods, which would have seen a woodland adventure play area added to the park, possibly in the area now occupied by Haunted Hollow. In addition to climbing nets and treehouses, the attraction would also have boasted illusions such as a "Magic Tap" that seemed to hover in mid-air and a "Bridge to Infinity".

Also on the drawing board for 2007 was "Just Add Water", which would have occupied the Ingestre Lake, which had hosted the pay-per-play Splash Kart Challenge since the exit of the Swan Boats in 2003. This interactive water playground would have featured a variety of themed floating platforms, many of which would be equipped with water cannons. Some sections of the playground would have been located below ground, with guests able to stand in bubbles that rose just above the water level. Battle Galleons was later installed on the lake instead.

Another proposal for the same season was Garden Vistas, a project to overhaul the Towers' famous landscaped gardens that had virtually no chance of receiving planning consent. A number of bizarre, interactive modern structures would have been added to the gardens, including "picture frames" through which guests would have photographs taken with iconic features such as the Choragic Monument.

More reasonable, but still dropped, was the Tea on the Lawn concept. This would have seen guests enjoying a traditional British "high tea" in front of the Garden Conservatory, or in the gardens at the rear of the Alton Towers Hotel.

The main entryway to the park, Towers Street, was considered for a major update during DIC's reign. The grassy "islands" in the centre of the street would have been replaced by themed features. One of these would have incorporated the existing iconic frog fountains, adding other aquatic elements and giant dragonflies. Another would have been themed around the Towers themselves, while one island would have resembled a beach, complete with buckets and spades.

Fans of wooden roller coasters were hugely excited in October 2006, when Alton Towers announced plans to install a "woodie" in the former Coaster Corner area. This would sit at the centre of an entire new land, which would also incorporate a water ride and a flat ride. Less ambitious than John Wardley's cross-valley design, the coaster would have been a family-oriented attraction similar in scale to Megafobia at Oakwood in Wales. Wardley was again said to be involved, but no manufacturer had been selected. The ride was described as being "medium-sized", although it would be much smaller than the previously-proposed wooden coaster.

The accompanying water ride would have been a Shoot-the-Chute-style ride similar to Tidal Wave at Thorpe Park, with riders boarding large boats before plunging down a drop into a splash zone below. In keeping with the marine life-themed codenames introduced during the DIC era, the plans were known as "Project Shark".

Though the new land was being proposed for the 2008 season, no plans were ever submitted to the local council and new owner Merlin instead opened the revamped Mutiny Bay in that year.

One of the last plans proposed by Tussauds before its takeover by Merlin (and submitted to the authorities just after the deal went through) was for a new water slide for the Cariba Creek water park. Coming hot on the heels of the approval of plans for the Extraordinary Golf attraction, the proposed new slide was designed to enhance the resort's offerings during the winter months, attracting more guests to the hotels. It was also hoped that it would help encourage day guests to extend their stay, visiting the water park in the late afternoon and early evening.

The slide was to be added to the outdoor area of Cariba Creek, to the south of the existing Splash Landings hotel. It would include a 42 foot (13 metre) tall launch platform, located close to the uppermost of the three Flash Floods pools. Guests would access the platform via the main area surrounding the Lagoona Bay pool. Less mobile and disabled guests would be carried to the top by a vertical platform lift.

Once they reached the top, guests would clamber into a rubber ring and slide down a steep flume to the opposite side of the outdoor area, emerging into a half-pipe style element which they would swoosh around before plunging into the bottom Flash Floods pool. The incorporation of the existing pool would reduce the amount of development required.

Alton Towers attempted to reduce the visual impact of the proposed slide – which was much larger than the existing slides in the outdoor area – by finishing the underside in dark green plastic. The launch platform would fit in with the rest of the Caribbean-themed Cariba Creek, with green painted timber boarding wallows and a shallow-pitched dark green corrugated sheeting roof.

Evidently, Merlin did not view expanding the water park's offerings as a priority following its takeover, and withdrew the planning application for the new slide. No new rides have been added to the water park since its debut in 2003.

When Merlin acquired the park, the Black Hole tent in X-Sector was an empty shell. The firm entertained a number of ideas for putting it back into use, before it was eventually removed in 2012 to make way for The Smiler.

One such concept was for Duelling Deadstars. In keeping with X-Sector's theme, this would be based around a shadowy experiment: "Subject yourself to the extreme turbulent forces of the Dead Star experiment - a secret underground facility built to research and monitor the atomic effects on body and state. Step forward and donate yourself to molecular science - experience atomic euphoria aboard these awesome machines."

The actual ride system was to be supplied by Technical Park. It would consist of two of the firm's Vortex flat rides, hence the "Duelling" moniker. Each of these rides would feature two 16-seater gondolas, both attached by arms to a V-shaped central structure. With the central structure rotating in a clockwise or counter-clockwise direction, the arms would be angled outwards. Simultaneously, the gondolas would also start rotating, each one in a different direction. Riders would face inwards, with their legs dangling beneath them, spinning rapidly and at times being in a near-vertical position. Special effects and lighting inside the tent would enhance the experience, as would the apparent danger of a collision with the neighbouring ride.

Another concept considered for the Black Hole tent was Area 51, themed around the top-secret US military installation in Nevada. It was to be very similar to the Nemesis Sub-Terra ride, which was subsequently built in Forbidden Valley. Riders would board one of ABC Rides' small miniature free fall rides, plunging around 7 metres towards the ground below. As with Nemesis Sub-Terra, it appears that staff members in costume would add to the atmosphere.

Merlin also looked into installing Kuka Robocoaster rides into the Black Hole tent. Launched in 2007, these are based on technology developed by the German manufacturer of industrial robots. The Robocoaster is the first robot licensed to carry passengers, who are seated in roller coaster-style seats on the end of a robotic arm. The system is used to simulate riding on a user-designed roller coaster in the Sum of all Thrills attraction at Walt Disney World's Epcot, and is also employed – mounted on a track – by the Harry Potter and the Forbidden Journey ride at Universal Orlando's Islands of Adventure. Alton Towers planned to house multiple Robocoasters in the tent, with the theme being based around riders being used as crash test dummies.

Prior to selecting freefall coaster Thirteen as its first major new roller coaster for the park, Merlin considered a variety of alternatives. One of these was a "tilt" coaster, building on a previous design for a spinning coaster with a trick track section that John Wardley had put together. This would have been used instead of the freefall drop that eventually made it into the final coaster, with the track suddenly tilting backwards, before the train sped off in a reverse direction.

Another option was a Tower Launch Coaster, to be manufactured by German firm Zierer. Guests would have been seated in small cars that could accommodate eight in two groups of four, and would then have been launched up a vertical hill – almost the opposite of the Oblivion ride experience. The ride would have been visually similar to the Gerstlauer Euro-Fighter model employed by The Smiler. Currently, only one example of a Zierer Tower Launch Coaster exists, at the Lagoon park in the US state of Utah.

Once again, designs for a wooden coaster were considered, running into the woods just as Thirteen does – but not making the trip across the valley. Concept artwork shows near-misses with the surrounding trees.

An innovative option that was investigated was a Vekoma Dragon Fly coaster, a concept put forward by the Dutch firm that has yet to be utilised in a real installation. The ride would have employed suspended trains which would swing as they navigated the circuit, in a similar style to existing coasters such as Vampire at Chessington World of Adventures. The twist, though, was that riders would be in a kneeling position, just as they are on motorbike coasters. The resulting experience would potentially have been akin to riding a floating "speeder bike" from the *Stars Wars* movies.

Several potential themes were put forward for the overhaul of the Ug Land area. These included the industrial-style "The Quarry", which would have seen Rita converted into "Rockblaster" and was an ideal fit with Robocoaster rides. Another possible theme, which could also have incorporated Robocoasters, was based around a world of machines. The Nemesis-style "Creatures" would have seen monsters emerging from the ground following the demolition of the Corkscrew, while "Ghost Rider" would have been a Wild West-themed area with a supernatural twist. A final, *Lord of the Rings*-inspired option was "Dragon's Lair", a fantastical realm complete with a fiery volcano. Concept artwork for all of these options, as well as the Dark Forest, showed far more elaborate theming than was ultimately installed.

Alton Towers conducted a number of customer surveys during the 2008 season regarding the potential additions. Ultimately, the Dark Forest theme won out, along with Intamin's freefall coaster design.

John Wardley has put several further designs for wooden coasters forward during the past decade, including one with a *Wallace and Gromit* theme. Another, designed in conjunction with Candy Holland, would have featured a "spooky horror circus theme".[498]

Despite these being dropped, Wardley has not given up on his dream of adding a wooden coaster to Alton Towers. He pushed the idea one final time for the park's 2013 coaster, saying in his autobiography: "We all knew that a traditional wooden coaster would be an absolutely perfect attraction for the park, and would thrill young and old alike."

However, Merlin's management did not approve. CEO Nick Varney has, on several occasions, explained why he does not believe wooden coasters are a good fit for the firm's parks. In a 2013 interview, he said: "I love wooden roller coasters as much as you do! The problem is that the general public doesn't 'get' what is so special about them and they therefore don't represent good investments because historically parks will not achieve the visitor uplift required to pay for them. It is, I agree, very frustrating." [499] Wardley views it as a chicken-and-egg situation: "I was convinced that once the guests had ridden such a ride they would love it and be very enthusiastic." [500]

Wardley was involved in the concept-generation stage for The Smiler, and laments the amount of time that wasted on ideas that were ultimately not pursued. "My favourite was a stand-up coaster that we designed to run around Katanga Canyon. It would have had a huge drop to it down into a hole that we were going to excavate. A very, very deep hole. It would have been very expensive and manufactured by B&M. Various people thought that we would never get planning permission for it."

Merlin's insistence on every ride having a unique selling point also caused problems. "They said 'what about putting people in a sort of ball that rolls along the track?', or 'what about a coaster that is part-above and part-below the track?'" One suggestion was for a ride with a train featuring multiple types of seats, including inverted coaster seats, stand-up coaster sections and some sit-down seats, so that guests could choose how to ride. Not surprisingly, these concepts didn't get far.[501]

As well as all-new rides, sometimes proposals are put forward for updates to existing attractions that do not go ahead. For example, after building Katanga Canyon and Gloomy Wood, Alton Towers recognised that the miniature railway could be an important transportation link between the new areas, as well as the Thunder Valley land. It submitted plans to add a second track (enabling two trains to operate at once), and to build a new station in Gloomy Wood, to be known as "Gloomy Halt". Ultimately, it dropped plans for a third station, and instead moved the Thunder Valley station closer to Gloomy Wood so that guests could easily reach both areas on foot. The circuit was shortened, instead of extended as originally planned. A second track was added, but that only provided a stay of execution for the railway before its closure at the end of the 1996 season.

When the Runaway Mine Train suffered an extended period of downtime followed the 2006 crash, the park revealed that: "There is some debate about whether or not we change the theme of the ride, but this is yet to be resolved." Rumours – never confirmed by the park – suggested that a deal had been discussed with the producers of the videogame SingStar, which would have seen guests singing along to popular tunes via microphones as they raced around the track. Not surprisingly, this idea was not pursued.[502]

Some rides that were eventually built could have looked very different. Before the X-Sector theme was settled on for Oblivion and its surrounding attractions, another theme dubbed "Port Discovery" was also considered – and Alton Towers still holds a trademark for the name. It would have seen the area decorated in a steampunk style, in an alternative future world that still utilised steam powered machinery. It was similar in style and name to the Discoveryland area at Disneyland Paris, and with the Black Hole also resembling Space Mountain the two concepts may have been considered too close for comfort. This didn't stop the park from revisiting the steampunk theme when it was designing Air, which would have seen the coaster's trains designed to resemble steam-powered flying machines. Another option for Air was a dystopian theme, complete with destroyed landmarks such as the Statue of Liberty. While this was dropped in favour of the eventual "oasis" concept, similar ideas were incorporated into the theme for The Swarm, the winged coaster that opened at Thorpe Park in 2012.

In addition to rides, Alton Towers has formulated several plans for accommodation on the site that have not come to fruition. The most ambitious of these was John Broome's plan for Alton Towers Village, which was dropped not long after Tussauds bought the park. The plans for the sprawling, 33-acre village appear to have been inspired by the Center Parcs resort that opened in Nottinghamshire's Sherwood Forest in 1987 (a second resort, at Elveden Forest in Suffolk, followed two years later).

Guests would be housed in 107 chalet buildings, each comprising two units (one on the ground floor, one on the first floor). Up to six people could be accommodated in a unit, with each featuring between two and four bedrooms, two bathrooms, a combined kitchen / dining room / living room and a balcony. The structures would be built with timber frames, with stone cladding added to enable them to "blend in with the natural setting of the area". The roofs would be covered with cedar shingles. The balconies would overlook water, with each of eleven "clusters" of chalets being based around its own small lake fed by natural springs within the area. Rockwork, streams and a tree screen would provide a "serene setting" for the clusters.

A private village store would offer day-to-day food supplies for self-catering visitors, newspapers and magazines, stationery, hardware and other essential items.

At the heart of the village would sit an enormous leisure complex, complete with a tropical lagoon and leisure pool, waterfalls and water slides - strikingly similar to the Cariba Creek water park that was eventually opened in 2003. As at Center Parcs, a variety of other activities would be on offer, with the centre also hosting saunas, a gym, a snooker room, several squash courts, a sports hall, an amusement arcade, a sun deck, a bar and a beauty parlour. A restaurant would overlook the surrounding area.

The glass-topped leisure centre, almost 100 feet tall, was one of the most controversial aspects of the design, although the plans promised that it would be similar in style to the existing monorail station, located nearby.

Broome's original application was for single-storey chalets, with a capacity of 500. Adding a second story enabled this to be boosted to 1,200 in a second application, which also added the leisure complex. A second phase would have included the construction of a golf course, a dry ski slope, a pub and a 56-

bedroom hotel. While the first proposal had been approved after being referred to the Secretary of State, the second was ultimately withdrawn by Tussauds. Instead, it built the Alton Towers Hotel, which opened in 1996.

The chalet village idea was revived by Merlin in October 2012, when it submitted plans for a "phased development of 150 lodges". The two-phase project would have seen the resort install a range of lodges, "holes" and "huts" to the north of its two existing hotels, with the site opening in 2014. The accommodation would resemble the Hobbit houses seen in the *Lord of the Rings* movie trilogy, but the plans had – predictably - faced opposition from local residents.

Situated on a 10-acre site to the north east of the existing Alton Towers Hotel and Splash Landings Hotel, the lodge development was to be smaller than Broome's chalet village. It would sit in a meadow surrounded by woodland, which is currently used for overflow parking during major events. The aim was to widen the variety of accommodation available at the resort, "in terms of size, format and pricing".

The first phase, to open in March 2014, would consist of 8 double lodges (each housing two accommodation units), 64 single huts and 5 holes. A further 9 double lodges and 47 huts would be added in the second phase, to open in March 2015.

The theme for the development was described as being "based on myths and legends and the increasing popularity of children's adventure stories and fairy tales." It would conjure up "images of accommodation in a far-off magical land that one might dream of staying in on a holiday".

Lodges would feature rounded windows, bent chimneys and strangely-shaped roofs, with giant fake mushrooms "growing" in the garden. Holes would be partly buried under vegetation, resembling something from children's TV series the *Teletubbies*. Huts would feature pitched roofs that reached right down to the ground.

Despite their differing appearances, all of the units would offer similar, "entry-level" accommodation. This would include a main room with a double bed and a small seating area, a wet room with a walk-in shower, and a separate sleeping area for children boasting bunk beds and a slide-out truckle bed. Children's play areas would be dotted around the site to keep little ones entertained.

Located close to the entrance of the site would be the arrival / restaurant building, covering 436 square metres and designed to resemble a crumbling old shack. This would host a reception facility, a small shop and a canteen-style restaurant with capacity for 150 indoors and 60 outside during good weather.

The lodge area was designed to be largely car-free. On arrival, guests would park in one of six visitor parking spaces close to the restaurant building. From there, they could use a golf buggy to transport their luggage to their temporary home. They would then park their car in an existing car park to the south. The only exceptions were accessible units for disabled visitors, which would feature their own car parking space.

The application was withdrawn in May 2013, although it could still be resubmitted at a later stage. A spokesperson for the resort said: "Even though future expansion of the Resort's accommodation remains a priority within the long term plan, a decision has now been made not to pursue this particular type of development at the current time and these plans have therefore been withdrawn."

Not all of the plans that have been publicised by Alton Towers over the years have been genuine. Two hoaxes in particular captured the imagination of the public and the media.

The first of these featured on the BBC's *Live and Kicking* show in 1995. The park, it was said, would open a new roller coaster dubbed "The Great White", which was to be located in and around the main lake. Riders would don wet suits before boarding the ride, as part of its circuit was to be underwater. Real, live sharks would swim in the lake, with riders protected by a cage around the coaster's trains. Bags of salt were shown on the shoreline, which would be used to convert the lake from freshwater to saltwater to accommodate the sharks. The broadcast date of the show was a hint as to the false nature of the report – it was April 1.

Merlin's takeover of the resort was followed by a flurry of publicity stunts designed to enhance its appeal to families. One of these, picked up by a number of major newspapers, was the claim that the park was planning to install a roller coaster designed for babies. Known as the "Babycoaster", the ride would feature teddy bear-shaped carriages and would travel at just 2 miles per hour to replicate the motion of being pushed in a pram.

Codenamed Project Giant Gurgle, the coaster was said to be aimed at babies aged over six months. The short, 196 foot (60 metre) circuit would be navigated in just 67 seconds. Morwenna Angove was on hand to explain the plans – and helpfully point out that the park already featured a number of rides for small children, saying: "As the UK's No 1, we are constantly evaluating a whole host of ride and attraction concepts to complement the fantastic combination of experiences already available at the Alton Towers Resort. Project Giant Gurgle is the latest concept to be considered and would fit perfectly amongst attractions already aimed at our younger guests, such as the Driving School and Heave Ho." [503]

Like so many planned rides before it, the Babycoaster was sadly never built.

Predicting the future for a theme park such as Alton Towers that operates in a competitive market in which technology and customer behaviour are constantly evolving is a near-impossible task. The history of the park demonstrates that long-term (and even short-term) plans put in place by its various owners over the years have frequently changed or been dropped altogether.

John Wardley is clear on his hopes for the park, however. Asked what he would most like to see added to the park over the coming years, his response was emphatic: "A woodie!"

Alton Towers has entertained tens of millions of people since the days of the fifteenth Earl of Shrewsbury. From the Great Sale to the asset-stripping of the 1950s, the Grand Fetes to Scarefest and the miniature railway to The Smiler, it has attracted hordes of visitors, as well as controversy. This unique attraction on a fascinating historical site looks set to continue to surprise and amaze for decades to come.

About the author

Nick Sim is the owner and editor of Theme Park Tourist, an independent theme park website that offers news, reviews, guides and discount listings. Since its debut in 2009, the website has grown to receive several million pageviews each month.

Having trained as a computer scientist, Nick worked for BT, the UK's leading telecommunications company, for 9 years. There, he led the Connected Home Research team, investigating future solutions for networking within the home. If you're a BT customer with a Wi-Fi Home Hub or a pair of powerline adapters, Nick's team probably tested them (so you can blame him if they don't work properly).

Theme parks have been an important part of Nick's life since he was six years old, when his parents took him on a trip to Pleasurewood Hills in Suffolk. He married his wife Natalie in 2009, after a romance that had spanned his entire adult life. Together, the pair have travelled the world, visiting many of its best theme parks along the way.

Nick and Natalie live in Ipswich, Suffolk with their sons Steven and Matthew.

Notes

[1] Michael J. Fisher, *Alton Towers: A Gothic Wonderland*, 1999, p.15
[2] Peter Scott, *A History of the Alton Towers Railway*, 1998, p.10
[3] Fisher, *Gothic Wonderland*, p.18
[4] Fisher, *Gothic Wonderland*, p.23
[5] The Graphic, July 29, 1871
[6] J. C. Loudon, *The History of Garden Design and Gardening*, 1834
[7] Scott, *Alton Towers Railway*, p.11
[8] Fisher, *Gothic Wonderland*, p.58
[9] Fisher, Gothic Wonderland, p.62
[10] W.A. Nesfield, unpublished, 1844 via Alton Towers Conservation Management Plan
[11] Fisher, *Gothic Wonderland*, p.73
[12] Fisher, *Gothic Wonderland*, p.29
[13] Fisher, *Gothic Wonderland*, p.85
[14] Fisher, Gothic Wonderland, p.117
[15] A.W.N. Pugin, *The True Principles of Christian Architecture*, 1841, p.51
[16] Fisher, *Gothic Wonderland*, p.120
[17] E. Rhodes, *The Derbyshire Tourist's Guide*, 1837
[18] Fisher, *Gothic Wonderland*, p.9
[19] *White's Directory of Staffordshire*, 1851
[20] The Standard, October 7, 1856
[21] Fisher, *Gothic Wonderland*, p.159
[22] Alton Towers Heritage website, http://www.altontowersheritage.com/heritage/article.asp?articleid=19
[23] Derbyshire Times, June 6, 1868
[24] The Times, October 4, 1870
[25] Staffordshire Sentinel, July 13, 1875
[26] John Abberley, *In Memory*, Staffordshire Sentinel, July 29, 2007
[27] The Mercury, August 11, 1893
[28] Nottingham Evening Post, August 7, 1895
[29] Fisher, *Gothic Wonderland*,, p.161
[30] The Mercury, August 10, 1894
[31] Nottingham Evening Post, August 7, 1895
[32] The Mercury, August 10, 1894
[33] Nottingham Evening Post, August 7, 1895
[34] The Mercury, August 10, 1894
[35] The Mercury, August 11, 1893
[36] Grantham Journal, June 29, 1901
[37] Nottingham Daily Guardian, 1907
[38] Modern Society, 1910
[39] Daily Express, November 8, 1905
[40] Daily Express, November 8, 1905
[41] Daily Express, November 8, 1905
[42] Daily Express, November 9, 1905
[43] Daily Mirror, November 8, 1905
[44] Daily Express, November 11, 1905
[45] Daily Mirror, November 10, 1905
[46] Daily Express, November 11, 1905
[47] Derby Evening Telegraph, August 5, 1931
[48] Derby Evening Telegraph, August 21, 1934
[49] Alton Towers Heritage website, http://www.altontowersheritage.com/heritage/article.asp?articleid=29
[50] Derby Daily Telegraph, March 27, 1929
[51] The Herald, June 30, 1928
[52] The Times, June 13, 1934
[53] Derby Evening Telegraph, July 28, 1933
[54] Fisher, *Gothic Wonderland*, p.11
[55] Fisher, *Gothic Wonderland*, p.162
[56] Alton Towers Memories website, http://www.altontowersmemories.net/page19.htm
[57] Alton Towers Memories website, http://www.altontowersmemories.net/page4.htm
[58] Alton Towers Memories website
[59] Derby Evening Telegraph, May 31, 1946
[60] Towers Times Magazine, October 1999
[61] Alton Towers Heritage website, http://www.altontowersheritage.com/heritage/article.asp?articleid=75
[62] *Alton Towers Guidebook*, 1870
[63] Scott, *Alton Towers Railway*, p.12
[64] J.M. Robinson, *1989*, p.167

[65] National Monument Record, 1951
[66] Fisher, *Gothic Wonderland,*, p.164
[67] *Alton Towers Conservation Management Plan*, 2012
[68] Historic Building and Monuments Act, 1953
[69] Scott, *Alton Towers Railway*, p.12
[70] *Alton Towers Guidebook*, 1970
[71] Alton Towers Heritage website, http://www.altontowersheritage.com/heritage/article.asp?articleid=30
[72] *Alton Towers Guidebook*, 1952
[73] Alton Towers heritage website, http://www.altontowersheritage.com/heritage/article.asp?articleid=30
[74] Scott, *Alton Towers Railway*,p.8
[75] *Alton Towers Guidebook*, 1957
[76] *Alton Towers Guidebook*, 1964
[77] *Alton Towers Model Electric Railway Handbook*, c.1960
[78] Towers Times Magazine, October 1999
[79] Daily Express, March 30, 1961
[80] Phil Gould, *Inland parks: Before they were famous*, 2012, Joyland books website, http://www.joylandbooks.com/themagiceye/articles/inland-parks-before-they-were-famous.htm
[81] Alton Towers Heritage website, http://www.altontowersheritage.com/heritage/article.asp?articleid=51
[82] The Mirror, May 18, 1974
[83] Daily Express, March 30, 1961
[84] National Fairground Archive, http://www.nfa.dept.shef.ac.uk/history/rides/looper.html
[85] Gould, *Inland Parks*
[86] *Alton Towers Guidebook*, 1970
[87] *Alton Towers Guidebook*, 1964
[88] Alton Towers Heritage website, http://www.altontowersheritage.com/heritage/article.asp?articleid=31
[89] Gould, *Inland Parks*
[90] *Alton Towers Guidebook*, 1970
[91] *Alton Towers Conservation Management Plan*, 2012
[92] Towers Times magazine, October 1999
[93] The Mirror, November 17, 1978
[94] The Mirror, May 31, 1975
[95] The Mirror, June 11, 1976
[96] The Mirror, August 5, 1978
[97] The Mirror, May 18, 1974
[98] The Mirror, August 18, 1979
[99] The Mirror, July 19, 1980
[100] The Independent, May 30, 1993
[101] Daily Express - June 14, 1982
[102] Daily Express - June 14, 1982
[103] Daily Express - June 14, 1982
[104] The Independent, May 30, 1993
[105] Daily Express - June 14, 1982
[106] The Independent, May 30, 1993
[107] Daily Express - June 14, 1982
[108] Daily Express - June 14, 1982
[109] Scott, *Alton Towers Railway*, p.13
[110] John Abberley, *Memories of Alton Towers and the Corkscrew*, Staffordshire Sentinel, October 11, 2008
[111] Gould, *Inland Parks*
[112] Daily Express, June 14, 1982
[113] Chris Johnson, Wardley interview
[114] The *Alton Towers Story*, DVD, 2008
[115] *Alton Towers Story* DVD
[116] Caroline Davies, *All aboard for the last Corkscrew*, The Guardian, October 26, 2008
[117] Towers Street forum, http://www.towersstreet.com/talk/talbot-street/corkscrew-memories/msg7164/#msg7164
[118] John Wardley interview, Park World Online, http://www.parkworld-online.com/news/fullstory.php/aid/1759/John_Wardley_.html
[119] Daily Express, November 1, 2008
[120] Daily Star, December 16, 2008
[121] Scott, *Alton Towers Railway*, p.13
[122] *Alton Towers Park Guide*, 1981
[123] *Alton Towers Guidebook*, 1990
[124] Towers Times website, http://old.towerstimes.co.uk/history/oldrides/talbotst.htm
[125] The Times, April 10, 1982
[126] Staffordshire Sentinel, February 8, 1984
[127] The Times, February 21, 1984
[128] Towers Nerd forum, http://towersnerd.com/community/index.php?/topic/1297-first-day-of-alton-magic/

Notes

[129] Towers Times forum, http://forum.towerstimes.co.uk/alton-towers-archive/what-was-the-black-hole-like/15/

[130] ITN news report, 1985

[131] Alton Towers park leaflet, 1988

[132] National Fairground Archive, http://www.nfa.dept.shef.ac.uk/history/ri des/enterp.html

[133] Towers Times forum, http://forum.towerstimes.co.uk/alton-towers-archive/from-festival-park-to-dark-forest/15/

[134] *Alton Towers Guidebook*, 1990

[135] Daily Express - March 25, 1986

[136] Bill Cotter, Vancouver's Expo '86, 2009, p.45

[137] Midlands Today news report, 1987

[138] Daily Express, March 27, 1987

[139] Towers Almanac website, http://www.towersalmanac.com/areas/ri des.php?id=34

[140] Rollercoaster Database website, ,http://rcdb.com/1460.htm

[141] Towers Times forum, http://forum.towerstimes.co.uk/alton-towers-archive/re-located-coasters/msg37636/#msg37636

[142] Tower Times forum, http://forum.towerstimes.co.uk/alton-towers-archive/re-located-coasters/msg37636/#msg37636

[143] Planning application 89/00047/OLD

[144] *Alton Towers Guidebook*, 1983

[145] Daily Express, March 27, 1987

[146] *Alton Towers Guidebook*, 1990

[147] *Alton Towers Guidebook*, 1990

[148] *Alton Towers Guidebook*, 1990

[149] *Alton Towers Guidebook*, 1990

[150] Towers Almanac website, http://www.towersalmanac.com/areas/ri des.php?id=83

[151] Alton Towers Heritage website, http://www.altontowersheritage.com/her itage/article.asp?articleid=31

[152] The Times, April 10, 1982

[153] *Alton Towers Story* DVD

[154] *Trentham History Timeline*, http://www.trentham.co.uk/media/14100 1/history-timeline.pdf

[155] *History, Gazetteer and Directory of Staffordshire*, Sheffield, 1851

[156] *Trentham History Timeline*

[157] Graham Bebbington, *Trentham Reflections*, 2005, p.108

[158] Bebbington, *Trentham Reflections*, p.87

[159] Scott, *Alton Towers Railway*, p.54

[160] Gould, *Inland Parks*

[161] Bebbington, *Trentham Reflections*, p.87

[162] Scott, *Alton Towers Railway*, p.54

[163] The Times, April 10, 1982

[164] Bebbington, *Trentham Reflections*, p.115

[165] The Times, July 16, 1982

[166] The Times, April 10, 1982

[167] *Memorable days out at the coolest pools*, Staffordshire Sentinel, August 2, 2008

[168] The Times, July 16, 1982

[169] John Broome, *Project Trentham*

[170] Trentham planning documents, 82/13607/OUT

[171] *Trentham History Timeline*

[172] Scott, *Alton Towers Railway*, p.55

[173] Derby Evening Telegraph, October 18 1979

[174] Derby Evening Telegraph, October 18 1979

[175] Derby Evening Telegraph, October 18 1979

[176] The Times, June 7, 1985

[177] Derby Evening Telegraph, October 18 1979

[178] *Domesday Reloaded – Britannia Park*, BBC History website, http://www.bbc.co.uk/history/domesday/ dblock/GB-444000-342000/page/7

[179] The Times, June 7, 1985

[180] The Times, November 29, 1984

[181] The Times, November 29, 1984

[182] The Times, June 7, 1985

[183] *Corby people recall steel works closure 30 years ago*, BBC website, June 1, 2010, http://news.bbc.co.uk/local/northampton /hi/people_and_places/history/newsid_8 715000/8715706.stm

[184] The Times, September 22, 1983

[185] The Times, January 28, 1985

[186] The Times, January 28, 1985
[187] The Times, September 7, 1982
[188] The Times, September 7, 1982
[189] The Times, September 7, 1982
[190] The Times, August 18, 1984
[191] Daily Express, August 19, 1988
[192] Daily Express, August 19, 1988
[193] The Times, April 10, 1982
[194] The Times, January 28, 1985
[195] Daily Express, August 19, 1988
[196] Daily Express, September 17, 1989
[197] Bob Thorogood, *Behind the Call of Duty*, 2006, p.227
[198] The Times, June 7, 1985
[199] The Times, April 16, 1983
[200] The Independent, May 30, 1993
[201] The Times, April 16, 1983
[202] The Times, April 16, 1983
[203] *In Pictures: Battersea Power Station*, BBC News Website, http://news.bbc.co.uk/1/shared/spl/hi/picture_gallery/05/uk_battersea_power_station/html/3.stm
[204] *Battersea's Powerful Story*, September 1, 2000, BBC News website, http://news.bbc.co.uk/1/hi/uk/906135.stm
[205] Keith Garner, *A Well Known Power Station*, Society of Architectural Historians of Great Britain Newsletter 71
[206] Daily Express, November 26, 2010
[207] The Times, April 16, 1983
[208] The Times, July 3, 1984
[209] *The Battersea* brochure, undated
[210] The Times, September 12, 1974
[211] Garner, *Well Known Power Station*
[212] Garner, *Well Known Power Station*
[213] *The Battersea* brochure, undated
[214] ITN News report, July 2, 1984
[215] The Times July 4, 1984
[216] The Times July 4, 1984
[217] Margaret Thatcher Foundation website, http://www.margaretthatcher.org/document/107009
[218] The Times, July 3, 1984
[219] The Independent, May 30, 1993
[220] BPSCG chronology, http://www.batterseapowerstation.org.uk/chron.html
[221] *The Battersea* brochure, undated
[222] The Times July 4, 1984
[223] The Times, June 9, 1988
[224] Daily Express, June 17, 1988
[225] Garner, *Well Known Power Station*
[226] The Times, July 3, 1984
[227] The Independent, May 30, 1993
[228] The Independent, May 30, 1993
[229] EDM number 1139, June 20, 1990
[230] Daily Express, November 26, 2010
[231] Garner, *Well Known Power Station*
[232] Financial Times, June 13, 1994
[233] Financial Times, February 25, 1993
[234] The Independent, February 28, 1993
[235] The Guardian, May 20, 2013
[236] The Independent, May 30, 1993
[237] Associated Press, January 23, 1989
[238] Associated Press, January 23, 1989
[239] John Wardley, *Creating my Own Nemesis*, 2013, p.18
[240] Season Pass podcast episode 103
[241] Season Pass podcast episode 103
[242] Season Pass podcast episode 103
[243] *John Wardley Looks Back*, First Drop magazine issue 72
[244] Wardley, *Nemesis*, p.85
[245] *Themes, Dreams and Scream Machines*, TV documentary
[246] Associated Press, January 23, 1989
[247] Chris Johnson, Wardley interview
[248] *Chessington Goes Bats*, unknown newspaper, 1992
[249] Associated Press, January 23, 1989
[250] John Wardley interview, Park World
[251] *Wardley Looks Back*, First Drop
[252] Wardley, *Nemesis*, p.130
[253] John Wardley email, Towers Street forum, http://www.towersstreet.com/talk/talbot-street/before-alton-towers/
[254] *Chessington Goes Bats*
[255] John Wardley email, Towers Street
[256] *Chessington Goes Bats*
[257] Daily Express, March 31, 1990
[258] Daily Express, March 31, 1990
[259] Daily Express, July 17, 1993
[260] Daily Express, July 17, 1993
[261] The Independent, October 24, 1993
[262] Daily Express, July 17, 1993
[263] *Bedfordshire Matters* issue 40, CPRE

Notes

264 Mail on Sunday, December 5, 1993
265 *Themes, Dreams* documentary
266 *Wardley Looks Back*, First Drop
267 Chris Johnson, Wardley interview
268 Season Pass Podcast episode 103
269 Season Pass Podcast episode 103
270 *Themes, Dreams* documentary
271 Towers Times forum, http://forum.towerstimes.co.uk/alton-towers-archive/forbidden-valley-(thunder-valley)/15/
272 *Themes, Dreams* documentary
273 *Marketing a Theme Park – The Alton Towers Story* documentary, 1998, TV Choice Ltd
274 Wardley interview, Park World
275 *Themes, Dreams* documentary
276 *Themes, Dreams* documentary
277 Season Pass Podcast episode 103
278 Season Pass Podcast episode 103
279 *Themes, Dreams* documentary
280 *Themes, Dreams* documentary
281 Wardley, *Nemesis*, p.135
282 Towers Times forum, http://forum.towerstimes.co.uk/alton-towers-archive/were-you-ever-scared-of-the-haunted-house/
283 Towers Times forum, http://forum.towerstimes.co.uk/alton-towers-archive/were-you-ever-scared-of-the-haunted-house/
284 Daily Express, May 29, 1993
285 Daily Express, May 27, 1995
286 Towers Street forum, http://www.towersstreet.com/talk/talbot-street/toyland-tours/
287 Towers Street forum, http://www.towersstreet.com/talk/talbot-street/toyland-tours/
288 *Wardley Looks Back*, First Drop
289 John Wardley, *Nemesis X* presentation, March 15, 2004
290 Wardley, *Nemesis X*
291 Wardley, *Nemesis X*
292 Season Pass Podcast episode 123
293 Chris Johnson, Wardley interview
294 Wardley, *Nemesis X*
295 Wardley, *Nemesis X*
296 Wardley, *Nemesis X*
297 Wardley, *Nemesis X*

298 The Independent, June 7, 1997
299 Daily Express, May 27, 1995
300 Wardley, *Nemesis X*
301 Chris Johnson, Wardley interview
302 *Marketing a Theme Park*
303 Rollercoaster Database website, http://rcdb.com/777.htm
304 *The Story of Alton Towers* DVD
305 Season Pass Podcast episode 103
306 Season Pass Podcast episode 103
307 Season Pass Podcast episode 103
308 Wardley, *Nemesis*, p.150
309 Season Pass Podcast episode 103
310 *Marketing a Theme Park*
311 Birmingham Mail, May 5, 2013
312 Chris Johnson, Wardley interview
313 Season Pass Podcast episode 123
314 Season Pass Podcast episode 123
315 Alton Towers Heritage website, http://www.altontowersheritage.com/heritage/article.asp?articleid=99
316 Alton Towers Heritage website, http://www.altontowersheritage.com/heritage/article.asp?articleid=99
317 Season Pass Podcast episode 123
318 Season Pass Podcast episode 103
319 Air reviews, Theme Park Tourist website, http://www.themeparktourist.com/guides/alton-towers/air
320 Chris Johnson, Wardley interview
321 Planning appl. 90/00008/OLD
322 Steve De La Mere website, http://www.stevedelamare.com/biography.htm
323 Daily Express, March 17, 1998
324 The Express - October 17, 1998
325 Pearson press release, http://www.pearson.com/news/1998/october/pearson-completes-tussauds-group-disposal.html
326 Wardley, *Nemesis*, p.151
327 Daily Mail, June 2, 2003
328 *Splash Landings photos*, Alton Towers Almanac website, http://www.cjbennett.com/ata_gallery/thumbnails.php?album=429
329 Daily Mail, June 2, 2003
330 The Guardian, September 12, 2003
331 The Telegraph, February 23, 2003
332 Wardley, *Nemesis*, p.155

333 *Transport Study*, Alton Towers Long Term Development Plan
334 Daily Express, December 8, 2003
335 New York Times, March 24, 2005
336 *Student Information Pack*, Alton Towers, 2012
337 *Transport Study*
338 Alton Towers Almanac forum, http://forums.towersalmanac.com/index.php?showtopic=13936&mode=threaded&pid=159623
339 Staffordshire Sentinel, November 18, 2006
340 *Transport Study*
341 Vardon PLC press release
342 Blackstone Group press release, May 23, 2005
343 Wall Street Journal, July 13, 2005
344 Fast Track (Sunday Times)
345 Reuters, March 5, 2007
346 Bloomberg, March 5, 2007
347 *Alton Towers sold in £622m deal*, BBC News website, July 17, 2007
348 *Park Life*, themarketer website, July 2010, http://www.themarketer.co.uk/archives/interviews/profiles/park-life/
349 *Park Life*, themarketer
350 Alton Towers targets short-break audience, March 6, 2008, Marketing Week website, http://www.marketingweek.co.uk/alton-towers-targets-short-break-audience/2059932.article
351 *Transport Study*
352 *Park Life*, themarketer
353 *Annual Review 2009*, Merlin Entertainments Group
354 *Transport Study*
355 Season Pass Podcast episode 122
356 *Park Life*, themarketer
357 Season Pass Podcast episode 122
358 Wardley interview, Park World
359 Season Pass Podcast episode 122
360 Wardley interview, Park World
361 Season Pass Podcast episode 122
362 Wardley interview, Park World
363 Season Pass Podcast episode 122
364 Wardley interview, Park World
365 Season Pass Podcast episode 122
366 Wardley interview, Park World
367 Wardley interview, Park World
368 Season Pass Podcast episode 122
369 Season Pass Podcast episode 123
370 John Wardley presentation to European Coaster Club, August 2013
371 Birmingham Mail, May 5, 2013
372 John Wardley radio interview, Bolton FM, February 20, 2013
373 Birmingham Mail, May 5, 2013
374 Wardley, ECC presentation
375 Daily Express, March 25, 2013
376 Chris Johnson, Wardley interview
377 Local Pinch Point Fund application, Staffordshire Country Council, http://www.staffordshire.gov.uk/transport/transportplanning/localtransportplan/a50toaltongrowthcorridor.pdf
378 Uttoxeter Advertiser, March 8, 1989
379 Uttoxeter Advertiser, March 8, 1989
380 Uttoxeter Advertiser, March 8, 1989
381 *Chronology*, BPSCG
382 Staffordshire Sentinel, April 21, 2003
383 *Keep the woodie petition*, http://www.petitiononline.com/cjw4sw5/petition.html
384 *Transport Study*
385 Staffordshire Sentinel, December 18, 2008
386 Staffordshire Sentinel, January 13, 2009
387 Staffordshire Sentinel, January 2, 2013
388 *Corporate Social Responsibility*, Alton Towers website, http://www.altontowers.com/uploadedFiles/Page_Content/About/CSR.pdf
389 Towers Times Magazine, October 1999
390 Towers Times Magazine, October 1999
391 Judge's ruling, Tussauds vs. Ropers, July 21, 2005
392 Daily Star, August 3, 2004
393 *Noise Report*, Alton Towers Long Term Development Plan, 2012
394 Staffordshire Sentinel, September 8, 2008
395 Staffordshire Sentinel, November 16, 2011
396 *Churchill China says former chairman Stephen Roper cuts stake in*

Notes

co, London South East, September 7, 2007

[397] *Roper climbs at Churchill China*, Citywire, December 7, 1999, http://citywire.co.uk/new-model-adviser/roper-climbs-at-churchill-china/a200836

[398] *Balancing nature of countryside with needs of industry*, Staffordshire Sentinel, August 8, 2004

[399] *'It feels like we're living in a factory'*, Staffordshire Sentinel, April 11, 2009

[400] Pits n Pots website article, October 26, 2008, http://www.pitsnpots.co.uk/2008/10/terry-craig-contact-pitsnpots-about-churchill-china-monstrosity/

[401] *Alton Towers Guidebook*, 1990

[402] Sunday Express, April 16, 2006

[403] Daily Express, November 19, 2008

[404] Towers Times forum, http://forum.towerstimes.co.uk/alton-towers-archive/the-mysterious-stuff-of-alton-towers/105/

[405] The Telegraph, May 28, 2013

[406] Morwenna Angove Facebook interview, https://www.facebook.com/note.php?note_id=422319651391&id=21765316200

[407] *Transport Study*

[408] telecompaper, May 13, 2002

[409] Daily Star, August 16, 2000

[410] *Student Information Pack*, 2012

[411] Daily Express, August 1, 2002

[412] The Mirror, January 4, 2007

[413] Staffordshire Sentinel, December 23, 2006

[414] The Independent, July 3, 1997

[415] *Alton Towers Guidebook*, 1990

[416] Daily Star, October 5, 2010

[417] The Times, October 5, 2010

[418] Towers Times Magazine, October 1999

[419] Towers Times magazine October 1999

[420] Daily Star, November 3, 2006

[421] *Alton Towers told off for BT Bash*, The Register, September 3, 2003, http://www.theregister.co.uk/2003/09/03/alton_towers_told_off/

[422] The Independent, July 1, 2006

[423] *A gay old time*, PinkNews, October 4, 2006

[424] Daily Star, July 12, 2006

[425] Daily Star, August 22, 2006

[426] The Guardian, August 3, 2006

[427] Daily Express, April 22, 2004

[428] *Gnomes abandoned at Alton Towers*, BBC News website, June 6, 2005, http://news.bbc.co.uk/1/hi/england/staffordshire/4613307.stm

[429] Daily Express, August 6, 2005

[430] Daily Star, April 4, 2009

[431] Daily Star, August 28, 2007

[432] Daily Star, June 16, 2009

[433] *Naked riders take tilt at record*, BBC News website, August 29, 2004, http://news.bbc.co.uk/1/hi/england/staffordshire/3602750.stm

[434] Daily Mail, August 9, 2010

[435] *Alton Towers 'bans' PDAs and smartphones*, neowin.net, May 28, 2008, http://www.neowin.net/news/alton-towers-bans-pdas-and-smartphones

[436] Daily Express, August 11, 2009

[437] Daily Express, July 30, 2010

[438] Daily Star, March 29, 2005

[439] Daily Star, February 14, 2010

[440] *Park Life*, themarketer

[441] Daily Star, January 22, 2010

[442] Daily Star, March 21, 2010

[443] Morwenna Angove, Facebook

[444] *Hit or Miss? Alton Towers promotes new rollercoaster using 'branded' sheep*, PRWeek website, January 23, 2013, http://www.prweek.com/uk/news/1167763/

[445] Towers Times Magazine October 1999

[446] Daily Express, September 13, 1982

[447] Daily Express, January 3, 2009

[448] Sunday Express, May 23, 2010

[449] Sunday Express, May 23, 2010

[450] Daily Star, April 14, 2010

[451] Staffordshire Sentinel, April 27, 1984

[452] Staffordshire Sentinel, April 27, 1984

[453] Staffordshire Sentinel, April 30, 1984

[454] Staffordshire Sentinel, May 17, 1984

[455] Staffordshire Sentinel, date unknown

[456] Alton Towers Memories website, http://altontowersmemories.net/page8.ht m

[457] *Visitors trapped on rollercoaster*, BBC News website, June 24, 2001, http://news.bbc.co.uk/1/hi/uk/1405525.st m

[458] Daily Express, June 14, 2005

[459] *Boy in hospital after rollercoaster accident*, BBC Newsround website, May 30, 2002, http://news.bbc.co.uk/cbbcnews/hi/uk/ne wsid_2017000/2017283.stm

[460] The Telegraph, July 25, 2008

[461] Daily Express, July 21, 2006

[462] Daily Express, July 21, 2006

[463] Daily Star, July 21, 2006

[464] Staffordshire Sentinel, October 6, 2006

[465] Towers Times Magazine October 2004

[466] *Crash closes monorail at theme park*, BBC News website, August 3, 2003, http://news.bbc.co.uk/1/hi/england/staffo rdshire/3120729.stm

[467] Staffordshire Sentinel, October 29, 2005

[468] Daily Star, July 26, 2005

[469] Daily Star, March 7, 2001

[470] Manchester Evening News, December 1, 1884

[471] *Student Information Pack*, Alton Towers

[472] Daily Star, January 1, 2011

[473] Alton Towers Jobs website, http://altontowersjobs.com/working-for-us/rewards-and-benefits

[474] Morwenna Angove, Facebook

[475] *Park Life*, themarketer

[476] *Park Life*, themarketer

[477] Towers Times forum, http://forum.towerstimes.co.uk/alton-towers-archive/any-ex-staff-from-1988-season/

[478] *The Magic Factory* documentary, BBC Learning, 2007

[479] *Marketing a Theme Park*

[480] *The Magic Factory*, BBC Learning

[481] Alton Towers Jobs website

[482] Daily Star, December 4, 2005

[483] *Your Money Their Tricks*, episode 1, BBC , July 3, 2013

[484] *We Are Social addresses Thorpe Park game-rigging*, Campaign Live, July 5, 2013, http://www.campaignlive.co.uk/news/11 89117/we-social-addresses-thorpe-park-game-rigging/

[485] *Park Mascots*, Towers Times website, http://old.towerstimes.co.uk/history/mas cots/

[486] Abberley, *Corkscrew*

[487] John Abberley, *The day Royals dressed up for theme park fun*, Staffordshire Sentinel, April 4, 2009

[488] Abberley, *Royals*

[489] Abberley, *Royals*

[490] Daily Star, September 23, 2011

[491] Staffordshire Sentinel, unknown date

[492] Jeffrey Seifert, *The first pipeline coaster - Ultra Twister*, RollerCoaster! Magazine, 2007

[493] Wardley, *Nemesis X*

[494] Wardley, *Nemesis X*

[495] Morwenna Angove, Facebook

[496] Wardley, ECC presentation

[497] *Lindstrand HiFlyer brochure*, http://www.lindstrandtech.com/2011%2 0Brochures/HiFlyer%20Brochure.pdf

[498] Wardley, ECC presentation

[499] *Nick Varney interview*, Chessington Buzz website, March 2013, http://www.chessingtonbuzz.co.uk/i nterviews/nick-varney-2013/

[500] Wardley, *Nemesis*

[501] Wardley, ECC presentation

[502] Staffordshire Sentinel, November 29, 2006

[503] The Sun, May 8, 2008

Printed by Amazon Italia Logistica S.r.l.
Torrazza Piemonte (TO), Italy